27·50

A HISTORY

OF

THE REIGN OF QUEEN ANNE

A HISTORY

OF

THE REIGN OF QUEEN ANNE

BY

JOHN HILL BURTON, D.C.L.

HISTORIOGRAPHER-ROYAL FOR SCOTLAND
AUTHOR OF 'A HISTORY OF SCOTLAND,' ETC.

IN THREE VOLS.

VOL. I.

University Press of the Pacific
Honolulu, Hawaii

A History of the Reign of Queen Anne
(Volume One)

by
John Hill Burton

ISBN: 1-4102-0196-1

Reprinted from the 1880 edition

University Press of the Pacific
Honolulu, Hawaii
http://www.universitypressofthepacific.com

In order to make original editions of historical works available to scholars at an economical price, this facsimile of the original edition of 1880 is reproduced from the best available copy and has been digitally enhanced to improve legibility, but the text remains unaltered to retain historical authenticity.

CONTENTS OF FIRST VOLUME.

CHAPTER III.

Domestic Affairs.

CHAPTER IV.

International Difficulties.

CHAPTER V.

The War in the Netherlands and Germany.

CHAPTER VI.

The War.

(Continued.)

CHAPTER VII.

The Union.

THE

REIGN OF QUEEN ANNE.

———•———

CHAPTER I.

𝕿𝖍𝖊 𝕭𝖊𝖌𝖎𝖓𝖓𝖎𝖓𝖌.

THE ACCESSION—THE CRISIS AND ITS TRANSIT—PERIL OF THE
ABJURATION BILL—THE EXPIRING PARLIAMENT—THE QUEEN
—HER DESCENT AND KINDRED—HER HUSBAND—HER FRIENDS
—MARLBOROUGH, DUCHESS SARAH, GODOLPHIN—THE CORRE-
SPONDENCE OF THE GROUP OF FRIENDS—HER CHILDLESS CON-
DITION AFTER THE DEATH OF THE DUKE OF GLOUCESTER—
THE NECESSITY FOR A PARLIAMENTARY REVISION OF THE SUC-
CESSION—THE ESTABLISHMENT OF THE HOUSE OF HANOVER
—HISTORICAL POSITION OF THIS HOUSE—THE CORONATION—
THE PROCESSIONS—THE CEREMONIES IN WESTMINSTER ABBEY
AND IN THE HALL—THE NEW PARLIAMENT—"QUEEN ANNE'S
BOUNTY"—ITS CONNECTION WITH THE QUEEN'S ZEAL FOR
THE CHURCH OF ENGLAND—HOW ITS OBJECT WAS DEFEATED.

ON the morning of Sunday, the eighth day of March,
in the year 1702, King William the Third died at
Kensington Palace. Even to the vigilant members
of the Privy Council who were assembled in the
palace to watch the event, the moment could not
be more distinctly fixed than by the words, "about
eight of the clock in the morning." Yet, both by
the theory of the constitution and by the statute law

of England, at the point of time when the last breath
left his lungs the reign of Anne began—a point as
impalpable and indivisible as that belonging both to
December and January, accepted by the Christian
world as marking the death of the old year and the
birth of the new. The councillors present, "after
some time, agreed to go in a body to attend her
Majesty Queen Anne at her palace at St James's, to
acquaint her Majesty with the decease of the late
king." They at the same time directed the accession
to be immediately proclaimed.[1] The Privy Council,
in their minute on the occasion, called the dead
sovereign "King William the Third of ever-glorious
memory." He was sorely missed by statesmen, who
believed in him as the only effective pledge for the
Protestant succession. But his was not a death to
cause many domestic tears. The embalming and the
usual funeral pomp took their course. It was with
a certain touch of good feeling that he was laid in
the same vault with his wife, Queen Mary, his love
for whom was the one romance that brightened a
hard nature, and a life of heavy responsibilities and
arduous duties.[2]

---

[1] Minutes of Privy Council, MS.

[2] "The estimate for the funeral, when designed 'from the Princesses'
Chamber next the House of Lords, was £3500;' but upon other orders
given by the Committee of Council for the funeral—viz., the great
withdrawing-room at Kensington to be hung with black cloth, the
great bed-chamber with purple cloth, a 'state and canopy of the same,'
a pall and canopy of purple velvet, a chariot that cost £300, eight
horse-cloths of purple cloth down to the ground, the great withdrawing-
[room] at St James's to be hung with the finest purple cloth, the Yeo-
men of the Guard mourning liveries, with 'cawles' and black fringes
for their partisans, crape bonnet-bands, black swords, gloves, &c., with
other things not thought of—the estimate amounted to £6268, 7s. 6½d."
—Calendar Treasury Papers, vol. lxxix. No. 100.

On the day of the death, Sunday though it was, Parliament met; and the work of a new reign began. The doctrine that the throne is never vacant—that the sovereign never dies—was not perhaps in logical harmony with a forcible change of dynasty and a parliamentary title which had to be confirmed and proclaimed by a coronation; but in the political conditions of the moment it was urgently expedient that it should prove successful. And it was successful; for no one was ever more effectively swept into the throne by the influence of divine right than the new queen was by her parliamentary title. Yet to all who were high in the political hierarchy there was a mighty crisis; and any possible external symptoms of interruption to the absolute tranquillity of the hour were watched with ardent anxiety.

As the crisis hastened to its climax, the pulsations of excitement and suspense radiated from London over the empire. The settlement of the crown might pass into peaceful reality; but a counter-revolution and a bloody civil war were not expectations to be derided as impracticable and visionary. There was one narrow question demanding a specific answer— Had the Abjuration Bill, for extinguishing the hopes of the Jacobites, received the royal assent?—was it an Act of Parliament? The curiosity that seeks to penetrate to the seclusion of palaces was, as usual, aroused in vain. There were, indeed, some things that it was well to keep shrouded in the dignity of mystery; and many of the secrets of the hour had died with their holders, before it was quite safe to let the world know them. There is thus some interest in knowing that the following morsels of

curious gossip were thought worthy to be preserved
among the private papers of the person to whom
they were addressed—that person being Daniel Finch,
Earl of Nottingham, who, as Secretary of State,
shared with Godolphin supremacy in the cabinet in
the early years of the new reign.   The writer of the
paper, whoever he or she may have been, speaks
somewhat obscurely and incoherently; but this ren-
ders the document all the closer in harmony with
the spirit of the moment.

March 10, 1702.

I am to tell you as much as I dare write. In the first
place, the Abjuration was passed on Saturday night, in such
a manner as never was done in any reign in the world. For
the king was in so ill a condition that he could not write his
name; therefore a stamp was put into his hand, and that,
by the help of others, lifted upon the paper, though the day
before it was said he had refused to sign it. When they
came to the Lords' House, all but the lord keeper said the
king was out of danger; but he of a sudden telling the truth,
struck the others to that degree, that if you had been there
to have spoke almost anything, they had not been able to
have done it. But the truth is, your friends are so enraged
to be left, that they absolutely neglected it, when, as Lord
D—— says, he is sure it might have been rejected. But Lord
Nor[mandy] said it was to no purpose to do anything, for he
had nobody to second him; and [it?] will certainly be disputed. Yet if you would come, and as absurd as you think it
for it to be now imposed, it has been moved in the House of
Commons, because that where the word William is, Anne
is certainly now understood. However, I am to tell you
that your opposers are so amazed and confounded, that as
soon as they are opposed they let all things fall; and there
never was such an opportunity to save this nation as now,
for all the best party are so transported to have an English
queen, that they will agree to all that is for her and her kingdom's interest. Among the mob, where one is concerned

there are forty rejoicing. The Duke of Leeds and Sir Charles Hedges are sworn of the Council; and for a secret I was told by a family that is partly Irish, that the king dying before he had made a new lord-lieutenant, and the commissioner there being by his authority, he remains so still. And he knows it; for since the king died he has in one particular acted by his secretary. Lord W[harton] has been to assure the queen of his zeal for the service, and was received just as he could have wished. One thing I can't omit, which is, that nurse Dod was with the queen yesterday morning, and from thence came to me. She said the queen asked her if my Lord Nottingham was in town; and she saying "No," the queen said she wondered he would go out of town just now; and to show you what an opinion it must give, when she came out the very bedchamber-women asked her why you would go, and said sure you was not against the queen." [1]

[1] Hatton Finch Papers, vi., British Museum, additional manuscripts, 29588, f. 14. On the occasion of this, the first of a probably large succession of references to the recent acquisitions in the manuscript department of the British Museum, I think it right to say a few words that may afford a hint to others in search of information. I was certainly astonished to find how rich the collection proved to be in materials peculiar to my own purpose, and equally astonished that their use had not been already exhausted. The value of the collection is not in what are properly termed State Papers, but in the private correspondence of statesmen and other eminences—private correspondence on affairs of State. Of public State Papers we may conclude that all of any importance or significance during our period are already published; and indeed it was the great grief of a reverend gentleman who, a century ago, wrote a history of the reign of Queen Anne, to find that, after toiling for months in the State Paper Office, everything of any significance that he copied had been printed and abundantly used.

It is a feature of such collections as the one I now refer to, that the papers—some of them mere scraps, others of considerable length—are apt to be unsigned. If they reached the person they were intended for, the writer was well known; if they went astray, then it was, on the whole, desirable that the writer should not be identified. Queen Anne's letters are all unsigned, and many of Marlborough's, Godolphin's, and Peterborough's; but the handwriting is, in these and many other instances, easily recognisable. I endeavoured in vain to discover the writer of the letter printed in the text. It was clear only that it must

The new reign announced itself by instant political activity. On the 8th of March, when the Privy
Council passed from the deathbed to St James's to
attend on the Queen, they were received by her with
a royal speech. It was noticed on this occasion, as
ever afterwards when she spoke in public, that her
voice was soft with a feminine melody, while, at the
same time, it was distinct and sonorous.[1] The speech
put, in the briefest terms, the proper assurances
about the maintenance of the settlement of the crown
in the Protestant line, and the preservation of religion, laws, and liberties. But the great point was
the commencement of a policy in harmony with the
prevailing impulse of the nation—" the importance
of carrying on all the preparations we are making

have been some one on familiar terms with so eminent a person as
Nottingham. There is a touch of the feminine in its tone.

Affording materials thus peculiarly affluent for the present purpose, it
appeared to me that the collection,—revealed in the catalogue in two volumes, published respectively in 1875 and 1877,—of recent acquisitions to
the Museum, is full of materials for enriching other periods of British history and history's coadjutor archæology ; such materials, for instance, as
chronicles, cartularies, county and other local histories, ecclesiastical and
corporate records, registers of courts of justice, and books of heraldry
and family history. The value of the collection is enhanced by the skil-
fully-adjusted and well-sustained organisation for access to the whole.
No one can work there without being sensible of the unfailing courtesy
of the custodiers of these treasures, and their readiness to assist in rendering them available to every one who seeks them for the purpose of
legitimate research.

[1] There was a tradition that Charles II., who was sensitive to beauty
in sound as well as sight, having early noticed this quality in his niece,
sent her to the best school for its culture. " He ordered Mrs Barry, a
famous actress, should teach her to speak, which she did with such success that it was a real pleasure to hear her." This, noted by Speaker
Onslow, is confirmed by Lord Dartmouth, who, in reference to her
speaking from the throne, says, "I never saw an audience more affected
—it was a kind of charm."—Burnet's Own Time, ed. 1833, vol. v. 2,
notes.

to oppose the great power of France," specifically declaring, "I shall lose no time in giving our allies all assurances that nothing shall be wanting on my part to pursue the true interest of England, together with theirs, for the support of the common cause." On the 11th she addressed a solemn speech from the throne to both Houses of Parliament. Her concluding words had in them a touch of warmth, as if courting reciprocity: "As I know my own heart to be entirely English, I can very sincerely assure you there is not anything you can expect or desire from me which I shall not be ready to do for the happiness and prosperity of England; and you shall always find me a strict and religious observer of my word."

But the assurance seems to have received more suspicious criticism than reciprocity. Why did she declare her heart to be entirely English? Was it to remind her people that they had been in the hands of one whose heart was entirely Dutch? And yet this slighting criticism was neutralised by another, hinting that the remark was not original and sincere, but adopted from the speech made by her father when his secret designs were inimical to all things thoroughly English. In a celebrated speech on a special supply for the support of his Government he had said, "I cannot express my concern upon this occasion more suitable to my own thoughts than by assuring you I have a true English heart, as jealous of the honour of the nation as you can be." [1] Then, the assurances by the new monarch that she would be found a strict observer of her word were found to

[1] Parl. Hist.. iv. 1359.

have a suspicious analogy to her father's reiterated assurances that he would make it his "endeavour to preserve this Government, both in Church and State, as it is now by law established;" and again, when, on a solemn repetition of these words, he had uttered an assurance that the repetition was intended "the better to evidence to you that I spoke then not by chance, and consequently, that you may firmly rely upon a promise so solemnly made."[1]

Parliament occupied the few remaining days of its existence in denunciations of certain pamphlets, and sermons preached on the 30th of January, the commemoration day of the execution of King Charles I. Of the mischievous influences that might be aroused by recriminating against a commemoration sermon, we shall in a few years find a brilliant example. Nothing more could be made of the pamphlets than that they were found to hint at dangers to the parliamentary settlement of the crown on the queen; but neither from the substance of the pamphlets themselves, nor in a cross-questioning of those who avowed themselves authors or publishers of the culpable pages, could a distinct announcement of where the danger might be found, be extracted.[2]   There

[1] Parl. Hist., iv. 1351-1353.

[2] As, for instance, when "the House went into consideration of the paragraphs in the 89 and 90 pages of the said book, which were read as followeth—viz. :

"'Whiglove.—I find we have miscarried in our great design : the train would not take. We were very hot upon it just before the Parliament met ; all the Whig coffee-houses rung, how necessary it was to break into the Acts of Settlement, and to exclude——'

"'Double.—Mum, Whiglove ; talk no more on that subject, I beseech you : fresh orders are issued out, and since we are not strong enough to make it go, we are now directed to say that never any such thing was intended by our party.'"—Cited from 'Tom Double returned out of

seemed more peril in an articulate story that among
the late King's papers there would be found evidence
of a plan to throw Queen Anne out of the succession
in consequence of dangerous communications that
passed between her and her father. By appointment
of the House of Lords, an august group of their
number examined the King's private repositories for
the satisfaction of Parliament, and found nothing to
justify the story. The Lords, on this, could only vent
their wrath on the distributors of the false story, while
they requested her Majesty to order Mr Attorney-
General to prosecute, with the utmost severity of the
law, the authors or publishers " of the above-mentioned or suchlike scandalous reports."[1]

The Parliament that had begun in August 1699,
sat to finish the business before it as the fourteenth
of William III. and the first of Anne. If there was
any peril in the strange conditions of the conferring
the royal assent on the Abjuration Act, this item of
critical legislation received a strengthening in the
necessity for a new Act applying it to a new reign.
The logic of the Abjuration Act was, that Parliament
having settled the succession to the crown, and demanded that all good citizens should loyally accept
the Protestant line of succession, they were required
to abjure the Jacobite line in this Act, bearing the

the Country; or, the True Picture of a Modern Whig,' &c. Another of
the House's critical attacks was 'The History of the last Parliament,
begun at Westminster in the Reign of King William, anno 1700,' of
which Dr James Drake admitted himself to be the author. Two pamphlets—one recommending that the Electress of Hanover and her son
should be invited into the country, and another professing to denounce
the Pretender—were among the productions deemed offensive in their
double meaning.—Parl. Hist., vi. 18-23.

[1] Parl. Hist.. vi. 7.

expressive title, "An Act for the further security of his Majesty's person, and for extinguishing the hopes of the pretended Prince of Wales, and all other pretenders, and their abettors."[1] The immediate apology for the Abjuration Act was Louis XIV.'s acknowledgment of "the Pretender." It had been adjusted that, in failure of any representative of either of the Protestant daughters of King James, the succession should open to "the excellent Princess Sophia, Electress and Duchess-Dowager of Hanover, daughter of the most excellent Princess Elizabeth, late Queen of Bohemia, daughter of our late sovereign lord King James the First;" "and whereas the French king, in hopes of disturbing the peace and repose of your Majesty and your kingdoms, and creating divisions therein, hath, since the making of the said Act, caused the pretended Prince of Wales to be proclaimed in your Majesty's said kingdom of France by the name, style, and title of James the Third," &c. ; and here it may be inferred that the promoters of the Act must have been conscious of adding sarcasm to defiance, since, if we follow the clause to its logical conclusion, it charges Louis XIV. with seizing the opportunity of his being unlawfully in possession of that part of the heritage of the English crown called France, for doing as he did.

This Parliament came to an end in a speech from the throne on the 25th of May. Parliament, indeed, had by a recent statute of its own, adjusted, subject to the sovereign's right of prorogation, the exact duration of its own life. It had become the constitutional rule that the Parliament died with the sove-

---

[1] 13 & 14 Will. III. c. 6.

reign. But the Revolution and the political conditions
of the time had shaken the efficiency of the fiction
that the sovereign never dies; and with a preamble
referring to "great dangers by the invasion of foreigners or by the traitorous conspiracies of wicked
and ill-disposed persons," it is provided that the
Parliament in existence at the king's death is immediately to assemble, and to exist "for and during the
time of six months and no longer." [1]

The definition of persons required to take the Abjuration Oath is an attempt, and a successful attempt,
to exhaust the gentry and the educated community.
It includes all holders of public offices, civil or military, members of the universities, teachers of youth,
clergy of all denominations, legal practitioners of all
grades: the only considerable body apparently omitted
is medical practitioners not having degrees; but as a
general remedy of omissions, the oath might be tendered "to any person or persons whatsoever." [2]

It was adjusted that the coronation should be performed on the 15th of April; and looking forward to
that event, the opportunity may be taken for a brief
retrospect of some conditions that give a strong
political influence to what, in the ordinary fixed conditions of succession to the crown, is merely an august
ceremonial. To count, indeed, that a coronation went
for anything more, was an outrage to the absolute
doctrine of divine right so influential during the
dynasty of the Stewarts. Though Anne acted as
queen whenever William by death ceased to be king,
yet it is an established fact that the eight successive

[1] 7 & 8 Will. III. c. 15.
[2] 14 Will. III. & 1 Anne. cc. 6 and 22.

monarchs after the Conquest did no regal act until, in each instance, the coronation sanctioned his admission as monarch.[1] The doctrine that the throne is never vacant, that "the sovereign never dies," was a subtle invention of the canonists for the purpose of conferring on the "divine right" doctrines the conditions and power of an exact science. Genealogy—or the exhaustion of male descendants in the ratio of seniority, then taking female descendants in the same ratio, before working out collaterals in the ratio of their vicinity—was an exact science ; and if it was to rule the succession to the throne, then divine right was also an exact science.   In the later calm period of uninterrupted hereditary succession the doctrine has met with approval, or at least acquiescence.   It is a convenient adjunct to the working of that which really is an exact science—the application of the rule of lineal descent which exhausts the sons or other nearest male descendants according to their seniority, and then does the same by the female.

Queen Anne's accession, however, followed no such abstract rule. Supposing her to have had no brother, King William's short period of sole government as thoroughly broke in upon the hereditary descent of the crown, as if he had not been the nephew of King James and the husband of his daughter.   In fact, Queen Anne's reign was part of a revolutionary pro-

---

[1] This was not generally known in our own country until, in 1830, John Allen published his learned little book, called 'Inquiry into the Rise and Growth of the Royal Prerogative in England ;' but it had been announced half a century earlier by the French archæologists— *see* 'L'Art de vérifier les dates des faits historiques, des chartes,' &c., iii. 798 *et seq.*   The conclusions on this matter are briefly told in the chapter on "Regnal Years of the Kings of England," in the 'Chronology of History,' by Sir Harris Nicolas.

cess, beginning with the Long Parliament and only subsiding as the house of Hanover became finally enthroned. In all its external conditions, however, Queen Anne's accession was as quiet and uneventful as that of any legitimate successor has been ; and it was signally acceptable to the nation at large. A slight disturbance of certain conditions tending to this happy conclusion, might have given civil war and a violent revolution instead of the peaceful succession. There were statesmen alive who remembered the death of Charles I., the Protectorate, the Restoration, and the Revolution ; and to all public men these were events perplexing the nation with fear of change. Hence the accession of Queen Anne, if it has not the interest attending on contest and bloodshed, has the interest attending on a narrow escape from these calamities ; and the conditions to which the world owes this escape seem worthy of minute attention.

It enhances the critical interest of these conditions that they only postponed the danger—they did not extinguish its causes. While they made the beginning and continuance of her reign easy and popular, events had occurred that limited the happy prospect to herself personally, and for the duration of her life. Already domestic calamities had passed it into absolute decrees of fate, that there were doubts and difficulties in the future, sadly weakening the hope of a final settlement without revolution and bloodshed.

A large body of the British people still believed that the son of King James was in reality what he was called in Acts of Parliament and otherwise, a " Pretender," not born to Mary of Modena, the queen.

With these, since her elder sister's death in 1694, the Princess Anne was the legitimate heir to the throne ; and her accession dated not from the death of her brother-in-law, who might be counted a usurper, but from an event a few months earlier—the death of her father on the 19th of September 1701. And so, had any of her many infants lived to make her a happy mother, the Stewart dynasty might have survived her. But, as we shall see, it was otherwise decreed.

There was little in Anne Stewart, either personal or intellectual, calculated, alone and unaided, to arouse interest or command admiration. Yet fate had so ordered that not only her position by birth and rank, but her personal qualifications, whether merits or defects—that, in short, all things about her—were endowed with sources of vast influence on the des-tinies of the British empire, and, through these, of the world at large. Hence the historian, to do his office properly, must bring the character and position of the new queen to the front, with an amount of pre-cision and detail that might not have been demanded for a sovereign of grander qualities and higher force of personal character.

When the genealogical sequence, giving succession to power or property, is established to the satisfac-tion of the world, any other element that pedigree can confer, has merely the decorative character of lustre. The value of this will depend on the prevail-ing habits and opinions of the age, and we shall see that the reign of the Revolution king had created an epoch of hard-working trade and money-making. To those, therefore, who could satisfy themselves that Anne legitimately held the monarchy that her father

had succeeded to, it was of little moment that her
mother was merely Anne Hyde, the daughter of one
who no doubt was an illustrious statesman, but whose
birth was in the rank of the middle class.[1] But if
a subject was to be taken into the royal family, it
was better thus than if the alliance had been less
unequal. Falling to any of the great territorial
houses already dignified by royal alliance—such as
the Howards, Percys, Stanleys, and Greys—it might
have alienated more of the support from that class of
potentates than it gained, and might have created
general suspicion lest a political power might arise
between the sovereign and the other elements of the
constitution, aristocratic and democratic. True, it
was remembered how Queen Elizabeth had exasperated the great houses by the advancement to the
highest offices of "mean persons" from her mother's
kindred and their ranks; but the political elements
had changed in the lapse of more than a century,
and the country had to deal with a woman who, had
she been of the daring and despotic character of Elizabeth, could not follow her example. Then the Hyde
family, though they had become great, were divided
among themselves. The Earl of Clarendon was a
steady Jacobite, and, though he took no part in active
politics, he declined to take the oath of allegiance to
his niece. Her other uncle, Rochester, took, as we
shall see, a share, but not a dangerous one, in the
service of his niece.

[1] The birth of the queen's grandfather is thus recorded : " The sixth
year of the reign of our most gracious sovereign lord King James, ann.
dom. 1608. In this year, the two-and-twentye day of February,
Henry Hide of Dinton, gent., had a son christened, named Edward."—
Lister. Life of Clarendon, i.

On the other hand, it would not have been matter of substantial gratification to the people to boast that their sovereign's mother inherited the blood of a foreign royalty attached to the wrong religion. Three Popish queens in succession had troubled the land with enmities and suspicions. If such a matter crossed people's thoughts, it would tell more against than in favour of Queen Anne, that her grandmother was Henrietta, the French wife of Charles I.

In the year 1683 the Princess Anne had been married to George, Prince of Denmark, the brother of King Christian V. He was forty-eight years old at the time of his wife's accession. The neutrality of his character, and the insignificance of his position, have given him something like a conspicuous place in history, since it is difficult to understand how one not incapacitated by mental disease, in the midst of the temptations to ambitious aspirations so closely haunting him, could have kept so utterly out of the notice of the world. On one occasion only is he known to have taken, or rather proposed to take, a step in active life—it was to accompany King William to the war in Ireland. But the sagacious leader, who knew that the prince's rank would throw him perpetually in the way, would take no such encumbrance to the serious task before him. The one thing for which Prince George is chiefly known to the world, is the occasion when his monotonous stupidity prompted the solitary jest that twinkles through the gloomy career and character of King James; and it came at the gloomiest moment of his days, when his family and kindred were one by one deserting him.[1]

[1] "What! is Est-il-possible gone too?" in allusion to the exclama-

But he brought with him a spiritual qualification so valuable in those critical times that it made his treatment of the things of this world a matter of no moment. So far as he could be anything in religion he was a Protestant—a member of the house that

tion by the prince as each desertion was reported. See the story at length in Macaulay's ninth chapter. If utterances like the following got notice and sympathy among those who had the destinies of the empire in their hands, the appropriate disposal of Prince George must have been a troublesome affair :—

"To begin with his Birth—Prince *George* of *Denmark* is second son of *Frederick III.*, late king of *Denmark*, and Uncle to *Christiern V.*, the present king. He was born at *Copenhagen* in *April* 1653, and in 1668 he went to Travel into several parts of *Europe*.

"As he came into the World with all the advantages of a Royal Birth and Education, so he has rendered both yet more conspicuous by his matchless Vertues. By these (tho' he is not crown'd) he hath a Title to all our Hearts.

"Thus the morning of his Life was clear and calm ; and ever since, his whole Life has been a continued Series of Heroick Actions ; which he began so Early that he was no sooner nam'd in the World but it was with Joy and Admiration.

"Even the first Blossoms of his Youth paid us all that could be expected from a *ripening Manhood ;* while he practised but the *Rudiments of War,* he out-went all other Captains ; and has found none to surpass, but himself alone. The opening of his Glory was like that of *Light.* He shone to us from far, and disclos'd his first Beams on distant Nations. He Fought several Battles in *Denmark, Sweden, Ireland,* &c. And wherever he charg'd in Person, he was a Conqueror. To describe all his Victories would require a Volume ;" and so forth.— The History of Living Men, or Characters of the Royal Family, the Ministers of State, and the Principal Natives of the Three Kingdoms ; being an Essay on a Thousand Persons that are now living, with a Poem upon each Life. Dedicated to his Royal Highness Prince George of Denmark. P. 33 *et seq.*

In the days when the penalties of sedition applied to any words tending to bring disparagement or ridicule on rulers and potentates, such a passage as this could surely have been proved to be seditious. Doubtless there is no case precisely in point, but strangely enough the arguments supporting Defoe's conviction for "The Shortest Way" fully apply to the logic of such a case—viz., that the words profess to be uttered in a just and commendable cause, but by their hyperbolical exaggeration they tend to arouse contempt instead of approval and respect.

had sent to Britain a Protestant queen, the wife of
James I., followed by three successive Popish queens.

It seemed to be thought necessary that something
in the shape of official dignity should be conferred on
Prince George, and he was elevated to that of "Gen-
eralissimo of all her Majesty's forces by land and
sea." The etymological structure of the title is questionable, and it had no practical meaning; for there
was no precedent for any powers or duties attached
to an office so named.

A time had been, however, when George of Denmark might have been a mighty person, as the sire of
a line of sovereigns. Again and again that hope
seemed realised, only to be blasted, plunging the
public life of England into ever-renewed anxieties.
The country had seen the two Protestant daughters
of King James married—the elder twenty-one years
old, and the younger nineteen. The hope attached
to Queen Mary died gradually away; but throughout
the married life of her sister, while she was yet the
Princess Anne, the hope had revived over and over
again, only to be blasted. The promised children
were so numerous that it is a question whether there
were more than seventeen. Of those who existed long
enough to die with the names they were baptised in,
there were six—Mary, Ann, Sophia, William, a second
Mary, and George.

One of them, William, created Duke of Gloucester,
lived for eleven years. His death in 1701, when
Queen Mary had been four years dead, was such a
political catastrophe as those only who remember the
death of the Princess Charlotte can in some degree
realise—in some degree only, for the death of the

princess did not devolve on the statesmen of 1818
the perilous duty, to be presently recorded, of searching the world for a successor to her inheritance.

This boy was one of the instances occurring from
time to time, when the fate of millions seems to be
bound to one fragile life. As the endurance of that
life was momentous, so there was a general concentration of all eyes and thoughts upon the boy's health
and progress. For a few years these gave confidence
to the national hopes. People heard of his precocious
capacities—his thirst for knowledge, and his marvel-
lous capacity of acquiring it. He promised to be a
hero as well as a sage. His chief enjoyment in the
intervals of his studies was in drilling and reviewing
a regiment of boys of his own age. He had a small
park of artillery, and the other military playthings
beloved by the boy in whom the nature of the ardent
soldier is growing. Tales were told of tournaments
and sieges in St George's Hall—one where the prince
received a wound and absolutely bled. He was likened to Prince Henry, the eldest son of King James
I. ; and when he died, it was remembered how this
elder brother of his grandfather might, had he
lived, have averted the disasters that so long des-
olated the land. But the two were very different.
Henry was a robust and ardent athlete ; but with
Anne's only son the mimicry of a soldier's life was
but the imparting of some touches of incident and
variety to the lethargic life of an unhealthy boy.

Perhaps acting the soldier and the hunter was a
wholesome variation of the dreary routine of mental
discipline under a succession of teachers, each endeavouring to pour into the child's intellect the whole

bulk of his own pedantic learning; but the story leaves a painful impression that, had the boy been let alone, he might have lived to be a good king.

Bishop Burnet, who was chief among his instructors, thus describes his own contribution to the child's acquirements : " I went through geography with him. I explained to him the forms of government in every country, and the interests and trade of that country, and what was both good and bad in it. I acquainted him with all the great revolutions that had been in the world ; and gave him a copious account of the Greek and Roman histories, and of Plutarch's Lives. The last thing I explained to him was the Gothic Constitution, and the beneficiary and feudal laws. I talked of these things at different times nearly three hours a-day." [1]

On the 24th of July 1700, the tenth anniversary of his birth was celebrated with due splendour. " After the ceremony was over, the Duke found himself fatigued and indisposed, and the next day he was very sick, and complained of his throat ; the third day he was hot and feverish." On the 29th, " the physicians who attended him thought it probable that he might recover ; but about eleven at night he was upon a sudden seized with a difficulty of breathing, and could swallow nothing, so that he expired before midnight, being ten years and five days old." [2]

---

[1] Own Time, ii. 211.

[2] There is a portrait of the Duke of Gloucester by Kneller, well known through an engraving by Houbraken. It has not the fulness inherited by his mother from the Hydes, and has more resemblance to the known portraits of the exiled Stewarts than to those of the boy's ancestors. It has a strong likeness to the portraits of his uncle, "the old

So by the death of an unhealthy boy the destinies of a mighty empire were set adrift. The uncompromising bigots of the divine right of kings, with sensations akin to exultation, saw here the dispensation of a quick and terrible judgment on the violators of a sacred law. Even those who had rejected the Popish and accepted the Protestant Stewart as a compromise, were uneasy, and remembered the conduct of Queen Anne at the period of her father's flight.[1]

A generation trained in the belief that no other dynasty throughout the world is so firmly rooted as

---

Pretender," taken in youth ; but with a like physical debility there is more intellectual spirit. A portrait of the mother and child by Dahl is, or recently was, in the National Portrait Gallery at South Kensington. There is an honest touch of the natural in its whole tone, refreshingly in contrast with the conventional State pictures of the period. It is attributed to the year 1695, when the boy was five years old. His face is delicate, but not unhealthy. There is, however, this peculiarity in it, that the eye catching it without premonition is apt to take it for the likeness of a girl.

[1] The belief that the death of Queen Anne's children was a judgment on her for her conduct to her father, lingered down to the present century, and appeared occasionally in quarters where it might not be expected, as, for instance, the following: " Every feeling of the heart rises in indignation against the unnatural deed, and seeks to hide it in that blaze of light which encircles the brilliant events of her reign. If heaven in this world ever interposes its avenging arm between guilt and happiness, may we not consider the loss of seventeen children as the peculiar penalty which it exacted from a mother who had broken the heart of the most indulgent father ? " This passage will be found in the Edinburgh Encyclopædia, conducted by David Brewster, LL.D., under the head " Anne " in the alphabetical arrangement.

The following passage is found in a quarter more congenial to such utterances: " Queen Mary II. and Anne, though apparently prospering in the sight of men, were not allowed to go unpunished by the just vengeance of God. Of Anne's seventeen children, not one survived to inherit the guilty parent's coronet."—The Descendants of the Stuarts : an Unchronicled Page in England's History, by William Townend (1858), p. 58.

the house of Hanover, has difficulty in realising the influence of one calamity treading on the heels of another; and how the "fear of change perplexing nations" drove statesmen, as well as those less highly endowed, to desperate or desponding conclusions. But if any of those who profess to penetrate and announce the secrets of omniscience were to argue from results, instead of classifying the calamities of the period as a judgment for sins and follies, it would be a more rational conclusion that they were administered in order that a great people might have the satisfaction of overcoming all, and of proving the flexibility as well as the strength of their political institutions.

With this death the fruits of the Revolution Settlement were lost, and its work had to be done over again. It stimulated the leaders of the party to rapid and decided action, that ominous events were reported from abroad. Louis XIV. had formally recognised the claim of the Pretender, and the quarrel that led to the war of the Spanish succession had broken forth. In a new settlement of the succession, the boy who had been sedulously trained at St Germains by monks and Jesuit fathers was not to be named, save in oath of abjuration and sentence of attainder. There was, then, a process unparalleled in any legislative assembly, alike for its boldness and the cold logic of its method,—an exhaustive analysis of the royal family in all its branches, until Parliament should reach the precise object it was in search of—a Protestant line. The promoters of this object determined to leave as little as possible to the intervention of accident. Since they were again to change the line of descent, let them do it securely, however far they went from home to achieve that object. It would not be securely achieved by offering the crown to any near relation of the Stewart family that would engage to live and die a Protestant. The monarchies of Europe were divided between Papal and Protestant dynasties; and it was in one of this latter, with its Protestant traditions of policy and alliances, that safety lay.

Next to the direct line were the descendants of Henrietta, the only daughter of Charles I. She was married to the King of Sardinia, and their descendants ramified through other Popish dynasties, including the royal families of France and Spain. It was necessary, therefore, to go a generation further back, and look to the descendants of King James, through his daughter Elizabeth, the unfortunate Queen of Bohemia. Of these, the first in order was the granddaughter of Elizabeth, married to the Duke of Orleans, and again running the search into the most dangerous of all quarters—the Popish and despotic monarchy of France, the "natural enemy" of Britain. Six other families of this line had to be passed over, until at last the analysis reached Sophia, Duchess of Hanover, a Protestant, the widow of a Protestant, whose son, also a Protestant, was forty years old, and a good soldier—a desirable recommendation to the destiny opened to him. Had no house properly qualified been found among the eight dynasties descending from the daughter of King James, the analysis must have gone back to the descendants of Henry VIII.

The momentous enactment creating the new dynasty is in these simple terms: " Be it enacted and declared by the King's most excellent Majesty, by and with the advice and consent of the Lords spiritual and temporal, and Commons, in this present Parliament assembled, and by the authority of the same, that the most excellent Princess Sophia, Electress and Duchess-Dowager of Hanover, daughter of the most excellent Princess Elizabeth, late Queen of Bohemia, daughter of our late sovereign lord King James the First, of happy memory, be and is hereby declared to be the next in succession, in the Protestant line, to the imperial crown and dignity of the said realms of England, France, and Ireland, with the dominions and territories thereunto belonging, after his Majesty and the Princess Anne of Denmark, and in default of issue of the said Princess Anne and of his Majesty respectively." [1] The clause is hidden among the many details of " An Act for the further limitation of the crown and better securing the rights and liberties of the subject," some of these being " rights and liberties " held to have been especially infringed by King William.

Few measures carry on the face of parliamentary record so little aspect of a party triumph, of a conflict and a victory. It was quietly passed as an inevitable affair of routine; and it was observed at the time that the Bill went through the usual stages in thin Houses. But all had been settled outside. Either it must pass as a matter of necessity, or it must be abandoned until a better opportunity came, probably as the result of a new revolution. To have opposed it would not have been merely the legitimate tactic

[1] 12 & 13 Will. III. c. 2.

of a usual parliamentary Opposition; it would have been a declaration of civil war.

Long after the crisis had passed away, there arose, even in the hearts of the devotees of divine right, a sense of legitimate security in the dynastic conditions of the throne. The conditions that superseded the Plantagenets by the Stewarts were certainly legitimate; but they were not satisfactory to Englishmen, who did not believe in "Father Fergus of a hundred kings," and could only carry the race of Stewart to the chief domestic officer of a sovereign of far inferior race to the Plantagenets—a sovereign whom, indeed, these claimed as a vassal. But the lustre of the Plantagenets had been tarnished by Elizabeth, whose mother was a commoner. Queen Anne brought the same blemish to the inferior race. Her mother, Anne Hyde, was respectable and respected. She had kept "the whiteness of her soul" under conditions that tripped others of far loftier birth. She was the Pamela of the palace—a lively instance of "virtue rewarded;" but this was no equivalent for the lustre of royal blood.[1]

[1] Such a union was not likely to be achieved in cloudless serenity; and indeed the storms it raised around the Court sadly disturbed the sunshine of the Restoration. Foul accusations were invented to blast the lady's fame, and had their oscillations of credit and utter contradiction. By a strange inversion of the conditions to be naturally anticipated, the charges got encouragement from her father; while her fair fame was upheld by the young King Charles, whose notoriety as a selfish voluptuary deserves to be lightened by this redeeming feature. The father's conduct was that of a man whose intellect is disordered by astounding revelations. For the calumnies, if they were true, "he would submit to the good pleasure of God. But if there were any reason to suspect the other"—that is, that his daughter was stainless and honestly married to the prince—he said to the Lords Ormond and Southampton, who had been sent by the king to soothe his irritation, "he was ready to give a positive judgment, in which he hoped their Lord-

The sovereign qualification was, however, restored
to the realm in its highest purity in the descendants
of the Guelphs, passing back through the house of
Este to connect themselves with some of the illustrious Roman Gentes. The new dynasty was, indeed,
by centuries, older in history even than the Plantagenets. It was natural to find that a race early renowned among the German potentates whom the
aggrandisement of Charlemagne incorporated with the
old Roman empire, could count an ancestry of credit
and renown more remote than the races of the North
seas, whose introduction to Central Europe was as
marauders, attracted by rapacity for the wealth accumulated through ages of civilisation.[1]

ships would concur with him, that the king should immediately cause
the woman to be sent to the Tower, and to be cast into a dungeon,
under so strict a guard that no person living should be permitted to
come to her ; and then that an Act of Parliament should be immediately passed for cutting off her head ; to which he would not only give
his consent, but would very willingly be the first man that should
propose it."—Life of Clarendon, i. 378, 379.

[1] We shall not easily find a more brilliant antithesis to the truth in
history than the doctrines about the Hanover succession, nourished—
and where that was safe, promulgated—by the Jacobites a hundred and
fifty years ago. They arose in pure sincerity—the growth of imperfect
methods in archæological inquiry and in the teaching of history. The
dignity of the Electorate was not palpable to those whose knowledge of
political institutions was limited to their own country, with a smatter-
ing from Greece, Rome, and perhaps France ; and it was a title very
open to depreciation. This process naturally culminated in Scotland,
through comparison with the illustrious race of Fergus. It found
expression in the mingled wailings and execrations of "the Jacobite
minstrelsy," where, in a sort of bathos of political comparison, it was
found at last safe to hold that the Elector of the Empire was something
akin to the Scots laird who held of the Crown : and once in the category of laird, the reduction to a humble grade of lairdship was simple
—as, for instance :—

> " Wha the deil hae we got for a king
>   But a wee, wee German lairdie?
> And whan we gaed tae bring him hame,
>   He was delving in his kail-yairdie."

The queen's relations on the mother's side neutral in politics by their position and opinions, her husband neutral by the limitation of his capacities, her children all gone, and those who looked to the heritage of her empire selected from among distant strangers, there was a peculiar isolation in her position ; and hence, perhaps, it befell that the queen's personal friends had far more influence on the destinies of her reign, than her husband or her nearest blood relations. If the pages that are to follow tell the accurate truth, this influence will be conspicuous in the tenor of our story. The growth of her friendships is touching in itself, as an effort to find something in the world dearer than greatness and power, and to enjoy a little of that simple life—so hard to be reached from the steps of the throne—where friends can confide their thoughts and aspirations to each other without their being trumpet - tongued by the unscrupulous parasites that haunt the steps of royalty. And if it was a weakness, it was grandly exercised— it gained for the recasting of Europe that one whose name is yet the greatest among warriors,—if we count in our estimate only those whose science and achievements we know with sufficient distinctness for comparison. It secured the greatest financial minister that ever ruled Britain ; and it was said—and apparently is true — that Marlborough, who had a powerful insight into character, would only undertake the command of the army if Godolphin were at the treasury to find and pay the money necessary for the effective support of the war. And yet, by the nation gaining both safety and glory through this, there was found in it the taint not only of royal

favour, but of "a family arrangement;" for the
lord high treasurer's son and heir was married to
the soldier's daughter and heiress, and it was in
Godolphin's line that the honours gained by
Marlborough were to last.

Every one who has glanced, however slightly, over
the history of this reign, becomes familiar with the
name and power of Marlborough's wife, the mighty
Duchess Sarah. The extent of the power held by
her in Court and Council is one of the points demanding caution in dealing with the history of the period.
It has many of the attractions of romance, creating a
tendency in the seekers of the picturesque to foster
it, till it becomes to the historical critic something
like what the gardener finds in some classes of plants
endowed with a rank prolificness that disturbs the
harmony of his distribution.[1]

[1] Take, for instance, the 'History of Great Britain from the Revolution in 1688 to the Accession of George I., translated from the Latin
Manuscript of Alexander Cunningham, Esq., Minister from George I.
to the Republic of Venice:' 2 vols. 4to (1787). Within the palace
the reign opens thus (i. 258) : "The queen, by the advice of Marlborough, who had now the chief direction of affairs, and made no difference between those who attended and those who did not, readily
excused all such persons as through excessive grief or regard to decency
did not appear that day at Court. From this circumstance men pre-
saged everything from the hands of the queen that was fair and honourable.

" In the first place, care was taken by public proclamation to order all
things to remain in the same state as they were in the time of the late
king. The queen commanded her magistrates and people to continue
in their duty as before, till such time as her Majesty should nominate
and appoint other magistrates, and give fresh directions for the government of the kingdom by her own authority. But within the palace itself
there was a very busy market of all offices of Government. For the
queen's relations being kept at a distance, all things were transacted by
the sole authority of one woman, to whom there was no access but by
the golden road ; and it was to no purpose for the Earl of Rochester to
set forth his own fidelity, duty, affection, and the rights of consanguin-

The best authority sets down that the marriage of
Colonel John Churchill with Sarah Jennings "must

ity." To the word "woman" the editor of the book appends in a note
"The Duchess of Marlborough." Then in the index, under the head of
Anne, he has, "Great influence the Duchess of Marlborough possessed
over her, i. 258." Then there is, "Marlborough, Duchess of, her
great influence over Queen Anne." Since so much meaning depends
on the words "one woman," it would have been desirable to see the
passage in the original Latin.

A sketch of the power of Sarah Jennings over the destinies of
Europe, by an eloquent French historian, may amuse us by its antagonism to our own associations with the character of the British constitution ; and yet in the historical facts referred to it is not easy to
deny that, as his countrymen say, the author has reason. The death
of King William is supposed to have made King Louis comfortable.
He was still girt for the great contest, were it necessary ; but he was
old, and preferred rest—and it seemed to have come. The Dutch, if not
backed by England, would be easily settled, and the emperor was too
poor to remain in the field without subsidies from England :—

"Mais la nouvelle Reine Anne étoit une femme foible et sans carac-
tère ; mariée au Prince George de Danemarck, homme plus insignificant encore. Elle se livroit toujours aveuglément à quelque confidente
qui acquéroit sur son esprit un absolu pouvoir. Elle étoit alors domi-
née par Sarah Jennings, femme de John Churchill, Comte de Marlborough, que Guillaume III. avoit, dès le premier juin précédent
nommé commandant en chef de toutes les forces dans les Provinces-
Unies, et son ambassadeur auprès des États Généraux. . . . La Reine
Anne le confirma dans les deux fonctions que lui avoient données son
beau-frère ; elle forma en même temps un ministère tout composé de
ses amis at à la tête du quelle elle plaça le grand Tresorier Lord Godolphin. Ainsi une intrigue de femmes donna à l'Angleterre son plus grand
général, et la plus haute gloire militaire a laquelle elle se fût encore
élevée."—Sismondi, Histoire des Français, xxvi. 328, 329.

Few women unambitious of renown in authorship have spoken to
the world through the printing-press so amply as Duchess Sarah has.
There is first the 'Account of her Conduct,' edited by Nathaniel
Hook in 1742, occasionally cited in these pages. In the same year
there were published 'A Review of a late Treatise entituled "An
Account,"' &c. ; 'A Continuation' of this Review ; 'A full Vindication of the Duchess-Dowager of Marlborough ;' and 'The other side of
the Question.' In 1744, 'Memoirs of Sarah Duchess of Marlborough ;'
and in 1745, 'The Life of the Duchess of Marlborough, with Remarks
upon her Will.' After the lapse of nearly a century there comes a
revival of interest demanding more of the same course of literature. In

have been in the beginning of 1678." [1] We must
assign to that period the rise of his favour with the
Princess Anne, for she and Sarah began their intimacy as playmates. Between Queen Mary and her
sister there was a strange and somewhat mysterious
quarrel—mysterious indeed, not from its secrecy, but
its odd publicity, making the reconciliation a State
affair. We find that Charles Hatton, on the 24th of
August 1693, writing in London, after telling the
"terrible news from Flanders," the battle of Steinkirk, the king wounded, and the Duke of Ormond
missing, goes on, "the great news is, the two great
sisters are reconciled, and my Lord Churchill hath—
as report saith—effected it; and that for his reward
he is to be declared General of the Forces. The
Princess of Denmark this day made her visit to her
sister. For joy of the reconciliation, the bells—which
have all this summer been very silent—ring very
merrily." [2]

Marlborough was more than fifty years old when
the curtain rose on the mighty theatre where he was
to be the chief actor. He had achieved a social reputation by his manly beauty and the charm of his

1838 we have in two portly volumes the ' Private Correspondence of
Sarah Duchess of Marlborough, illustrative of the Court and Times
of Queen Anne, with her Sketches and Opinions of her Contemporaries.' 'Memoirs of Sarah Duchess of Marlborough and of the Court
of Queen Anne,' by Mrs A. T. Thomson : 2 vols. 8vo (1839). ' Letters of Sarah Duchess of Marlborough, now first published from the
Original Manuscripts at Madresfield Court, with an Introduction : '
8vo (1875).

Perhaps as affluent in interest as the whole array of bulky volumes
here noted is one of minute dimension, edited in 1788 by Lord Hailes,
called ' The Opinions of Sarah Duchess of Marlborough, published
from Original Manuscripts.'

[1] Coxe, i. 11.   [2] Hatton Correspondence, ii. 195.

accomplishments. The great high priest of "the graces" bowed to him as one endowed with these crowning glories of human perfection.[1] There were stories abroad—more or less pungent, according to the genius of the narrator—of his having in his early days set his power of fascinating the female heart to purposes that would be counted discreditable to any young gentleman trained in a well-ordered home of the present day. Many difficulties impede any inquiry whether these are true or false, the chief difficulty being that in their day such accusations lay so lightly on a courtier's character that there would have been a puritanical pedantry in seriously contradicting them. The prevalence of the same spirit must, if they be true, furnish a palliation for them; and we must make allowance for a youth trained in the profligate Court of Charles II., as we make allowance for the young criminal trained in the rookeries of thieves and prostitutes. When the victim of such training

---

[1] Chesterfield handed down to posterity his judgment that Marlborough "possessed the graces in the highest degree — not to say engrossed them." "He had no brightness, nothing shining in his genius. He had most undoubtedly an excellent, plain understanding, and sound judgment; but these qualities would probably have never raised him higher than they found him, which was page to James II.'s queen. But then the graces protected and promoted him." The graces were Chesterfield's stock in trade, made in his own manufactory, where the pure, nude, raw material of the Grecian "Charites" was, by aid of paste, pomatum, powder, and lace, converted into the person presentable to good society. Chesterfield's judgments may therefore be taken as the trader's exaggerated estimate of his own article. The same kind of estimate was much better expressed by Hoby, the illustrious London bootmaker, when he attributed the successful career of the Duke of Wellington to the sound appreciation that prompted him always to wear "Hoby's boots." The exquisite fitting of these had no doubt an influence in relieving the mind from disturbance by uneasy sensations in the body.

shakes off its slough, and comes into the honest light
of day, making himself a good citizen by the force of
his own character, he justly earns the applause of
men; and this should not be denied to one shaking
off degradations, though these had polluted a higher
sphere of life. Marlborough was a faithful husband,
and dearly loved his beautiful wife, who had now
been his own for twenty-five years. She was the only
earthly being who affected him with anything of the
nature of fear. It was not such as in her fits of
furious passion she scattered around her in her sovereign's Court. It arose out of that deep sense of
thankfulness in believing himself to be the sole occupant of her ardent heart: and it was a belief tinged
with the misgivings arising in the very preciousness
of a blessing lest it might some time be lost—lest
fervid love might cool into indifference; and in that
cynical and mocking circle where their early wedded
life was spent, indifference was in good taste, and was
a trifle among the casualties that might befall the
husband of a beautiful wife. If one feels an inward
satisfaction in following and recording so grand a
career as that of Marlborough in the reign of Queen
Anne, it is also a satisfaction not to be responsible
for an investigation and final estimate of his conduct throughout the twelve previous years. It seems
lawful, however, to remark, that his bitterest accusers
have drawn on old principles of personal fidelity not
applicable to a large body of the statesmen of the
period. King William himself signally exempted
him from the application of this rule of political
ethics by appointing him to two offices of transcen-
dent trust—the one where the destinies of Europe

were in his keeping as the representative of Britain in the Grand Alliance, the other as governor and tutor to the child who was heir to the throne.

With legitimists such as the old Jacobites—if we have any such among us—the revolutionist is condemned by his one act. He cannot make himself worse as an "apostate from his own vile creed "— nay, he may have some claim to be credited with penitence. The legitimist is bound to the absolute laws of an exact creed : the revolutionist claims freedom of choice ; and if he has made a mistake in one selection, he may try another. But it is one of the calamitous results, that must always make grave men pause on the border of political convulsions, that a revolution takes generations for its firm completion. It is pleasant to be relieved of the responsibility of testing the evidence for the charge against the young officer of having revealed to the Jacobites the expedition against Brest in 1694, and hence causing the fatal slaughter of many of his companions in arms at the Bay of Camaret. It would be an endless element of confusion in political morality were we to burden the consciences of statesmen and soldiers with the blood that their conduct may have drawn ; but of this difficulty we are relieved by the knowledge that many others had given intimation of the intended descent, and among them Godolphin.

Regarding Marlborough's political conduct and warlike career we have throughout abundant information. We see, also, what he was as a husband and a father ; but we have scarcely any admission to him in his social circle. In this very silence, indistinctly broken by such vague generalities as Chesterfield affords to

us, there is a sort of silent hint that he was not one
who bore his "heart upon his sleeve." Evelyn says
of him that " he is a very handsome person, well-
spoken and affable, and supports his want of acquired
knowledge by keeping good company." [1] But the
genial discourser on sylvan life and beauty gives us
something infinitely more valuable in a brief note of
a casual meeting with the rising warrior. On the
9th of February 1705, after noting his eightieth
birthday, he says : " I went to wait on my Lord
Treasurer. There was the victorious Duke of Marlborough, who came to me and took me by the hand
with extraordinary familiarity and civility, as for-
merly he was used to do, without any alteration of
his good-nature. He had a most rich George in a
sardonyx set with diamonds of very great value :
for the rest very plain. I had not seen him for some
years, and believed he might have forgotten me." [2]

Between Marlborough and Sidney Godolphin there
had been at the commencement of the reign a long and
close intimacy. In the year 1698 they became allied
by marriage—Francis, the only son of Godolphin,
taking to his wife the Lady Henrietta Churchill.
The event is significant, as carrying evidence of the
interest taken in it by the Princess Anne. She
desired to endow the young couple with a gift of
ten thousand pounds ; and we are told that " the
Countess of Marlborough would not, however, accept
more than five thousand, though the establishment of
the young couple was ill adapted to their rank." [3]

If to these domestic adjustments we are to attri-
bute Godolphin's career as a statesman, we are in-

---

[1] Memoirs, ii. 78.   [2] Ibid. 84.   [3] Coxe, chap. vii.

debted to them for the greatest master of finance and pecuniary economy that ever held rule in Britain. He was attached to the Treasury in the reign of Charles II., and there he found the true sphere for his genius. He brought much scandal on himself by his active co-operation in drawing the subsidy from France; and it could be no vindication of the political baseness of that affair, that he loved the national treasury as a miser loves his hoard, and might not too scrupulously examine the sources whence it was fed. He was not—according to the practice that had become usual, and is now a fixed principle of the constitution—placed at the head of a commission as First Lord. To give power and dignity to his position, the old State office of Lord Treasurer was resumed. He did not repose on his dignity, but was eminently a hard worker—never letting the most trifling item of expenditure pass unexamined if it involved a principle or opened a novel source of expense.[1]

[1] Whoever desires to study with minuteness Godolphin's practice at the Treasury, will find abundant materials for his purpose in the two volumes containing the 'Calendar of Treasury Papers' from 1697 to 1707, contributed by Mr Joseph Reddington to the collection issued by the Master of the Rolls. Marlborough's name is of frequent occurrence, but anything connecting it with undue favour will be looked for in vain. He may possibly, on the other hand, find evidence that the mighty influence of Marlborough was not strong enough to break through a Treasury rule. The "Cardonnel" who appears in the following was Marlborough's secretary and close personal friend: "A Petition of James Cardonnel to the Lord High Treasurer." He had purchased the place of Court Post from William Van Hulse, Esq., which he desired to resign in favour of Henry Andrews, Esq., son of Sir Matthew Andrews, praying that a patent might pass from the same. There is also a memorandum reminding his lordship that the Duke of Marlborough had prayed his lordship's favour to do the same. "*Minuted*, 14th August 1704. My Lord Treasurer conceives there is intended to be a pecuniary consideration for the parting with this

It is usual to speak of Godolphin as a heavy-built,
lumbering, phlegmatic man, in intellect an exception
to the abounding wit and versatility of the statesmen
of Queen Anne's day.   There is an unlucky tendency
to promote this opinion in the one portrait whence
his aspect is generally known.   It is engraved by
Houbraken from a painting by Kneller, and being
one among the "heads of illustrious persons" published by Birch, it has been the natural source whence
engravers of historical portraits have taken their
ideas of the Lord Treasurer.   It certainly has an
aspect of the pompous solemnity unbrightened by
intellect that is popularly supposed to be the attendant of corporate eminence ; and this tone is enhanced
by his holding the mystic symbol of his office—the
Treasurer's white wand.   The form and expression of
his countenance seem to be more distinctly marked
for us in marble among the monuments of Westminster Abbey.   Stone is not so apt as canvas to
give us the niceties of expression ; yet here there is a
decided tone of high breeding—or, as it is otherwise
expressed, of blood and culture.   The uneuphonious
name of Godolphin has been traced by etymological genealogists to certain words of Celtic origin
signifying a white eagle.   The association of this
derivation with the grave Lord Treasurer makes a

place ; and her Majesty has made an order that no place shall be sold."
—Calendar of Treasury Papers, p. 289.

   On 7th March 1706 there is issued a "warrant of the Chamberlain of
the Household to John Charletin, Master of her Majesty's Jewel Office,
for the supply of a new silver trumpet to Mr John Seignier, trumpeter
to the third troop of Guards, who was appointed to attend on the Duke
of Marlborough abroad this campaign." This bears an indorsement
testifying to the minute scrutiny of Godolphin : "Query, what's become of the old one ?"—Ibid., p. 422.

ludicrous antithesis, since its appropriate application
would be to some vaunting Roderick Dhu or ferocious
Irish chieftain.

As the communion between the Queen and the
Duchess was to be absolutely free by disentanglement
from all courtesies of etiquette, it was decided that
this could be best accomplished by the use of fictitious
names, expressive of the equality of the untitled—the
Queen to be Mrs Morley and the duchess Mrs Free-
man. If by an act of her royal will the queen decreed
this plan of masquerade, she effectually abolished the
etiquettes of precedence without leaving an excuse
for insolence. We thus understand what was uttered
to the Duchess at a time when Marlborough threatened
to resign his command : " As for your poor unfortunate Morley, she could not bear it : for if ever you
should forsake me, I should have nothing more to
do with the world, but make another abdication; for
where is a crown when the support of it is gone ? "
And here there is a faint touch tending again to re-
kindle compassion for a lonely heart striving after
morsels of comfort. " Unfortunate Morley " was a
name she took in her little cabinet of intimates ever
after the death of her son.[1]

---

[1] Here is a short but pungent letter written by the queen at a point
of time between her father's death and her own accession. It affords
an example of the familiar intercourse of the four :—

For the Lord Godolphin.

" WINDSOR, Tuesday night.

" I can not lett your servant goe back without returning my thanks
for the letter he brought me, & assureing you it is a very great satisfaction to me to find you agree wth Mrs Morley conserning y[e] ill-
natured, cruel proceedings of Mr Caliban, w[ch] vexes me more then you
can emagin, & I am out of all patience when I think I must do soe

As it had been arranged, so the august ceremony of the coronation was observed on the 1st of April; and London for a day doffed its sombre neutral colours, and blazed forth in a more than oriental splendour—for however it might suit their tastes or desires, no Eastern despots had wealth enough to marshal before the world the glories of an English coronation. The brilliancy was enhanced by the vivid power of the national colour—the red. As the family livery of the Court, it had become the prevailing uniform of the army. Here it was seen in full bloom; for it was the etiquette of the coronation that the clothing of all partaking in it should be new, as casting off the past with all its mournful associations, and adopting the joyous present. The Household troops, drawn up in new scarlet uniforms, had the chief share in the predominant colour; but either in scarlet or crimson, it was distributed among high officers of law and State, among corporate officers, and even among the clergy. But the most gorgeous and attractive of colours may become oppressive by unvaried uniformity; so, in the feminine element, there was relief in a party-colouring of rich costumes, and the host of lackeys and other subordinates offered an ample variety of gaudy hues.

There were historical conditions, indeed, that gave oriental traditions to all this exceptional gorgeousness. The anointing, the orb, the crown, the ring,

monsterous a thing as not to put my lodgings in mourning for my father. I hope if you get a coppy of ye will Ld Manchester says he will send over, you will be soe kind as to let me see it, & ever believe me your faithful servant."—Mus. Brit., Addl. MSS.

The "Princess Anne" among her familiars called King William "The Monster, Caliban, Dutch Abortion."—Coxe, Marlb., i. 48.

and other mystic symbols, are believed to have been of oriental origin, and assumed by the emperors of the Eastern empire as suited, by their conformity with traditions of royalty and supremacy, to secure the reverence of the oriental natures. They tend to symbolise not so much the sovereignty of a limited territory, as the supremacy over all the world arrogated by the Cæsars. In their transference northwards they became mixed with homely Gothic customs and ceremonies, many of them being whimsical symbols or tenders of homage for the enjoyment of lands, dignities, or offices; and it had become the general tenor of the disposal of the symbols, that instead of being rendered as a gift or sacrifice by the person tendering, they were bought at the public cost and allowed to remain in the possession of that person. Thus the chief butler obtained a gold cup and cover, with the wine remaining "below the bar." The Lord Mayor of London tendering a cup of wine to the sovereign at the coronation-feast obtained the gold cup it was served in, and the Mayor of Oxford received in somewhat the same manner a gilt cup. The office of napier being attached to a manor held in grand sergeantry by a noble house, it was the custom for the holder when he had done his office and the feast was over to take possession of the table-cloths and other linen; and he must have found it a better prize than the holder of the manor of Heydon, who, having to hold the basin, ewer, and towel for the royal hand-washing, got possession only of the towel. The pomps and ceremonies of the Court were not congenial with the powers predominant in the middle of the seven-

teenth century. In June 1643, "on a motion in the
Commons that the Dean, Sub-Dean, and Prebend of
Westminster Abbey should be required to deliver up
the keys of the treasury there where the regalia
were kept, that the place might be searched and a
report of it made to the House,"—on a question
whether in the case of refusal to render up the keys
the repositories should be broken open, it was carried
by a majority of one—42 to 41—"for breaking open
the doors." [1]

The genial task of giving effect to this resolution
seems to have been assigned to the terrible Henry
Martin ; and he, being a man addicted to grotesque
ribaldry, crowned and enrobed George Tuthers, the
doggerel poet, who " did march about the room with
a stately garb; and afterwards, with a thousand apish
and ridiculous actions, exposed those sacred ornaments to contempt and laughter." [2] The exact fate
of the regalia is not on record, but we know that
all disappeared except the coronation-chair. That,
enclosing the stone of destiny like a fossil, was a
peculiarly ponderous piece of furniture; and for all its
affluence in picturesque traditions, it was of little
available value.

The dispersal of the other symbolic treasures of
the crown is proved by the arrangements for replac-
ing them for the coronation of Charles II., with the
aid of a committee of persons presumed to be experts
in the archæology of such symbols. We are told by
him who took the foremost place in this work :—

" And because, through the rapine of the late unhappy

[1] Parl. Hist., iii. 118.   [2] Wood. Ath. Oxon.

times, all the royal ornaments and regalia heretofore preserved from age to age in the treasury of the Church of
Westminster, were taken away, sold, and destroyed, the
committee met divers times, not only to direct the remaking
such royal ornaments and regalia, but even to settle the form
and fashion of each particular; all which do now retain the
old names and fashion, although they have been newly made
and prepared by orders given to the Earl of Sandwich, Master
of the Great Wardrobe, and Sir Gilbert Talbot, Knight Master
of the Jewel-house.

"Thereupon the Master of the Jewel-house had order to
provide two imperial crowns, set with precious stones—the
one to be called St Edward's crown, wherewith the king was
to be crowned, and the other to be put on after his coronation, before his Majesty's return to Westminster Hall.
Also, an orb of gold with a cross set with precious stones;
a sceptre with a cross set with precious stones, called St
Edwards; a sceptre with a dove set with precious stones;
a long sceptre or staff of gold, with a cross at the top, and a
pike at the foot of steel, called St Edward's staff; a ring
with a ruby; a chalise or paten of gold; an ampul for the
oil, and a spoon.

"The Master of the Great Wardrobe had also to prepare
new robes of State, for the old had disappeared." [1]

The regalia of England are in a style of decorative
art common to the period of Charles II. Perhaps it
might have been better had the ancient symbols been
reproduced in absolute facsimile. But in the impossibility of accomplishing this, it is well that it
was not attempted. The age was signally deficient
in a minute knowledge of archæology, while it was
proficient in the various forms of decorative art;

[1] "A circumstantial account of the preparations for the coronation
of his Majesty King Charles the Second, from an original manuscript
by Sir Edward Walker, Knight Garter, principal King-at-Arms at that
period: 1820."

and the regalia of England are a fine example of this proficiency.

Though thus aided by restored symbols, the coronation of Charles II. was still deficient in some of the old-established ceremonies. His brother James, however, set himself to restore them all, and made a thorough investigation through the survivors of those who had assisted at the coronation of his father, and persons learned in Court etiquette. He was sorely disturbed in spirit by the religious character of the ordeal through which he must pass if he would reign in England. It was not only that he had to take the oath to protect the religion by law established— being that of Protestant Episcopacy—but the sacred symbols of anointing and investiture, that had been of old performed by holy priests, would be performed on him by the hands of a heretic calling himself Archbishop of Canterbury. Order would readily be taken at the Vatican that no such trifle should stop a true son of the Church on the steps of the throne of England; and it is supposed that he had secretly procured a papal dispensation as an antidote to the pollution he was to endure. But perhaps it was with the view of strengthening the antidote that he thought it desirable to restore the ceremonials that had been practised under Catholic unity. He managed—it does not exactly appear how—to obtain one exemption in his own favour; he evaded the Communion, and so escaped desecration through the misconsecrated elements.

Of old it had been the practice for the sovereign to sleep in the Tower on the night before the coronation; and the procession thence to Westminster Hall swept nearly from the east end of London to the west. In the days of the Roses and the Barons wars, possession of the Tower was a practical symbol of monarchy, more significant than all the symbolic machinery of the coronation. Further, it made a great part of the ceremony of the coronation a city affair; and where the position of a new monarch was dangerous or doubtful, and influential bodies had to be propitiated, the corporate authorities of London were of mighty avail. The coronation procession then passed through all the long intervening line of street. At the coronation of James I. the procession was evaded, because eastern London was assailed by the plague. The fears of a similar dispensation impeded the restoration of the long march when his son Charles was crowned. The significancy and interest of the procession had died out; and as it was not convenient, so it seemed unnecessary that it should be undertaken by Queen Anne.

All the elements of the old procession were preserved, but it merely wound from Westminster Hall into Westminster Abbey. The several groups had to be marshalled in the inverse order of Court precedence, the most insignificant taking precedence of all, and each expanding in dignity until the climax of royalty was reached. This is the necessary law of such a solemnity. The spectators are gradually lifted up to behold passing before them the several grades, up to the highest in the land; and then, when the sovereign is beheld, there is nothing more to feast the eye. If the order were that of Court precedence, the whole significance of the affair would be over with its first appearance. The first group, then, that emerged before the assembled crowd was "the queen's herb-woman, with her six mades," all attired like Dresden shepherdesses. Their function was to strew the path of those who followed with flowers. The next was the beadle of Westminster, and the high constable of the same. Then came animation into the scene by a long array of drummers, fifers, and trumpeters. The first group endowed with official consequence presented the six clerks of Chancery. Legal station expanded till it reached the Bench; and then came the Church, from the assistants in the chapel royal to the Dean of Westminster. The peerage began with the barons and bishops; and each peer and peeress carried a coronet, usually made for the occasion. The last, and of course highest, in the peerage were a curious relic of the old Continental domains of the Plan-tagenets—"two persons to represent the Dukes of Aquitain and Normandy, in crimson velvet mantles lined with miniver, powdered with ermine, each of them his cap in his hand, of cloth-of-gold, furred and powdered with ermine." Where princes of the blood might have been, Prince George of Denmark marched, "his train borne by his master of the robes;" and it was noted that both here and in the homages and other etiquettes within the Abbey, he was treated simply as the most illustrious subject of the queen. It was further noted that all was studiously arranged to let him know that the husband of Queen Anne was not to become what the husband of her sister had been. After dignities were exhausted, came perhaps the most significant feature in the august ceremonial—the procession of those who bore the symbols devoted to the occasion—the bearers of the golden spurs, Prince Edward's staff, the various State swords and sceptres, the crown, the chalice, the Bible, the orb, and the paten. Then came "the canopy, borne by sixteen barons of the Cinque Ports, over the queen, attended by gentlemen pensioners; the queen in her royal robes of crimson velvet furred with ermine and bordered with gold lace, on her head a circlet of gold, wearing the great collar and George, her train borne by a duchess in her robes, assisted by four ladies and the queen's lord-chamberlain—supporters the Lord Bishop of Durham and the Lord Bishop of Bath and Wells."

The infirmities of the queen rendered even the short walk from the Hall undesirable; and "she had the conveniency to be carried in a low open chair." The ceremony of the train-bearing was not thus defeated, a length of cloth being thrown out behind the chair, and carried by the noble ladies who did duty as train-bearers. Parliament being in session, the number thus entering the Abbey was increased by the members of the House of Commons. Within the church—the queen standing on "the theatre," or raised stage where the throne was placed—the first act was "the recognition." In this the queen turned her face four times to the assemblage—to the east, south, west, and north successively, the archbishop in each direction proclaiming, "Sirs, I here present to you Queen Anne, undoubted queen of this realm, whereof all you that are come this day to do your homages and service,—are you willing to do the same?" The response, "God save Queen Anne!" was uttered with a mighty shout throughout the echoing arches, followed by a blast of trumpets, and this by the choir singing the anthem, "The queen shall rejoice in Thy strength, O Lord; exceeding glad shall she be of Thy salvation." All the choral elements in the service of the Church of England contributed on the occasion to a musical festival that had been enriched from time to time by such artists as Purcell, Blow, Child, Lawes, and Turner ; it had not yet received the touch of the mighty Handel. In performance it had its chief character from the voices of the well-trained choir of the chapel royal. The text traditional to Christian religious services was remembered—"Thou shalt not appear before the Lord thy God empty;" and the queen made oblations in old customary forms, one of them being a weighty ingot of gold.

The sermon was preached by John Sharp, Archbishop of York, on the text from Isaiah, "Kings shall be thy nursing fathers, and their queens thy nursing mothers." He began thus: "I am aware how much time the following solemnity will take up; and therefore I mean to give as little interruption to it as possible, being very sensible that the shortness of my sermon will be the best recommendation of it." The hopes thus raised were fulfilled; for the reading of what stands in print would hardly require ten minutes : and yet it is a very full though concise precept on the reciprocal duties of sovereign and people in a constitutional kingdom. The sermon was followed by two transactions more significant and solemn than State ceremonies—the parliamentary test and the coronation oath. These sanctions were among the many items of legislation ingenuously designed for keeping King James and his son from the throne; and it was at the accession of his daughter Anne that they became a feature in the ceremony of the coronation. It may be proper to repeat them at large. The words of the " Test," otherwise called " the Declaration," are : " I do solemnly and sincerely, in the presence of God, profess, testify, and declare that I do believe that in the sacrament of the Lord's Supper there is not any transubstantiation of the elements of bread and wine into the body and blood of Christ at or after the consecration thereof by any person whatsoever; and that the invocation or adoration of the Virgin Mary or any other saint, and that the sacrifice of the Mass— as they are now used in the Church of Rome—are superstitious and idolatrous. And I do solemnly, in the presence of God, profess, testify, and declare that I do make this declaration, and every part thereof, in the plain and ordinary sense of the words read unto me, as they are commonly understood by English Protestants, without any evasive equivocation, or mental reservation whatsoever, and without any dispensation already granted me for this purpose by the Pope, or any other authority or person whatsoever, or without any hope of any such dispensation from any person or authority whatsoever, or without thinking that I am or may be acquitted before God or man, or absolved of this declaration, or any part thereof, although the Pope, or any other person or persons or power whatsoever, should dispense with or annul the same, or declare that it was null and void from the beginning." [1]

---

[1] The Declaration is not easily found in the statute-book. It is set forth in an Act of the year 1677, 30 Charles II., chap. i., called " An Act for more effectually preserving the King's Person and Government

The coronation oath was established by statute immediately after the Revolution. In the preamble that the oath administered at the coronation "hath heretofore been framed in doubtful words and expressions, with relation to ancient laws and constitutions at this time unknown," assent is required to the following propositions :—

" Will you solemnly promise to govern the people of this kingdom of England and the dominions thereto belonging according to the statutes in Parliament agreed on, and the laws and customs of the same ?

" Will you, to your power, cause law and justice in mercy to be executed in all your judgments ?

" Will you, to the utmost of your power, maintain the laws of God, the true profession of the Gospel, and Protestant reformed religion established by law ? And will you preserve unto the bishops and clergy of this realm, and to the churches committed to their charge, all such rights and privileges as by law do or shall appertain unto them or any of them ?" [1]

These obligations by the sovereign to her subjects —the counter-equivalent of the oaths of allegiance taken by the subject as holding public office, or under other specified conditions—might be out of harmony with the divine-right doctrines of half a century earlier; but they were in accordance with the old notions of the coronation as an occasion when the rights and obligations of both the high contracting parties were adjusted and sworn to.

by disabling Papists from sitting in either House of Parliament." It was imposed on the sovereigns succeeding William and Mary by the " Act declaring the Rights and Liberties of the Subject, and settling the Succession of the Crown."—1 William & Mary, chap. 36.

[1] 1 William & Mary, chap. 6.

These important preliminaries being completed, the queen "in King Edward's chair, placed in the middle of the area before the altar, was anointed, and presented with the spurs, and girt with the sword, and vested with her purple robes; and having received the ring, the orb, and sceptre," homages and established courtesies followed, with the Communion taken by the queen,—of course according to the Church of England. It was remembered that, as we have seen, her father had evaded this rite, offensive to himself; but he had been unable to substitute anything for it that might have been offensive to others. Lastly, the queen "being vested in her robe of purple velvet," the procession was recast for its return, in the original order, to the Hall, the queen "wearing her crown of State, and the peers and peeresses and kings-of-arms their coronets." In the final benediction, after the crowning was completed, among the blessed destinies besought for the new queen there was one that, if it raised gloomy associations in the crowd rendering the responsive "Amen," must have shot a pang to the heart of the poor queen. It was in these words: "The Lord preserve your life and establish your throne, that your reign may be prosperous and your days many; that you may live long in this world, obeyed and honoured and beloved by all your people; ever increasing in favour both with God and man; and have a numerous posterity to rule these kingdoms after you by succession in all ages." Perhaps few were present who would not have felt relief in the omission of the last specific item in the blessing; but it was one of the unhappy

alternatives where the omission only aggravates the
significance of what is omitted.

That great English institution, the dinner, was not
neglected.   It was in busy preparation in the Hall
during the absence of the company in the Abbey.   The
House of Commons made no fixed, invariable element
in the coronation : but as they were present they
must, like casual guests, be hospitably entertained ;
so they were accommodated with a separate table in
the Exchequer.   It was an item of scant hospitality
that the sovereign's hereditary champion could not
join the other high officers of the Crown at the social
board, being engaged on duty, and that duty was the
one element of discordant tenor exceptional to the
occasion.   It must have been under some obdurate
traditional usage that while the sovereign and her
guests sat at meat, and in their presence, the champion should throw down his gauntlet of defiance.
"Just before the second course, Charles Dymoke,
Esq., her Majesty's champion, in complete armour,
between the lord high constable and earl marshal
.   .   .   performed the challenge ; after which the
kings-of-arms and heralds proclaimed her Majesty's
style in Latin, French, and English."

Whether, even to many of those seated at table,
the great festival afforded the feeling of ease and
satisfaction, the cordial frankness, of English hospitality, there were, besides the champion and the
heralds, others of various social grades, on whom lay
the weight of duties of a servile and domestic character, yet burdened with tragic traditions of times
and places wherein sovereigns ate and drank in dread
of poison.   "The lord the server, with the lord his

assistant, went to the dresser of the kitchen, where the master of the horse to her Majesty, as sergeant of the silver scullery, called for a dish of meat, wiped the bottom of the dish, and likewise the cover within and without, took assay of that dish, and covered it; then delivered that dish, and the rest of the hot meat, to gentlemen pensioners, who carried it to the queen's table in manner following: first, two clerks comptrollers in velvet gowns, two clerks of the green cloth in the same habit, the master of the household, the cofferer of the household, six sergeants-at-arms with their maces—two abreast."

Follows another group thus: "Three great officers in their robes of estate on horseback—viz., the earl marshal of England, the lord high steward of England, the lord high constable of England; six sergeants-of-arms more, with their maces; the comptroller of her Majesty's household, with his white staff; the treasurer of her Majesty's household, with his white staff; the queen's server.

"Then the dishes of hot meat were carried up by the gentlemen pensioners, bareheaded, and placed on the table by the lord carver, with the help of the lord the server and his assistant.

"Then the mess of dillygrout was brought up to the queen's table by Mr Leigh, in right of his claim as lord of the manor of Addington, in Surrey, who was knighted that day."[1]

---

[1] Authorities. An Account of the Ceremonies observed in the Coronations of the Kings and Queens of England: 1760—4to. The History of the Reign of Queen Anne digested into Annals, vol. i. p. 25 *et seq.* The Round Table—the order and solemnities of the Crowning the King and the Dignities of his Peerage: 1820—8vo. Collections relative to claims at the Coronations of several of the Kings of England,

The whole came to an end at eight o'clock in the evening, when the queen retired to St James's, no doubt heartily tired.   That night all London blazed with bonfires and illuminations, amid ringing of bells and the cheering of enthusiastic crowds.   It was observed that as an occasion of public rejoicing and a token of cordial popular acceptance, this coronation ceremony was a contrast to both the two coronations best remembered,—that of the queen's father, and of her sister; and yet there was so little of harmony in the conditions rendering these unpopular, that each was more antagonistic to the other than the spirit of Queen Anne's coronation was to either of them.

Before passing from the Court and the personal character and position of the sovereign, it may be in harmony to deal with an early and characteristic instance of the queen's religious prepossessions—the devotion of the first-fruits and tenths of benefices to the augmentation of small livings.   The history of the fund thus applied is briefly this: To secure for the Vatican out of the incomes of the clergy, the whole

---

beginning with King Richard II.   A Key to the Regalia; or, the Emblematic Design of the various forms observed in the Ceremonial of a Coronation, by the Rev. Jonas Dennis: 1820.   A Faithful Account of the Processions and Ceremonies observed in the Coronation of the Kings and Queens of England, &c., edited by Richard Thomson: 1820. Chapters on Coronations: 1838.   Regal Records; or, a Chronicle of the Coronations of the Queens Regnant of England, by J. R. Planché: 1838.

One is surprised by the light cost of so much splendour.   The estimate was about £10,000; "but there being several tradesmen in the office, put in by Lord Preston, who had great sums due to them, and had put down the prices higher, they were discontinued, and it then amounted to £7439, 8s. 5¼d."—Calendar of Treasury Papers, vol. lxxix., No. 100.   One sees the economising hand of Godolphin in this.

amount for the first year of the possession of a bene-
fice, and the tenth part for the other years, was one
of the papal claims not always effectively exacted.
At the Reformation it was transferred to the Crown,
and thenceforth rigidly exacted.   A bill came to the
Commons, with a special message from the queen,
and her strong interest in the matter is evidently the
source of a certain rhetorical character in the preamble
of the Act : " Whereas a sufficient settled provision for
the clergy, in many parts of this realm, hath never
yet been made, by reason whereof divers mean and
stipendiary preachers are in many places entertained
to serve the cures and officiate there, who depending
for their necessary maintenance on the goodwill and
liking of their hearers, have been and are thereby
under temptation of too much complying and suiting
their doctrines and teaching to the humours rather
than the good of their hearers, which hath been a
great occasion of faction and schism and contempt
of the ministry.—And forasmuch as your Majesty,
taking into your princely and serious consideration
the mean and insufficient maintenance belonging to
the clergy in divers parts of this your kingdom, has
been most graciously pleased out of your most religious and tender concern for the Church of England
—whereof your Majesty is the only supreme head on
earth—and for the poor clergy thereof—not only to
remit the arrears of your tenths due from your poor
clergy, but also to declare unto your most dutiful and
loyal Commons your royal pleasure and pious desire
that the whole revenue arising from the first-fruits
and tenths of the clergy might be settled for a perpetual augmentation of the maintenance of the said

clergy in places where the same is not already sufficiently provided for;" that mysterious entity of the
English constitution—a corporation—was created by
the statute for giving effect to its object. The statute
of mortmain, prohibiting perpetual alienations of
estates for ecclesiastical purposes, was repealed to the
extent of legalising such alienations when made to
the corporation.[1]

The Act of Henry VIII., vesting the fund in the
Crown, provided that a royal commission should be
issued "from time to time to search for the just
and true value of the said first-fruits and bene-
ficies," and so of the tenths. The suspension of this
statute was part of the reaction towards the Church
of Rome in the reign of Henry's daughter Mary.
The revival of the Act under her sister Elizabeth
was accompanied by a special "search for the just
and true value." And the statute for the occasion
proclaims that the ascertained value was justly answered and paid by "the prelates and clergy of the
realm to the great aid, relief, and supportation of the
inestimable charges of the Crown." But the injunction in the Act to make valuations from time to
time dropped out of sight, and the valuation was
never repeated. Hence the valuation stood in 1703
as it had been made in the reign of Elizabeth. There
was not only no such revision under the Act of Anne,
but a few casual words were dropped into it that effectually precluded such a revision. A section of the
Act relieving the clergy from a complex multiplicity
of bonds for the payment of their allotments, pro-
vides that "from and after the 25th day of March in

[1] 2 & 3 Anne. ch. 11.

the year of our Lord 1704, one bond only shall in
such case be given or required for the four payments
of the said first-fruits, which said first-fruits, as well
as the tenths payable by the clergy, shall hereafter be
answered and paid by them according to such rates
and proportions only as the same have heretofore
been rated and paid."

It has been remarked that in consequence of this
clause, " as the old and insufficient rate of payment
was fixed and made perpetual, the most religious
queen went to her grave without seeing any effect
from her bounty ; as, in consequence of the encum-
brances upon the fund, and the impossibility of increasing its produce, it was not till 1714 that the
governors of the bounty were able to make their first
grants."[1]

And when there came a fund to be allotted it did
not help the humble working clergy.   The small-
ness of the revenue of the charge was the criterion,
without bringing in to the calculation the amount
of duty to be performed, or asking whether any
duty was rendered for the humble revenue drawn.
As part of the result, it is noted that " the governors go on therefore increasing the incomes of two
small livings, in order to make each of them capable
of supporting a resident clergyman, while after as
well as before the augmentation, one incumbent may
hold them together, reside in neither, and allow
only a small part of the accumulated income to a
curate who performs the duties of both."[2]

The Church of England has not often been justly
subject to a charge of excessive zeal.   It has had its

[1] Edinburgh Review, Feb. 1823, xxxviii. 152.   [2] Ibid., 157.

zealots—High Church and ritualism on the one side, Low Church and evangelicism on the other. But these have been elements tending rather to modify than exasperate the collective ardour of the Church at large. Of all the great religious communities it is, take it for all in all, the one that has least attraction to the fanatic, and affords him least satisfaction when he gets within it. Yet the zeal of Queen Anne for the Church of England at large amounted to something like fanaticism, and exercised a powerful influence in the protection of the Protestant succession. The simple power of such fanaticisms, when it does not happen that they are accompanied with other symptoms of a powerful nature—as they were, for instance, in Cromwell—is a political force not perhaps sufficiently admitted in all histories. It at once converts the weakest into the strongest nature. It overcomes all overcomable opposition and fights with fate itself.

The following statement by the Duchess of Marlborough is important in its reference to the conduct of the queen at the commencement of her reign ; but it has had the effect of leaving a false impression of her political creed.

"Hitherto my favour with her Royal Highness, though it had sometimes furnished matter of conversation to the public, had been of no moment to the affairs of the nation, she herself having no share in the councils by which they were managed. But from this time I began to be looked upon as a person of consequence, without whose approbation at least neither places, nor pensions, nor honours, were bestowed by the Crown. The intimate friendship with

which the queen was known to honour me afforded
a plausible foundation for this opinion ; and I believe,
therefore, it will be a surprise to many to be told
that the first important step which her Majesty took
after her accession to the government, was against
my wishes and inclinations I mean." Here she
refers to the appointment to office of Normanby,
better known as Duke of Buckingham—Jersey, Nottingham, Sir Edward Seymour, Rochester, and Sir
Nathaniel Wright, and proceeds : "These were men
who had all a wonderful zeal for the Church ; a sort
of public merit that eclipsed all others in the eyes of
the queen. And I am firmly persuaded that, notwithstanding her extraordinary affection for me, and
the entire devotion which my Lord Marlborough and
my Lord Godolphin had for many years shown to
her service, they would not have had so great a
share of her favour and confidence if they had not
been reckoned in the number of the Tories."[1]

The word "Tories" deposited in this explanation
a cause of false interpretation. "Tories," as the term
came afterwards to be used as applicable to a party
who opposed the constitutional Whigs without being
Jacobites, did not then exist,—it was the contest
between the Marlborough and Godolphin party, and
the Bolingbroke and Harley party, that brought
them into existence, and transferred that name to
them. The "account" begins with transactions forty
years old at the time when it was published. And
its being put into readable form by a man of letters
rendered it all the more apt to take the nomenclature
that had become rooted in the public mind by a

[1] Duchess of Marlborough's account of her Conduct, 1742, 124, 125.

growth of forty years' duration. The Duchess, indeed, unconsciously expresses the anachronism in her use of the party term when she says of the queen " as soon as she was seated on the throne, the Tories— whom she usually called by the agreeable name of ' The Church Party,' became the distinguished objects of the royal favour."[1] What we should be content to take in the well-instructed and vigilant Sarah's defi- nition, is the absorbing influence on the queen of zeal for the Church of England, so as to prepare our- selves for the effects of this zeal on the destinies of the nation, and on the content or discontent of her subjects at large.

[1] Duchess of Marlborough's account of her Conduct, 1742, 124.

CHAPTER II.

The Religious World.

AT the period of the queen's accession, here and
there throughout the empire—chiefly in Ireland—
there were people who believed that the divine right
of a sovereign reigning over them could only be
certified by the papal benediction of the oil used in
the anointing at the coronation ; others held that the
true sovereign was infallibly indicated in the divine
rule of primogeniture. Perhaps there were believers
that the power of adjustment lay with Parliament.
There were others—far more numerous—who passed
no judgment on the abstract question, but were

thankful that Parliament had acted, and acted wisely. There was a body of infallible men—chiefly dwelling in the moorlands of the south-western counties of Scotland—who held the test of legitimate sovereignty to be an oath of adherence to the Solemn League and Covenant, and who were in a condition of chronic penitence and lamentation for the sins of the land that bent under an uncovenanted sovereign. The Church of England sat perhaps more lightly on the heart than any of these motive creeds; but the queen herself, and many of her subjects — chiefly among the clergy — thought adherence to the Church of England essential to the sovereign of England. And she especially felt and acted as one who was legitimately placed on the throne for the protection and promotion of that Church. Without passing judgment on it as an abstract principle, it may be admitted that this assurance in the royal mind protected the empire from many dangers.

As the Dissenters—or "Nonconformists," as they were more commonly called—are, throughout our narrative, a political power, it may be well here to note their position and conduct in the earlier years of Queen Anne's reign. They were growing in numbers and influence; but it was the infirm growth of a feeble vitality that might be extinguished in any hard contest. The mighty organisation of Methodism was neither in existence nor in expectation; for John Wesley was an infant in the cradle in the midst of the short contest about occasional conformity; and his father had abandoned his charge as a dissenting minister to become a High Church clergyman.

All but an exceptional few of those who professed themselves Protestants not of the Church of England clustered into three groups—the Presbyterians, the Independents, and the Baptists. There were, to be sure, "the people called Quakers," perhaps larger in number than any of the three. But they were a peculiar people, standing aloof; and if it might not be said that their hand was against every man, yet every man's hand was against them. The Quakers, indeed, left on the opening of the reign a distinct mark, that between them and the other Dissenters there was no community of interests or sympathies. Among the many addresses lamenting the departure and hailing the succession, "the Dissenters in and about London presented also an address, which was the more remarkable because all the non-conformers except the Quakers joined it. The queen, in her answer, assured them of her protection, and that she would do nothing to forfeit her interest in their affections,—which words were afterwards remembered when the royal assent was given to the Schism and Occasional Bills." [1]

Taking a "Dissenter," in the strict sense, to be one who has separated from his friends on some special points of difference—who will be delighted to rejoin them if they will drop the cause of quarrel or scandal—the Quaker could not be aptly called a dissenter. The community of "Friends," to which he belonged, had bound themselves together by an organisation that discarded, as far as they could, all the traditions of a common origin that even those

[1] Parl. Hist., vi. 7, where it is cited from Tindal. I am not aware of any other authority for this exchange of courtesies.

who had gone farthest away from the Church of the
middle ages carried with them. While all others had
more or less in common indicative of relationship
and common parentage, the Society of Friends was
like an erratic formation bursting through the whole,
standing erect above the surrounding country and
courting every storm. Iᴛ would be difficult to
say which of the denominations of the day hated
them most thoroughly. It was difficult to sympathise
with them in their sufferings, or to denounce those
who persecuted them ; for they themselves seemed to
court persecution, as aspiring to the crown of martyrdom. Their casting themselves in the way of those
who hated them most was, in fact, a sort of retalia-
tory persecution ; for when the most bigoted of the
Puritans crossed the Atlantic to isolate themselves
in pious communities, unpolluted by the presence of
the various abominations that embittered life to them
in Britain, did not the most abominable of all, dog
them to their place of refuge, courting martyrdom,
and obtaining it in full measure ? The general silence
of British history about the cruel persecution of the
Quakers in New England, is an emphatic testimony
to their isolation from the sympathies of their kind.
Among the scanty allusions to the affair, one tells
how a message went from some of " the Dissenters of
the three several denominations, transmitted to New
England, in approval of some laws there against the
Quakers." [1]

The stern resoluteness of the Quakers was crossed
by a quality as peculiarly their own as everything
else about them. Their uncompliability was neutral,

[1] Life of Calamy, ii. 34.

not active. They would not comply with the injunctions of the powers that be, but they would not offer resistance to those powers with the arm of the flesh. It was a meeting of extremes, where resistance united itself with passive obedience. To King James the Second, any element of this blessed quality was so delightful that he had wild dreams about converting this neutral power into alliance with his own objects of active subjugation. For purposes totally different from his, however, this power of inertness was mightily effective. It gave the Quakers a strength possessed by no other communion. As they would not fight they could not be beaten. They hence turned the world round to serve them. A solid mass of human beings, unconformable to many of the established usages secular as well as religious, was a grievous clog on the free movements of the complicated machinery of British social and political life. This erratic unconformability was all the more provoking and troublesome that the Society of Friends were not only in general good citizens, but counted among them men who had both capacity and inclination for conducting the active affairs of life. So early as the Act of Toleration of the year 1689, the Quakers were favoured above all other men. A declaration of fidelity was prepared for them instead of the oath of allegiance; and a short general acknowledgment of belief in Christianity exempted those who officiated at their places of worship, while dissenting ministers were required to subscribe the Thirty-nine Articles of the Church of England.[1] The laws passed from time to time to extract from Quakers, without injury to

[1] Act I., W. & M., c. 18, §§ 8 and 13.

their consciences, the payment of taxes and the performance of other duties of the citizen, hold a considerable place in the statutes of the realm.

One illustrious member of the fraternity, for all the abnegation of pomp and power laid on him as a faithful "Friend," yet virtually acted the statesman. William Penn, fifty-six years old at the time of the accession, lived the life of an active public man through our whole period. He possessed a subtle power—noted in the fraternity by those who have come across them in business transactions—of doing things equivalent to, though not coming within the absolute definition of, the things prohibited. It is a becoming use of this faculty when we find him addressing Marlborough as " my noble friend," — an epithet that, coming from such a source, was a higher courtesy than the " your grace " and " my lord duke" from the common herd.

Of the three communities forming the bulk of the Dissenters, the Presbyterians, if not the greatest in bulk, were the strongest in the effectiveness of their ecclesiastical organisation. The Baptists were a small body, imperfectly organised. The Independents or Congregationalists abjured a collective organisation, whether hierarchical or republican; and their strength had been shown rather in the destruction of the co-operative action of other bodies than in the formation of a common scheme of action among themselves. The Presbyterians could proudly look back to the day when the potency of their organisation carried the Covenant in triumph over the three kingdoms, binding them together, with all their inhabitants, in that "solemn league and covenant" which was the final authorised accomplishment of God's will. The Independents came down with the sword in their hand on this beautiful organisation and hurled it into chaos. But it was a day of wrath when all things were confounded; and though the Presbyterians had to endure dire humiliations after the Restoration, yet this was a convulsive epoch that in its turn had subsided, and the power of the Presbyterian system was gradually waxing again.

Those who put reliance in this power were not without reason. Of all organisations in the Christian Church, Presbytery is, next to the Romish hierarchy, the most powerful. In places entirely isolated from external aid and countenance, it is far more accomplished in organisation than any other Church. With their simple apparatus of government and ceremonial, those that sought refuge beyond the Atlantic equipped themselves at once as ecclesiastical communities. The rapidity of their organisation was conspicuous by contrast with the adherents of the mighty Church of England, who, when they parted from the monarchy, parted also from the hierarchy, and had to wait, through difficult and dubious negotiations, until the year 1783, when the apostolical succession was communicated to the clergy in the United States— not from the Church of England, where political difficulties stood in the path—but from the humble and oppressed remnant of Episcopacy in Scotland.

But if the Presbyterians of England were better organised and saw a brighter future than their fellow-Dissenters of other communions, they were far below the proud position of their fellow-Presbyterians in the north. It was not merely that there, from political conditions, they had become supreme, and could dictate to the civil power its dealing with other religious bodies. Even those dissenting from the Establishment took a prouder position than any claimed by English Nonconformists. Perhaps there is no way of better appreciating the nature of Dissent in each of the countries separately than by looking at them together, and seeing in what they have differed as well as in what they have agreed.

In Scotland, every body of men who dissented from the Establishment professed to throw it off as departing from the good old ways, and to be themselves the representatives of the Establishment in still pursuing the good old ways it had deserted. Hence, however few and poor, and in all worldly things insignificant, they nourished a spirit of haughty exclusion towards their old comrades, handing them over by a sort of comprehensive excommunication to the doom of the uncovenanted. Such was the lofty position successively taken by the Cameronians, the Macmillanites, the Secession, and the Relief. The spirit of all was well expressed in the phraseology of the latest and largest secession from the Church of Scotland, when they threw back on those they left behind the title of "The Residuary Church." The same spirit animated sub-secessions from the successive seceding bodies, as when the anti-Burghers drew away from the remnant of the Secession and established themselves as the only true Church of Scotland; and again, the phenomenon was repeated even in the separate portions of the small body thus divided, for a portion of the Burgher community were constrained to sever themselves as "The Old Light

Burghers," who denounced the brethren whose indul-
gence in certain accursed innovations earned for them
the denunciatory epithet of "New Lights." Then,
again, the anti-Burghers, who dissented both from old
and new light, found themselves left behind by the
departure from among them of "The Constitutional
Associate Presbytery." These being the furthest removed from the Establishment, denounced by all the
others in succession, claimed the privilege of standing
before the world as the sole representatives of the
True Church.

There was intolerance throughout all, and each
new swarm was more intolerant than all those it
had left behind. They took with them the traditions of the Covenant. They were the champions of
that Covenant which, in the Solemn League, the three
nations, England, Scotland, and Ireland, had sworn
to adopt and obey. That oath was still binding on
all the inhabitants of the British empire, true though
it was that the multitude had forsworn it, and the
Church of Christ was for the time represented by
only a small chosen band of true believers.[1]

---

[1] How intolerantly and domineeringly these small sects could express
their views is well exemplified by the following utterance of a period
later than Queen Anne's reign :—

Question. "Should not Episcopalians have the benefit of toleration
in Scotland (as was pleaded in Assembly, 1724) as well as Presbyterian
dissenters in England? Should not every man live according to the
light of his own conscience, &c.?"

Answer. "A toleration of all religions is the very cut-throat and
ruin of all true religion, and contrary to our blessed Lord's example,
given for purging and keeping pure His house : it is what Satan boldly
pursues for and glorifies in as the only bulwark of his kingdom. As
for Presbyterians being tolerated in England, if they were standing
upon their ancient basis, valiantly contending for the glorious reformation that nation attained, and is sworn in the most solemn manner to
maintain in opposition to Prelacy and all other heresies and errors, &c.,

The Nonconformists of England took up a less arrogant position, and were more gently dealt with by those who were nearest to them in the Establishment. They had "tender consciences," demanding gentle handling. They were "weaker brethren," the objects of charitable allowance by the strong and orthodox. Their demeanour in some measure accepted of these unflattering courtesies; for their desire was towards the great bulk of the Christian world around them forming the Establishment, and it was a grief to them that they could not overcome the small barrier that excluded them. In Scotland the smallest sects would hold that they were the only adherents of that true presbytery that was of "right divine," as the Romanist maintained the divine infallibility handed down by St Peter to his successors; and the High Church of England men held by the divine pedigree of apostolic succession. But the English Dissenters were shy of such a rivalry, and the arrogators of aught in the shape of divine right were few among them.[1]

they, in that case, had a just title and claim unto the ancient Establishment, when Prelacy was trodden under foot; and even as the matter is with them, they ought, if sound in the faith, with the Apostle Paul to plead the truth and soundness of their doctrine, who, though frequently under persecution, did always plead against toleration—Gal. v. 11, 12."—Plain Reasons for Presbyterians Dissenting from the Revolution Church in Scotland, pp. 72, 73.

[1] Calamy, with reference to the publication in 1704 of his 'Defence of Moderate Nonconformity, in Answer to the Reflections of Ollyffe and Mr Hoadly,' says : "That I might know the utmost that could be said against the latitude into which I had run, I sent it with a letter to Mr Williams, begging he would let me have his strongest objections against my scheme. This I then rather did because I knew he was in his judgment for the divine right of presbytery, though there were but very few of our ministers that I ever could discern to be of that mind."—Life. ii. 30.

Daniel Defoe, who could give no description without imparting to it a touch of picturesqueness, thus describes " The English Protestant Dissenter," and in doing so must be understood to speak of and for himself :—

" The Dissenter is an Englishman that, being somewhat desirous of going to heaven—having heard his Church of England father and schoolmaster and the minister of the parish talk much of it,—begins seriously to inquire about the way thither ; and to that purpose, consulting his Bible and his conscience, he finds that, in his opinion, there are some things in the established way of worship which do not seem to correspond with the rule he has found out in the Scripture.

" Now I shall not examine here whether the man thus scrupulous be in the right, or whether the Church be in the right—it does not at all belong to the case in hand.

" But the man being fully convinced that he ought to worship God in that way, exclusive of all others, which is most agreeable to the will of God revealed in the Scripture : and being, on mature consideration also, and after sincere endeavours to be otherwise satisfied fully convinced that the established way is not so near to that rule as it ought to be, ventures the displeasure of the civil magistrate in dissenting, in pure obedience to the commands of his conscience and of that rule which bids man obey God rather than man—firmly believing that 'tis his duty so to do, and that the compass and extent of human laws do not reach to bind him in matters of conscience—at the same time living in charity with all the rest of the world whose consciences do not require the same restriction, and peaceably submitting to the laws and government he lives under, as far as either his right as an Englishman or his duty as a Christian can require." [1]

To the bulk of Englishmen of a serious class—and the Dissenters were to a man "serious"—"schism" was a heavy charge to be imputed, and a heavy weight to be felt on the conscience. The doubts and troubles of many pious writers of the day are directed always as amply to this dificulty as to the great essential questions of orthodoxy in faith. To Dissenters of Scotland—Covenanter, Cameronian, or Macmillanite—there was no such dubiety. The word schism was not much in use among these fraternities, but if any one were bound to find a meaning for it, he would apply it to all who differed from himself and his set. A time had been, indeed, when the English Presbyterian could have fairly denounced as schismatic any one who questioned the Confession of Faith, or offered disobedience to the Directory of Public Worship. So it was in the glorious days of the Westminster Assembly, when it was laying down the creed and constitution that were immediately to hold rule over all Protestantism, and ultimately over all Christendom. But that was an affair of sixty years ago, and the glorious fabric had been scattered to the winds by storm after storm sweeping past from divers points in the political horizon.

The great men who gave life and lustre to that Assembly had now long gone to their rest. As in the

---

[1] An Inquiry into Occasional Conformity : writings of the author of The True-born Englishman, i. 388.

traditions of some great battle, after all the veteran leaders have been removed, those who fought as raw recruits become memorable as each arrives at old age and drops away,—so the skirts of the departing Assembly men were honoured. The last of them who lingered among men was great enough to dignify the end of all, though his greatness was not in ecclesiastical matters—this was John Wallis, the mathematician, grammarian, and teacher of the deaf to speak.[1]

Apart from natural regrets for the historical lustre that had departed with the skirts of the potent Assembly, the Presbyterian dissenters were reminded of incidental misfortunes in their present lot when they thought of the men of the old time. The leaders in the Assembly had been educated at the universities. So, too, had many of the succeeding generation of Nonconforming ministers, some of whom still lived. Of these were Calamy, Howe, and Bates.

The restrictions that excluded their followers were too much in harmony with the long pressure of the narrow interests of " the college," on the catholic spirit of " the university," as an institution where all souls thirsting after knowledge might come and drink their fill. No doubt profound classical scholars and skilful mathematicians were bred by the universities of England ; but it could not be otherwise where so affluent an apparatus for teaching and studying was available. But co-operating with the internal economy that

---

[1] October 28th this year (1703) died Dr John Wallis, Savilian Professor of Geometry in the University of Oxford, and last surviving member of the Assembly of Divines.—Calamy: Own Life, ii. 21.

made the colleges available as a right only to the
very wealthy, the exclusion of Dissenters served to
make university education one of the distinguishing
badges of a class, rendering it an object of ambition
rather to attach Oxon. or Cantab. to the name, than
to prove the high tone of the education by the knowledge and accomplishments it has imparted. The
tendency of all this was, until in recent times a wiser
spirit began to prevail, that the frequenters of the
universities were a social caste, dividing the male
population of England into university men and the
others; so that any exhibition of the acquirements
peculiar to Oxford or Cambridge respectively, by one
who had not acquired them at their legitimate source,
partook of the nature of a pretence,—like a man of
meagre means making exhibition of the attributes
of wealth, as by hunting or horse-racing.

That there were three bodies standing under the
common shade of nonconformity, does not appear
to have made any one of them stronger than it
would have been alone. Then, at the time of our
making their acquaintance, the great Antinomian
controversy had been raging through each and all
of them. The reproach of Antinomianism held a
slightly sarcastic inference of superstitious tenden-
cies; and those who were assailed by it retaliated
with a charge of Socinianism, inferring the deeper
reproach of a tendency to infidelity. Here there was
room for wider and deeper hatreds than any that
could arise where a taste for simplicity was offended
by pomps and ceremonies, or the possessor of a
tender conscience was unable to reconcile some
item in his brother's creed with the precepts of

Scripture. Hence, wherever there was a considerable body of Dissenters, there were opposite parties casting at each other words harder and bitterer than any that the Established Church had thrown at either.

The laymen who made the congregations of Dissenting ministers were generally, as they have been in later times, men endowed with the plain but substantial virtues of the middle-class Englishman. They were moral in their lives without professing the painful austerity of the earlier Puritans ; they were peaceful citizens when let alone, and men of their word in their business transactions. They were industrious and frugal, and as many of them were able men of business, they had a tendency to accumulate wealth. In London, where there were many capitalists among them, they were a powerful body ; and by a discreet use of the privilege of occasional conformity, they often held rank and office in the city and the parochial corporations.

The wealth of the Dissenters enabled them to purchase influence and respect, but such tributes were tinged by a slight infusion of the venerable prejudice of the Christian against the rich Jew, and of the Mohammedan against the Parsee. It did not reconcile the haughty Churchmen to the wealth of these neighbours that it enabled them to contribute to public benefactions, and even to aid the State itself in raising loans, and in facilitating the commerce in the national stock.

Another use made by the Dissenters of the fruits of their industry gave a still more offensive feature to their liberality. It was frequently an object

of their pride that their pastor should be well endowed in worldly goods, and so stand in invidious contrast with the pecuniary condition of his
neighbour who represented the Establishment.   It is
true that the curate or the equally humbly endowed
incumbent of a "small living" was qualified to rise
to a bishop's throne and affluence, or for the enjoyment of a rich deanery.   But there were multitudes
who knew that the chance of such a fortunate consummation was a virtual nullity ; and then, close at
hand, was the minister of the meeting-house, whom
the parochial incumbent was bound in clerical etiquette
to despise, living on the easy competence provided for
him by an attached and generous flock.[1]

[1] Tom Brown, in his usual happy way, gives life and individuality to
the attractions of the Nonconforming interest in the eyes of a worldly-
minded scholar selecting his lot as a pastor.   In the search after some
" curacy, vicarage, or parsonage," he reflects thus : "I may possibly meet
in a short time with some rich impropriator, who receives two or three
hundreds a-year in tythes, who may, out of Christian charity or generous
liberality, vouchsafe to promise me ten pounds a-year besides a Sunday
pudding."   "But to put the best case, we shall suppose a vicarage or
parsonage to become vacant of an hundred pounds value in common
estimation, and the poor painful priest, standing fair in the opinion of
the neighbourhood, is recommended to it : it is ten to one but there
is an abigail in the patron's house that must be married."   " If there
be not anything of that here, and all must be done by hard silver or gold,
or something equivalent, as a lease of tythe or the like—I am certainly
ruined.   The oath of simony will be a continual scourge to me, and
I may wear away my unhappy life before I shall receive the money
I have paid or engaged to pay."   Then there are fees and costs for
wax and parchments, composition for first - fruits.   "The church-
wardens tell me that they have a sequestration upon my living, and
the profits are at their disposal till I have taken it off : and withal,
that a considerable sum of money has been disbursed by them for
the service of the cure during the vacancy, which must be repaid them."
We follow him home to "an old rotten house ready to fall upon his
head," whence he continues his story.   "Besides tenths to be yearly
paid to the king, and the charges of visitations, by way of procurations,
synodals, and I know not what more ; the charge of my attending upon

The Dissenters were to a man champions of the Revolution Settlement, but even this claim was slightly tainted in the eyes of the Churchmen who competed with them for the same merit. The Church

my superiors when they are pleased to command me ; the charge of entertaining officers, and I know not how many sorts of men coming to me upon public business,—I shall find a charge to lie heavily upon me from my own parish. Hospitality must be kept, and none of my parishioners must go from me with dry lips," and *per contra*. " When I come to demand my dues for defraying that charge, and the maintenance of my family, I shall find it a hard matter to get them. If I be minded to farm out my tithes, my parishioners will bid me half the worth of them. If I take them in kind they will cheat me of little less than the half. And that which will vex me most of all, I must not dare to tell them of their injustice, for if I do I shall certainly have their ill-will, and as many mischievous tricks played me as they can possible."

These items of sordid servitude are occasionally put in contrast with the happier field selected by the student for his own Christian labours.

" If a church will not call me I can call a church, and without a penny charge receive the profits thereof, being king, bishop, archdeacon, and everything myself. I shall be wholly on the gaining side, and not one person the better for my preferment."

" Suppose me then in a congregation as their pastor, teacher, holder-forth—call it what you please. You must know that they will be a select number of people (not like your churches, a herd made up of a few sheep and a multitude of goats), most of them of the sweet female sex (whose kindness towards their spiritual pastors or teachers is never less than their zeal for what they teach them), scattered up and down here and there in several of your parishes. And for the better edification of these precious souls, it will be in my power to choose the place of my residence or abode ; and if I do not choose a convenient place 'tis my own fault. Instead of an old rotten parsonage or vicarage house, I promise myself forty, fifty, or threescore good houses, where I shall be entertained with such fulness of delight, yea, and empire too (not like your pitiful curates or chaplains that must sneak to the groom or butler), that even the gentlemen that pretend to make gods of their landlords will be apt to envy me : and if I resolve to enter into the matrimonial state, I shall be strangely unfortunate if, instead of an abigail, I meet not with some opulent widow, or some tender-hearted virgin of no ordinary fortune." " No obligation to hospitality will lie upon me, and I shall be troubled with few visitors but such as will bring their entertainment with them, if they send it not before them :

had provided the army and gained the victory of the Revolution. It cannot be doubted that the Dissenters of England, and the Presbyterians of Scotland who became the Establishment, had resisted the temptation of the indulgences, and refused to acknowledge that a repeal of the penal laws uttered by the king alone was a valid act of government. But some slight influence from what in Roman history was called the Fabian policy adhered to them. They had obtained gifts from the politic king, and some of them were yet enjoying offices which had been conferred on them when King James made his futile efforts to convince them and the rest of the world, that it was his design to treat them as well as he treated his fellow-Romanists, and to establish a general toleration and equality of rights among all classes of Christians.

Then, on his other side, the Churchman had to take an estimate of another class of Nonconformists who were called Nonjurors. Of lay Nonjurors we hear almost nothing; but the clergy who chose that path were very conspicuous. To them the High Churchman, who despised the Dissenting minister, would sometimes look with reverence, as to one who trod a path higher and holier than his own. The representatives of the class were, of course, those five bishops who, out of the seven that had been committed to the Tower, had lost their temporal rank

I shall not be liable to pay one penny out of my income to bishops or chancellors, to church or poor—no, nor to the king and queen. And what a happiness, think you, will this be, to live under a Government and enjoy so much good under its protection, and not part with one farthing towards the support of it."—Dialogue between Two Oxford Scholars, published in the Works of Mr Thomas Brown, i. 6-11.

and emoluments because they would not take the oath of allegiance, which indicated an adoption of the Revolution Settlement. They endured bondage rather than submit to a decree which their allegiance to their Church taught them that a king had no right to impose on them. They sacrificed the world and its gifts rather than depart from their allegiance to that same king, in the functions which they held that he and he alone could legitimately exercise.

The death of King William was the loss of their champion and protector to those adherents of the Church of England who, as a distinction from the "High Church," were called the "Low Church" party. They were those whose attachment to the Church went no farther than conformity—the bare acceptance of its hierarchy and ceremonies. It was natural that two bodies of men so significantly severed in popular nomenclature should prepare for war against each other. There followed a conflict stained by follies and malignant passions. In its historical development, however, one can see its slow but sure tendency to strengthen the Revolution Settlement, and that chiefly through the influence of the condition, that the High Church counted on the sympathy of the queen. This familiarised the opponents or dubious friends of that Settlement to the rule of a sovereign who, near as she was to the line of legitimacy and divine right, had nothing higher than a parliamentary title.

The contest began in a blow aimed at the Nonconformists or Dissenters. King William had been dead little more than half a year—the first Parliament of Queen Anne was but three weeks old—when the Commons were stirred by the "Bill for preventing Occasional Conformity." The "conformity" which, though only occasional, carried the privilege of permanence, and therefore was offensive to the zealous and steady Conformists, was conformity with the provisions of the celebrated Test and Corporation Acts. The Test Act had been memorable in history by fulfilling the design of its promoters in driving the Duke of York from the post of Lord High Admiral, and supplying him with a significant hint that, unless he abandoned his championship of Popery and arbitrary power, he would not be permitted to retain the higher place at the head of the State that was likely to become his by hereditary succession. It was called "An Act for preventing Dangers which may happen from Popish Recusants." With the verbosity of definition deemed necessary in statutes of a penal character, it comprehended every Government office, and enjoined that the holder of it shall take the Oaths of Allegiance and Supremacy, and "shall also receive the sacrament of the Lord's Supper, according to the usage of the Church of England," "in some parish church, upon some Lord's Day, commonly called Sunday, immediately after divine service on Sunday." Conditions of time and place were provided for facilitating the detection of defaulters; and if the occasion passed without the compliance being recorded, the defaulter's office was forfeited. There was a declaration, too, of belief—"that there is not any transubstantiation in the sacrament of the Lord's Supper, or in the elements of bread and wine, at or after the consecration thereof by any person whatsoever." All the phraseology of the Act expressive of alarm and denunciation was levelled against Papists and Popery.[1] But the substantive qualification for office of taking the Sacrament according to the usage of the Church of England, and within a parish church, technically excluded all who, from whatever motive, failed to pay this homage to the Church of England.

The Corporation Act dates from the beginning of the reign of Charles II. It required from all magistrates and officers of corporations an abjuration of the Solemn League and Covenant, " and that the same was in itself an unlawful oath, and imposed upon the subjects of this realm against the known laws and liberties of the kingdom." Forty years after the Restoration there were few champions of the Covenant in England. But there was a further condition that all corporate officers must have taken the Sacrament according to the rites of the Church of England within a year before acceptance of office; and here the Nonconformists in a body were struck.[2]

But the blow was not political death to them. They were not excluded from office for creed or opinion. If they chose to perform certain conditions they were as eligible to office as the stanchest Churchman. All that was necessary was, at proper time and place, to receive the sacrament of the Church of England. Many gave this testimony of conformity, and had satisfactory reasons to give for it. They could be in friendship with the Church of England, though not of it. Both acknowledged one common enemy in Popery, and both were alive to

[1] 25 ch. ii. c. 2.   [2] 13 ch. ii. stat. 2, chap. i.

the policy of comforting and supporting each other against the common danger. It was a good thing for the Churches, standing on the common ground of Protestantism, to hold communion and Christian intercourse with each other in matters not involving the essentials of faith and consequent salvation. If the Dissenter was faithful, in all essentials, to his own creed, it mattered not that on occasion he partook of the ceremonials of another denomination of Protestant Christians.

So one class of Occasional Conformists justified themselves. But to those who were more fundamentally rigid, there was an ampler justification. As they did not believe in any saving efficacy from the acts they were required to perform, these acts were not to them religious observances. They were merely civil conditions of qualification for office. To those who indulged themselves in this vein it was a support and refuge to reflect on the consolatory words of Elisha, when Naaman hinted the probable necessity for bowing himself down in the house of Rimmon.

The Churchman's answer to both reasonings was, that the Corporation and Test Acts were passed to reserve the sources of public emolument for his own sole enjoyment; and here stepped in the Occasional Conformist, by a legal quibble and an act of palpable insincerity, to reap a share in the spoil. There was still a third class of Casual Conformists, less odious to him than to the serious classes of Conformists. These were the very considerable body who had little or no religion, and who were as ready to participate in the rites of the Church of England as to perform any other duty of an uninteresting kind. These were the objects of sweeping general attacks on the growing immorality and infidelity of the age; but they lived on, enjoying their emoluments in personal peace, all the rancour of attack being against those who seriously professed religion, but a religion of the wrong kind.

Calamy, in narrating a conference with Bishop Burnet at the climax of the Occasional Conformity contest, says : " We told his lordship, that the communicating with the Church of England was no new practice among Dissenters, nor of a late date, but had been used by some of the most eminent of our ministers ever since 1662 with a design to show their charity towards that Church, notwithstanding they apprehended themselves bound in conscience ordinarily to separate from it ; and that it had been also practised by a number of the most understanding people among them before the so doing was necessary to qualify for a place."[1]

Among the casual but instructive traces of a sympathy between the Low Churchman and the Nonconformists, it is something to find the sincere mind of Calamy deriving comfort in these words of the restless casuist Chillingworth : " If a Church, supposed to want nothing necessary, require me to profess against my conscience that I believe some error, though never so small and innocent, which I do not believe, and will not allow me her communion but upon this condition — in this case the Church, for requiring this condition, is schismatical, and not I for separating from the Church." And

[1] Historical Account of my own Life (2d ed.) i. 473.

as an example : " If there were any society of Christians that held there were no antipodes, notwithstanding this error I might communicate with
them. But if I could not do so without professing their belief in this matter, then I suppose I
should be excused from schism if I should forsake
their communion rather than profess myself to believe that which I do not believe."[1]

It is perhaps rather curious than important to
find instances where the secular pomps of the Occasional Conformist in the office that his conformity
had enabled him to fill are transferred to the conventicle. The most conspicuous among these incidents is a few years older than the period we are
now in, but it worked itself into the history of
that period as a picturesque object of violent criticism from both sides. It is thus told : " In November 1697, King William, passing through the
city, Sir Humphry Edwin, Lord Mayor this year,
carried the sword before him, according to custom,
in a gown of crimson velvet.

" This gentleman not only worshipped God publicly with the Dissenters according to his usual custom, but carried the regalia with him, which very
much disgusted many of the Church of England.
Tragical were the exclamations and complaints
made on this occasion. Among others, Dr Nichols
tells the world that, ' to the great reproach of the
laws and of the city magistracy he carried the
sword with him to a nasty conventicle that was
kept in one of the city halls ; which horrid crime

[1] Quotation from " Religion of Protestants, a Safe Way to Salvation."
—Calamy : Own Life, i. 228.

one of his own party defended by giving this arrogant reason for it, that by the Act of Parliament by which they have their liberty, their religion was as much established as ours.'" Calamy, at the conclusion from this his translation from the Latin of the angry High Churchman, remarks apologetically,— "Many heartily wished that this action had been waived, as tending to enrage, yet were utterly to seek for the horridness of the crime. Nor could they discern the great arrogance of the plea when the religion owned in churches and meetings, having the same object in worship, the same rule of faith and life, the same essential principles, and the same aim and creed, cannot differ in any capital matter. The allowance of the law is of necessity a sufficient establishment. However, this measure drew unhappy consequences after it, both in this reign and in that which succeeded.'"[1]

How easily Dissent could shake hands with Establishment is curiously exemplified in an incident coming under the close personal notice of Calamy. His neighbour and fellow-Nonconformist, Mr Oldfield, had been offered a solid preferment in the Church, through the intervention of a friend who owned a cure in the Establishment. Oldfield, after maturely considering the offer, was constrained to reject it, but as it would be a decided advancement to his friend whose living was less lucrative, he naturally put the question, Why not take it yourself? No. His friend had undergone a change of opinion since he had entered on his present charge. He could not repeat what he did then. There was nothing in the duties

[1] Calamy : Own Life, i. 400, 401.

of his charge to offend his conscience, but there would be in the ceremonial and obligations incident to the acceptance of any new charge. It might be difficult to admit the sufficiency of so narrow a scruple were it not strengthened by the substantial nature of the sacrifice rendered to it.[1]

We must suppose that in such instances had the scruples come before the time of taking orders in the Church of England the orders would not have been taken, but the scruple was not strong enough to drag the acceptor back. On the other hand, there was little disposition to stigmatise the passing from Dissent into the Establishment; and it did not always earn the character of vile and treacherous apostasy so apt to be attributed to such defections by narrow and exclusive religious communities. Such communities are generally fastidious in securing their church edifices and other temporalities from all risk of passing into heterodox hands; and hence, while under the impression that because they take no endowments from the State they are free from the authority of the secular arm, they often become entangled in costly and harassing litigations, dragging their ten-

---

[1] He would fain have yielded to the temptation "in hope of his doing good, and being more useful than he had any prospect of being in the state he was in ; yet, as for the changing of his living he must be excused ; adding, that though he had no scruple remaining when he took possession of his living, against giving his assent and consent, and was not willing to lose the capacity of service he was in by that means, yet, as to giving his assent and consent now, he had such objections against it as he could not get over."—An Historical Account of my own Life, &c., by Edmund Calamy, D.D.: i. 266. The editor of Calamy's life remarks that the same incapacity to accept promotion overtook Dr Samuel Clarke. He was satisfied to remain rector of St James's, but as to further preferment, "he would take nothing which required his subscription to the Thirty-nine Articles."

derest mysteries through scornful criticism on questions of ownership of lands and buildings. It has been noted that the titles to the church edifices of Dissenting bodies at that period were often so adjusted as to facilitate absorption into the Establishment on the removal of existing impediments to an ecclesiastical fusion.[1]

Calamy tells us how, in his capacity of spiritual adviser, he was consulted by a gentleman " who has publicly declared himself in his judgment on the side of the Nonconformists as to their capital plea of a further reformation both as to worship and discipline, and has publicly communicated with them at the Lord's Table as well as with the Established Church, and has pleaded for such interchangeable communion with each party as requisite to the supporting that little charity that there is yet left amongst us." The practical question on which he sought solution and assurance was, " whether such a gentleman may with a safe conscience for a while withdraw from all the worshipping assemblies of the Nonconformists, in hope and prospect of a considerable public post in which he may (probably) be capable of doing much service to the public, and particularly of serving the

---

[1] It naturally occasionally happened that the transference of the property to the Establishment had not the unanimous assent of all concerned—pastor and flock. The great pulpit orator, Daniel Burgess, lost his chapel in Drury Lane—a spot he loved as best suited for the exercise of his powers, since it was in Queen Anne's reign, as it remained long afterwards, the centre and headquarters of the profligacy of London. The building does not now exist, but its site is easily recognisable, as it stood between the dreary little churchyard of Drury and the theatre. When the building passed to the Establishment it was repaired and decorated, and the raising the funds for this purpose by a theatrical performance, gave Defoe an opportunity for enlivening the town with a witty lampoon.

cause of charity by his interest and influence." After much meditating and balancing of possible results to the cause of sound religion, the honest divine came to the conclusion " that such a gentleman would better maintain his own reputation and more effectually secure his general usefulness, and particularly be more capable of serving the cause of charity among us, by a continued open adherence to his professed principle, and public acting according to it, than by a politic compliance with such as lay nothing less to heart than religion."[1] This occurred in the year 1706. The date is of some interest, as at an earlier period the conditions might have pointed to Harley. But he had cleared himself of all entanglements years earlier, and in 1706 was Secretary of State.

In the autumn of 1702, Mr Bromley moved the Commons to consider " the shameful practice of occasional conformity which had introduced men of republican principles into the chief places of profit and trust, and was likely to be fatal to the Government and Church established, if recourse were not had to such measures as were capable of eluding its design."

Leave was given to Bromley, who was member for the University of Oxford, along with Annesley, who represented the University of Cambridge, and Henry St John, to bring in a Bill " to Prevent Occasional Conformity." On the 17th of November it was read a second time, and committed. The preamble was,—" As nothing is more contrary to the profession of the Christian religion, and particularly to the doctrine of the Church of England than per-

[1] Calamy : Own Life, ii. 56-59.

secution for conscience sake." And to establish a harmony between this announcement and the legislation it announced, it is set forth as a desirable object to give full effect to the Toleration Act of 1689, which had been evaded by Dissenters finding their way into the offices, whence it was the intention of the Toleration Act to exclude them. To complete the object of the Toleration Act, by accomplishing this exclusion, the Bill provided that every person qualifying for and obtaining office, who afterwards attends a religious meeting or conventicle, where there are present more than five persons, besides the family of the house where it is held, is to forfeit a hundred pounds, and five pounds for every day of exercising the functions of his office after such attendance.

Several amendments on the Bill were carried in the Lords, the most important being the reduction of the penalty from £100 to £20. A free conference was adjusted, but the two Houses could not be brought to a concurrence, and the Bill dropped.

In the session of 1703 the Bill was again carried in the Commons, but lost on a second reading in the Lords. The debate there was adorned by a speech from Bishop Burnet, coming down to us in a shape so closely in harmony with the opinions expressed in his books that we may count it among the very rare authentic examples of the parliamentary oratory of Queen Anne's reign.[1]

---

[1] Speaking of the meaning of the term "occasional conformist," he said : "I myself was an occasional conformist in Geneva and Holland. I thought their Churches were irregularly formed under great defects in their constitution, yet I thought communion with them was lawful, for their worship was not corrupted ; but at the same time I

Calamy tells us that "the Archbishop of Canterbury—Tenison—made a warm speech upon this occasion, in which among others there were these expressions: 'I think the practice of occasional conformity, as used by the Dissenters, is so far from deserving the title of a vile hypocrisy, that it is the duty of all moderate Dissenters upon their own principles to do it.'" [1]

In this second defeat the champions of the measure were interrupted but not stopped. They pursued their one object with a singleness of purpose and a tenacity that drew people's eyes towards them as to a

continued my communion with our own Church according to the liturgy of this Church with all that came about me. And if the designs of some of the promoters of this Bill should be brought about, and I driven beyond sea—unless, among other unpardonable people, I should be first knocked on the head—in that case would communicate with the foreign Churches. So I think conformity with a less perfect Church may well consist with the continuing to worship God in a more perfect one. It remains, then, a point of opinion which Church or society is the more and which is the less perfect. In this I am very sure our Church is the more perfect and regular, and that the separation is founded upon error and mistake, and that true edification is among us and not among them. But some of them, by an unhappy education, think otherwise, and in this they are certainly to blame as they are in every part of the separation. But if it is intended to tolerate them under their other mistakes, I do not see why this should not be tolerated likewise, since it is much less dangerous than the other practices that are not at present complained of."

The bishop in his peculiar gossiping way gave the House of Lords the following note of the relations to each other of Churchmen and Dissenters in and around Salisbury :—

"In my diocese, those who are Occasional Conformists out of principle, who sometimes go to church and go sometimes to meetings, are without number, who yet have no office and pretend to none. I confess I do not desire to press it too hard upon them, that they may not do both ; but this, instead of keeping them from meetings, hinders them from coming to church."

[1] Life, ii. 26. There is no report of this speech in the Parliamentary History, but it will be found in a pamphlet referred to farther on.

body who had separated themselves from the ranks
of ordinary political parties to give themselves over
to the devoted pursuit of a separate object. They
gained at this time the name of the High Church
party, opening a new division in ecclesiastical politics
sufficiently famous as High and Low Church.[1] High
Church was in a few years to have its triumph from
causes not yet anticipated, but meanwhile the Occasional Conformity project had to be fought through
difficulties. The empire was throughout shaken by
various disturbing influences. There was the great
war abroad, and the war at home between the two
Houses in the Aylesbury Election case. There was the
Scotch Jacobite plot of 1703 ; and more formidable,
the Act of Security, severing the realms on the death
of the queen.

On the 14th of November 1704 leave was again
given to bring in a Bill against Occasional Conformity.
On this occasion the irrepressible Mr Bromley and his
followers conceived a grand idea in the tactics of parliamentary conflict. The nation had thrown itself into
the great war, in the conviction that nothing but the

[1] The passage here following from the speech by Bishop Burnet just
referred to is instructive, as showing us that, at the time when he
spoke, the beginning of the year 1704, the nomenclature of " High
Church" and "Low Church" was only working itself into articulate
meaning. " One author, who has wrote two books on behalf of this
Bill, is known to be the furiousest Jacobite in England, and does not con-
ceal it even in those books. In one of these he says he is once called
an 'High Churchman.' These are new terms of distinction. I know
no High Church but the Church of Rome ; and that author, L——
[Lestrange], has in another book showed us how near he comes to that
Church when he proposes that a treaty may be set on foot between our
Convocation and the Assembly of the clergy of France ; and that we
should abate the Regal supremacy and they the Papal, and then he
fancies all other matters could be easily adjusted ; so here we see who
are to be called High Church."—Parl. Hist., vi. 162.

prostration of France would save the Protestant religion and the remaining liberties of Europe. After a crisis of intense anxiety, the victory of Blenheim showed that the grand object was accomplished, if the ordinary human means were taken to keep what was gained. Foremost among these was the money which England only could furnish. It was needed for many purposes—to keep Gibraltar, which had just been gained, but more essentially to give effect to a treaty by which the King of Prussia was to supply a contingent of £8000 for the relief of the Duke of Savoy; and if the necessary funds were not available, all might yet be lost. Here, then, was the opportunity. Mr Bromley concluded an address by moving, "That the Bill to Prevent Occasional Conformity might be tacked to the Land Tax Bill."

The announcement of such a project points to the conditions of a time when parliamentary tactics had not achieved the adjustment now long so effectively secured, which enabled the three forces—the Crown, the Lords, and the Commons—to work smoothly together, and avoid the scandal of attempts to trip each other up. Tacking was a remnant of the old policy of Parliament to seek redress of grievances and secure conditions on the occasion of voting a supply to the Crown. It had been sometimes used in the reign of Charles II., but even then never so palpably with the view of bullying the whole forces of the Legislature to further the objects of a section as on this occasion. But as it was a factious attempt, so it was left in the hands of the faction that devised it. Some questions of secular politics had become mixed with the cause of the Dissenters. In the corporations especially, there were instances where the balance of power might be shaken so as to affect seats in Parliament if the Dissenters were politically paralysed. The nature of a tack suggested more dangerous suspicions. Its object was to compel the Lords and the Crown to pass the Bill with its tack to obviate all the ruin that must attend the stopping of the war. But what if the Lords and the Crown, as desperate as the Commons, should accept the alternative and reject the Bill? It was believed that many Jacobites rather lamented than gloried over Marlborough's victories, as blasting the hopes they nourished of aid from France. These considerations drew off a portion of the supporters of the original Bill; and "upon the division the tack was rejected by a majority of 251 voices against 134."

The Bill, with the severity of its penalties modified, was carried in the Commons and sent up on the 14th of December to the Lords. There it perished by a majority of 71 to 51 against the second reading.[1]

---

[1] The sources of information on the dispute generally are gathered up pretty amply in the Parliamentary History (vi. 59-369). There is an animated account of the whole contest in a pamphlet with this title: "The Proceedings of both Houses of Parliament in the years 1702, 1703, 1704, upon the Bill to Prevent Occasional Conformity, interspersed with Speeches for and against the Bill, most of which were never before printed. London: printed by Baker, at the Black Boy, in Paternoster Row, 1710." This pamphlet is more discursive than the account in the Parliamentary History, and its discursiveness professes to be in support of the measure and the laudation of its champions. But there is a grotesque excess of zeal in this laudation, apt to remind one of "The Shortest Way with the Dissenters." The loss of the tack in the Commons having been told, a list of the minority who voted for it is prefaced thus: "Since it may be looked upon by succeeding ages as a piece of injustice to the present not to give them the names of such as have rendered their memories pretious to posterity by asserting the

The excitement about the Occasional Conformity seemed to be at its climax when it caught an additional impulse from the renowned pamphlet called 'The Shortest Way with the Dissenters.' This struck a responsive nerve in all ecclesiastical parties—Romanists, Nonjurants, High Churchmen and Low Churchmen of the Establishment, and all grades and classes of Nonconformists. It had something of a bewildering character, that drove the excited readers into false positions. There is no doubt that it raised terror and wrath among the Dissenters. It is said, on the other hand, that some High Churchmen received it with warm sympathy and loud applause.[1]

cause of God in so noble a manner as those who were for tacking the *occasional* to the *money* Bill, I shall not quit the proceedings of this remarkable year without subjoining the following list." It is noticeable that in this pamphlet the oration by Bishop Burnet in the House of Lords is printed at full length, as if to afford an immediate contrast between its dignified spirit of toleration and the narrow bigotry of the "Tackers." The treatment of Episcopacy in Scotland is told with clearness and vigour. The avowed moral of the story is to let Churchmen see how dangerous the Dissenters might become in England if they were to rise through toleration to the supremacy enjoyed by their Presbyterian brethren in Scotland. But it is possible to believe in a broader latent policy of inviting the High Churchmen to consider whether they had been doing as they would be done by. It is observable that the pamphlet bears the date of 1710, when the High Churchmen were waxing in strength until they were able at last to carry the law for the suppression of Occasional Conformity.

[1] It is seldom easy to find strict historical evidence either for or against such rumours. Oldmixon, who is bitter on Defoe, and calls this "the smartest of all his venomous libels," says "it passed some time as the genuine work of a rank Tory, and met with applause in our two famous universities. A bookseller now living, having an order from a fellow of a college in Cambridge for a parcel of books, just at the time of publishing 'The Shortest Way,' put up one of them in the bundle, not doubting it would be welcome to his customer; who accordingly thanked him for packing so excellent a treatise up with the rest, it being, next to the Sacred Bible and Holy Comments, the best book he ever saw."—History, ii. 301.

Again the excitement drew new life when a suspicion began to creep abroad that it was a hoax, and the suspicion of perpetrating it naturally alighted on that restless pamphleteer Defoe, who had long declared himself to be the champion of the Dissenters. He had already marched into the battle-field of pamphleteering controversy in a tone of quiet earnestness not conformable with his usual tone, in rebuke of those who had yielded to the temptation of Occasional Conformity. It might have been fairly anticipated that one endowed with his easy political virtue would have found refuge in some one of the vindications of Occasional Conformity. But he was not of the men that may be counted on. He was stimulated by a wilful waywardness akin to honesty. Put Occasional Conformity in what shape his vindicators might, he would have none of it.[1]

Much critical laudation has been bestowed on the subtlety of the sarcasm that could thus deceive the zealots into folly. But it is scarcely a sound com-

---

[1] " Nothing can be lawful and unlawful at the same time. If it be not lawful for me to dissent, I ought to conform ; but if it be unlawful for me to conform, I must dissent. Several opinions may, at the same time, consist in a country, in a city, in a family, but not in one entire person. That is impossible." What, then, shall the Dissenter who aspires to office do ? "Let him boldly run the risk, or openly and honestly conform to the Church, and neither be ashamed of his honour nor his profession. Such a man all men will value and God will own. He need not fear carrying the sword to a conventicle, or bringing the conventicle to his own house. But to make the matter a game—to dodge religions, and go in the morning to Church and in the afternoon to the Meeting—to communicate in private with the Church of England, to save a penalty, and then go back to the Dissenters, and communicate again there,—this is such a retrograde devotion that I can see no colour or pretence for in all the sacred books."—A Discourse upon Occasional Conformity. Collection of the writings of the author of The True-born Englishman, i. 313, 315.

mendation of any literary effort that, but for an accidental discovery it might have missed its aim. It might have gone down through a short period of angry contest into oblivion with thousands of other better utterances of its day. Such a fate does not appear to have been averted by any revelation made by Defoe himself—indeed he was fully aware that to be the known author of such a pamphlet was to be in peril.

Defoe was not an accomplished satirist, in the sense of leaving behind the touch of the poisoned sting, that in either of his contemporaries, Swift or Tom Brown, would have revealed the work of his hand. Defoe turns about his victim with a resistless but good-humoured jocularity, showing his strength rather than his venom. On this occasion the accomplishments of the satirist had to give place to those of the mimic or personator, where Defoe was supreme. He metamorphosed himself for the time into the haughty High Churchman, " whose reddening cheek no contradiction bears ; " as years afterwards he metamorphosed himself into the shipwrecked sailor, whose dreams are disturbed by the pitiful prattle of his parrot, and who looks aghast on the footprints on the sand.

'The Shortest Way' is a work of high rhetorical art, modelled after the example set by him who imagined the speech of Antony over the dead body of Cæsar. The beginning is calm, gentle, charitable, with a touch of sadness over the fate of those steadfast clergymen who had either to sacrifice their worldly fortunes to their loyalty, or wrong their consciences by accepting the oath to the Revolution

Settlement. There is a touch of inevitable yet half-suppressed indignation when the case of the Church in Scotland is casually noticed. "If any man would see the spirit of a Dissenter let him look into Scotland; there they made entire conquest of the Church, trampled down the sacred orders, and suppressed the Episcopal government with an absolute, and, as they suppose, irretrievable victory." "Pray, how much mercy and favour did the members of the Episcopal Church find in Scotland from the Scotch Presbyterian government? I shall undertake for the Church of England that the Dissenters shall still receive as much here, though they deserve but little." It was naturally unlikely that readers were here to recognise the hand of him who, when he spoke for himself, ever commended the moderation exemplified by the Presbyterians of Scotland when they gained their victory over their enemies in the Revolution Settlement.

In these and suchlike casual sallies the pent-up wrath takes vent, until the sympathising reader is keen to have it all; and at last he is gratified, for it can be no longer restrained. The "hot and cold objector" mutters "cruelty" and is answered.

"'Tis cruelty to kill a snake or a toad in cold blood, but the poison of their nature makes it a charity to our neighbours to destroy these creatures—not for any personal injury received, but for prevention; not for the evil they have done, but the evil they may do."

"Serpents, toads, vipers, &c., are noxious to the body and poison the sensitive life—these poison the soul, corrupt our posterity, ensnare our children, destroy the vitals of our happiness, our future felicity, and contaminate the whole mass."

When the secret was discovered there was a cry for the punishment of the man who attributed such opinions to the High Church party. It has been maintained that punishment in such a case was signally illogical, since passages of a like tenor could be found in the writings of High Churchmen, especially those of their champion Sacheverell; and that they were mistaken for the utterances of some one among the High Churchmen only indorsed the fundamental truth of the charge implied by the pamphlet, that it spoke their true sentiments. But if there is to be punishment at all for clever lampoons and other passages of controversial party warfare, it might be as well vindicated in this as in many other instances. If it was true that Sacheverell said such things, was he not held to be a criminal for doing so, and was it not an offence for one citizen to fabricate criminal utterances, so that other citizens might be charged with them ? A blow had been struck at a party waxing strong and intolerant, and there was retaliation in the usual way. Indicted at the Old Bailey for a seditious libel, he believed that his safest course lay in a simple plea of guilty. Whether or not he was led to expect leniency he did not obtain it. His punishment was to stand three times in the pillory, and then be imprisoned until he should pay a fine of two hundred merks, and find security to keep the peace for seven years.[1]

Defoe had friends, personal or political, sufficiently sincere to afford him a guard of honour on the occa-

[1] See Life and Times of Daniel Defoe. i. 70.

sion when he stood in the pillory. It depended on the temper of the times whether in London this was a service of danger. They were able to protect him from injury and insult. This was in the summer of the year 1703. Had it been seven years later there would have been imminent risk that he and his champions might have been torn to pieces by a High Church mob.

At this point it becomes necessary to reveal a document that must touch the fame of Defoe in the eyes of all who may not believe that the chief advisers of the sovereign had conspired with her to blacken it. The document is a private letter from Godolphin to Nottingham, and it tells its own story with a distinctness and precision rendering unnecessary either explanation or comment.

"Mr William Penn came to tell me he had acquainted my Lord Privy Seal that Defoe was ready to make oath to your lordship of all that he knew, and to give an account of all his accomplices in whatsoever he has been concerned, provided by so doing he may be screened from the punishment of the pillory, and not produced as an evidence against any person whatsoever. And upon my acquainting the queen with this just now at noon, her Majesty was pleased to tell me she had received the same account from my Lord Privy Seal, and seemed to think this, if there were no other, occasion for the Cabinet Council to meet here to-morrow, and has commanded me to tell you so." [1]

One can imagine a touch of comic risibility gleaming in Defoe's thoughts when he succeeded in sending

[1] 17th July 1703. Mus. Brit. Addl. MSS., 29589, 628.

the sternly earnest Quaker on such an errand. Though unsuccessful in averting his fate, it amply proves how important a person the London tradesman had become. Penn was then in the full blaze of one of those visitations of sunshine from the Court that so strangely broke in on the sombre tenor of his life. The two chief ministers of the Crown take council with the queen, and there is to be a special meeting of the Cabinet. There will be the less to surprise us in this affair when we make better acquaintance with Defoe, and perhaps find that, whatever wealth of virtues he possessed, scrupulosity as a public man was not among them. In the sequel we are told on the same authority that, " as to Defoe, the queen seems to think, as she did upon your first acquainting her with what he said, that his confession amounts to nothing. However, she is willing to leave it to the Lords of the Committee to let the sentence be executed to-morrow, or not till after Sunday, as they think proper." [1]

[1] 22d July 1703, ib. f. 44. The following memorandum takes significance as having been indorsed by the Duke of Leeds :—

" Daniel Defoe, the author of the review, is no Frenchman, but born here in England, bred an hosier, and followed that trade till he broke for a considerable sum. His creditors run him into an execution of bankruptcy, he having fraudulently, as they seem assured, concealed his effects ; so that his reputation among the fair dealers of the city is very foul. He is a professed Dissenter, though reckoned of no morals. He wrote a libel, as soon as her Majesty came to the throne, called ' The Shortest Way with the Dissenters.' He personated the Churchman, and under that disguise would, by the villanous insinuations of that pamphlet, have frightened the Dissenters into another rebellion. My Lord Nottingham, then Secretary, hunted him out, proved him the author, and had him pilloried for it. That is the ground of his fury and rage against a loyal and Church Ministry. This makes him so zealously engage and so seditiously express himself against the queen's employing honest men. He is certainly paid well for his pains by a party, for he bestows the copy, which hardly bears the expense of the press. He lives on Newington Green, at his father-in-law's house, who

Before we deal with the events bringing up the great issues between England and Scotland, some casual disturbing elements in the latter may be noted as a portion of the religious difficulties of Britain. The Episcopal Church party were regaining heart after their defeat. The suffering Episcopal clergy adopted a humble address to the queen, representing the deplorable condition of the National Church "since the suppression of the truly ancient and apostolic government of the Church by bishops," and lamenting over the disgrace brought on a Christian land, wherein those consecrated to the altar lacked bread and were dispersed as wanderers. They sought mere toleration. Nothing ever written could be more reasonable than their appeal. But in the career of a nation, when swept by a frenzy of rage and terror, reasonable claims may arise of a kind that it is disastrous to proclaim, and perilous even to whisper. The simple word Episcopacy was associated with national memories not only of the odious but of the perilous. The bloody work of what tradition called "the Killing times" had not in the moment of signal triumph been avenged in blood. Unlike the sanguin-

is a lay elder of a conventicle there."—Mus. Brit. Addl. MSS., 28094, f. 65.

Defoe denied that he kept a hosier's shop, and called himself a "hose factor." He had probably established a connection with the wool-producing districts for bringing their knitted produce to the London market.

Nottingham writes to Godolphin : "The person who discovered Daniel Foe—for whom a reward of £50 was promised in the 'Gazette' —sends to me for his money, but does not care to appear himself. If, therefore, your lordship will order that sum to be paid to Mr Armstrong, I will take care that the person shall have it who discovered the said Foe, and upon whose information he was apprehended."—25th May 1703. Calendar Treasury Papers, ii. 153.

ary Huguenots, from whom they drew their inspiration, the Presbyterians of Scotland had been signally moderate to the enemy at their feet. The " curates," as the Episcopal clergy were called, were no doubt "rabbled ;" and this was an unpleasant ordeal to those who had been accustomed to hunt the rabble.

At this juncture, indeed, the safety and comfort of the scattered remnant of the hierarchy depended chiefly on the weakness that kept them passive and silent. This lay not entirely in the inferiority of the number of their followers; for in some of the northern counties the friends of Episcopacy predominated so as to be able to resist the intrusion among them of Presbyterian pastors. But whether few or many, they wanted a faculty of cohesion and combination sufficient for collective action. On the other hand, under the fostering care of the Revolution Settlement, the Presbyterian organisation had waxed strong. It was proving itself to be the most powerful of priestly arrangements for an isolated community. Episcopacy did not come into existence to supply the spiritual wants of independent states. It grew, indeed, out of conditions that made each national church a mere brigade, to be, with all others, at the command of the Bishop of Rome. Presbyterianism took its strength from the opposite direction — from its peculiar element, rooted, as it were, in the solid earth, and feeding the growing structure with healthy life, till it flourished like a green bay tree.

Thus Presbyterianism was strong in Scotland, but not strong enough at this critical point to be careless about the tenor and object of any curative measure likely to give vitality to Episcopacy. In fact,

a new element of danger — an element of indefinite
force—had just appeared.   Episcopacy was the great
ruling feature that made England now foreign to
Scotland.   Casting Episcopacy on the ground again as
it had been cast by the Westminster Assembly was the
great achievement that Scotland had succeeded and
England had failed to accomplish by the Revolution.

It was rumoured that there was something in the
air more formidable than the mere bleating of the
sheep in the wilderness.   The queen, known to be
an ardent devotee of the Episcopal Church of England, had written something about the Episcopal
remnant in Scotland.   It was in the form of a letter
to her Secret Council of Scotland, and the Estates
were determined to see that letter in open Parliament.   It revealed to them a document adjusted to
the emergency with great sagacity.   The antithesis of
the fixed ecclesiastical conditions of the two countries
is at once emphasised in the opening sentences.
" We do, in the first place, recommend to your care
the Church, now established by law, in its superior
and inferior judicatures—such as sessions, presby-
teries, synods, and general assemblies ; as also in the
exercise of their holy functions, and what concerns
their persons and benefices."   Then follows : " We
are informed that there are many Dissenters within
that kingdom who, albeit they differ from the Established Church in opinion as to church government
and form, yet are of the Protestant reformed religion."
The High Churchmen of England were just then gird-
ing for a war of extermination against their own dissenters by the Bill for suppressing that middle party
who sought refuge in Occasional Conformity.   The

letter further announced : " It is our royal will and
pleasure that they should be directed to live suitably
to the reformed religion which they profess, submis-
sively to our laws, decently and regularly with relation to the Church established by law, as good Christians and subjects, and in so doing that they be
protected in the peaceable exercise of their religion,
and in their persons and estates, according to the
laws of the kingdom." Surely it must have been painful to the crowned champion and devoted adherent
of Episcopacy, as represented in the Church of England, to sue thus humbly for a sister Church. And
yet the appeal received the most humiliating of
repulses in the shape of silence.[1]

---

[1] The letter is not set forth in the minutes of the Estates, where it is
said that, having been demanded, "the said letter being accordingly
brought in and read, was immediately returned to the clerk of the
Privy Council."— Act. Parl., xi. 47. I find the letter quoted at
length in a broadside of the period.

CHAPTER III.

Domestic Affairs.

THE duty of the historian takes its pleasantest shape
when he finds a continuous evolution of causation
accompany events in their chronological succession.
But it is sometimes necessary to drop the chain of
causes and effects winding into each other; and so it
is when some great event, portentous to mankind, is
not the result of man's passions and actions, but a
dispensation such as we can neither create nor obviate,
and cannot even foreknow. Such was "the storm"
of 1703. Its causes are hidden among the undis-
covered secrets of the structure and physiology of
the universe, and beyond its own immediate disasters,
it left no seeds to ripen into like events. It stands
alone in history as "The Great Storm." It made
itself felt all over Europe, but it especially swept the
British Islands on the night of the 26th of November

1703. London being the greatest assemblage in the realm of people, edifices, and wealth, gave it the largest surface for attack, and bore the most numerous and emphatic marks of destructiveness. The fragile houses built in the area that had been swept by the fire were tossed about like houses of cards, and caused many cruel tragedies, while there were also some curious and grotesque escapes of people whose perilous position seemed absolutely to doom them. There were inundations of the rivers, and the Thames swept through Westminster Hall. On the shores of all the roadsteads lay drowned bodies with fragments of wreck and heaps of drenched cargo. Even the ships, built with superfluous strength to meet the exigencies of war, suffered.

We have from a thoroughly competent authority, this account of the rough and almost fantastic handling of a portion of the English navy posted off the coast of Holland. " ' The storm ' drove the Veigo, Rochester, Swan, and Newport, with about twenty of the transport ships, from their anchors ashore in the country, where some of them will never get off. It put the Veigo upon the west pier head at Helvoetsluys, when the men had just time to save their lives and down she sunk. The rest of her Majesty's ships are got off and safe. The Russel was drove from her anchor, with Sir Cloudesley Shovel, and after beating over the Hynder sand, put ashore about three miles to the westward of Helvoetsluys. We have got out all our guns and stores, and have some hopes of saving her hull. We have yet no news of the rest of the ships with Sir Cloudesley Shovel, nor of Admiral Cullemberg. . . . There are about 150 sail of merchant-ships lost in the Downs and Yarmouth Sands with their men. The poor Prince of Hesse Darmstadt has lost all his servants but five, and all he has in the world, in a ship driven out of the Downs and lost upon the Ely Island, on the north coast of this country."[1]

A calamity that seemed to touch the power of the navy was matter of instantaneous and unanimous action in the Commons, who would have to vote the remedy ; and they promised to find the money for the cost of immediate restoration, giving assurance "that they could not see any diminution of her Majesty's navy, without making provision to repair the same ; wherefore they besought her Majesty that she would immediately give directions for repairing this loss, and for building such capital ships as her Majesty should deem fit, and to assure her Majesty that, at their next meeting, the House would effectually make good that expense."

Irreparable and inestimable mischief was dealt to many monuments of national architecture, and among these, conspicuous for its noble beauties and their defacement, was the chapel of King's College at Cambridge. The wind seemed to enjoy a furious revelry in pitching down the steeples of churches, and rolling up the leaden roofs, as a skilful draper rolls his web of cloth. Masses of brick and stone were torn from the Palace of St James's ; and it was noted that the queen, with her husband and her maids of honour, rose at midnight, and formed themselves into an anxious group, as if it were becoming that the sove-

[1] Admiral Sir George Rooke—The Hague, 23d December 1743.— MS. Mus. Brit.

reign should be on the watch while powers so awful
and mysterious were dealing destruction among her
people.

Through all these incidents the hurricane showed
no respect of persons, but another seemed to point at
distinction and selection. The Bishop of Bath and
Wells, along with his wife, was killed in the episcopal palace, crushed under a stack of chimneys.
Now this bishop was Richard Kidder, who had
acquired his bishopric when the sainted Bishop
Ken had abandoned it as a sacrifice to his resolution
to abstain from the Revolution Oath, though he was
one of the immortal seven who went to the Tower in
protestation against interference with his ecclesiastical
conscience from the opposite side. It is creditable
to the fundamental good sense of England at the
period, that allusions to the possibility that the whole
terrible affair of the storm was a special organisation
for manifesting, with all attributes of sublimity and
horror, the divine vengeance for the expulsion of the
Nonjuror, are rare.

John Evelyn was a sufferer from the storm, and
refers to his own losses and those of his friends in
his delightful book, 'Sylvia; or, a Discourse of
Forest-trees.' After casual allusion to superstitions
about the groaning of storm-shattered forests, he
comes home and finds,—"But, however this were,
methinks I still hear—sure I am that I still feel—
the dismal groans of our forests when that dreadful
hurricane subverted so many thousands of goodly
oaks, prostrating the trees, laying them in ghastly
postures, like whole regiments fallen in battle by the
sword of the conqueror, and crushing all that grew

beneath them. . . . The public accounts reckon no less than 3000 brave oaks in one part only of the Forest of Dean blown down; in New Forest, in Hampshire, about 4000; and in about 450 parks and groves, from 200 large trees to 1000 of excellent timber, without counting fruit and orchard trees *sans* number;—and proportionally the same through all the considerable woods of the nation. Sir Edward Harley had 1300 blown down; myself about 2000, several of which, torn up by their fall, raised mounds of earth near twenty feet high, with great stones entangled among the roots and rubbish."[1]

"The great storm" is an incident now more than a hundred and seventy years old. Throughout that long period no elemental riot has occurred sufficiently egregious to invite a comparison with it. Thus, as time passed, it became ever more and more distinguished in the isolation of its own unrivalled grandeur. Does this give us a right to expect exemption —to count that the last of such outbursts of elemental wrath is past? Hardly. In the law of storms science has done little more than to warn us of the approach of the enemy, so that we may take such steps for defence as may fall within our power. Yet there have arisen, though feebly and dubiously, some

[1] Sylvia, ii. 350.
The Irish have their own peculiar way of dealing with exciting occasions. An absentee landowner receives the following morsel of intelligence :—
"Dec. 11, 1703.—Mr Dixon writes me word that the great storm has blown down one of my barns, and that my tenants are run away. The latter I expected long ago, and endeavoured to persuade him to be beforehand with them, but could not prevail, and so have lost above a year's rent and the damage occasioned by the storm will be at least £20 more out of my way."—Ellis Correspondence, MS., B.M., No. 28,932. f. 114.

comfortable suggestions that the conditions affording material for the brewing of a storm of a character so comprehensive no longer exist, having been absorbed by the widening area of cultivation on the surface of our islands. It has been observed that in all the more recent occasions of elemental destruction the cause has been found to exist in some local specialty—mountain torrents, swamps, sudden thaws on the mountains; and in regions of perpetual snow, the mysterious movements of the glacier. The destructive floods, for instance, in the rivers flowing from the Grampians in the year 1829 had a special local cause, giving a lesson that might have been better studied than it has been. Why was it that a rainfall,—only a little above the heaviest that had occurred in previous years, and passed peacefully to the sea in swollen rivers,—had not only swept away bridges and drowned villages, but had actually torn mountains to pieces? It was because the cisterns of water quiescent in the hearts of the mountains had burst their stony sides, under the curious law of hydraulic pressure. That is part of the dynamics of the elements now thoughtfully studied, because money can be made by acquaintance with it. The engineer, with a pump, a tube, and a few gallons of water, can take by it the power of fifty horses; and possibly some ten per cent of rainfall above that of other years might give power sufficient for rending mountains.

Let us turn to a contemporary storm of a different character. There had passed, almost silently, from the last Parliament elected under King William into the first elected under Queen Anne, a quarrel between the two Houses of the English Parliament, destined to become memorable in the history of the constitution. It is known in history as the Aylesbury Election Contest, and in law-books as the case of Ashby against Zouch. Before it started into life as a contest between the two Houses, the affair seemed to have been buried among the thousands of squabbles raised in a general election. The writ for the Parliament was issued on the 26th of December of the year 1700, and the Parliament assembled on the 6th of February 1701. Whoever has taken the trouble of mastering the debates on this critical question, will feel little inclination to echo the words of those careless narrators who speak of it as an unseemly squabble between the two Houses, or a collection of arid speeches on profitless questions of form. Perhaps nowhere, within the same compass, is there crowded so much instruction and exemplification on the framework of our constitution as in the two great debates that arose out of the election on that occasion of a burgess or member of the Commons, representing the pleasant little town of Aylesbury, in the county of Buckingham. The discussion was enriched by contributions from the greatest lawyers of the age —Sir John Hawles, who had been solicitor-general to King William ; Dormer ; Sir Joseph Jekyll ; three men who, each in his turn, sat on the woolsack — Cowper, King, and Harcourt. There were political eminences, as Loundes, Strickland, Lord Hartington, Sir Edward Seymour, and Sir Christopher Musgrave ; and less distinguished than these, at the time, were three names destined to fill the car of fame—Harley, St John, and Walpole.

The record of the debate has an eminent interest,
from its peculiarity as the first significant political
discussion or dispute that began and ended in peace.
The constitutional discussions of the seventeenth
century were all swayed and characterised by bitter
enmities, actual war, and imminent danger. In the
days of the Long Parliament it was war for very
existence between prerogative and privilege; and the
latest dispute of all ended in driving a king from his
throne.

A writ had been issued to the sheriff of the county
for the election of two burgesses to represent Aylesbury.   The sheriff directed his precept to certain
constables with whom the execution of the precept
lay. The burgesses being assembled, Matthew Ashby,
the plaintiff, maintaining that he was duly qualified
to vote, tendered his vote for two candidates—Sir
Thomas Lee and Mr Mayne; but the constable
refused to receive it.   Ashby then brought an action,
tried at the assizes, where the end was a verdict in
his favour, with damages amounting to £5.   The
case was carried to the Queen's Bench, where this
judgment was reversed; and the elector, whose vote
was rejected by the constable, was found to have no
claim for damage on that account.   The franchise
on which the claimant tendered his vote had been
adjusted by the Commons.   In the words of Sir
Joseph Jekyll, "Before the action was brought there
was a resolution of the House of Commons that the
right of election for the borough of Aylesbury was in
the inhabitants not receiving alms.   It is from that
resolution the plaintiff hath taken his rise, and hath
brought his action; for by his declaration he makes

his case to be, that he was an inhabitant of that borough, not receiving alms, and that the constables falsely and maliciously obstructed and hindered him from giving his vote at the election there." [1]

The hero of this parliamentary contest was so close to the condition of penury that would have sunk him below the franchise, that, being a poor ostler struggling for a sordid living, he became chargeable on the parish while his name was yet the keynote of a mighty parliamentary struggle, — a struggle that might never have burst on the world had the poor ostler made his descent into pauperism more rapidly.

The case came to its climax when, on a writ of error, the judgment of the Queen's Bench was reversed by the House of Lords. This final finding by the Lords was favourable to freedom of election, since it opened up the question whether the constables could reject the vote of an adult male inhabitant of the borough, not in receipt of alms when he tendered his vote. But this was an act done by the Lords disposing of a question of membership in the Commons. It could not be denied that many incidental powers in the hands of divers persons might influence an election. The courts of law, in keeping the elector in possession of his territorial qualification, the sheriff taking steps for obedience to the writ, and the constables in receiving and recording the votes. But over all this, when the question settled itself down upon the issue of possessing a seat in the House, the Commons professed to be a club entitled to reject or accept their companions within the sacred precincts. They could

[1] Parl. Hist., vi. 271.

not decide a question of territorial possession. They could not put a witness on oath as that is done by a court of law. They could not find one disputant before them liable to pay damages to another. But when all these preliminary steps were disposed of, and the result came in the decision that some one had or had not a right to sit among them, then their supreme power over their own composition started into activity. This anomaly was a curious fruit of that jealous, separate independence that drove royalty from their door. The sovereign could not stand on the floor of the House of Commons, and consequently, the Commons could not make themselves a court of law and justice, because all such courts are animated by the royal presence and power, and the presence of the sovereign is a presumption of law in all of them, as it has been sometimes a reality in the House of Lords. The sovereign sought counsel in the administration of justice among the judges of his supreme courts, and among the members of the House of Lords. But he sought no counsel in the other House, because he was jealously excluded from it.

It was admitted that from the first irregularity or illegality at the hustings, the Commons could do nothing towards a remedy until the case became ripe for the Lords to correct it, and then the Commons could speak and say,—You shall not; it is our function. But when their jurisdiction did open, it went back over all the stages to justify the vote that had been rejected by the constable, and decide how the election would be affected by the admission of that vote, though it could not mulct the constable in damages for rejecting the vote. This position was stated at

an early stage of the dispute, was maintained throughout, and after all adjustment appeared to be buried
in helpless complexities, it was uttered in this distinct shape :—

"Nor can any elector suffer either injury or damage
by the officer's denying his vote; for when the elector
hath named the person he would have to represent
him, his vote is effectually given both as to his own
right and privilege and as it avails the candidate in
his election : and is ever allowed when it comes in
question in the House of Commons, whether the officer had any regard to it or no." [1]

While eloquence flowed at St Stephen's, there came
some practical hints that the elements of aggression
and contest referred to by the orators were finding
employment. It was maintained that if the affair
lay with the House of Commons, that august body
would be content to establish purity of election; but
where would be the end if all concerned in an election had an action at law against some public officer ?

"Suppose, as at Westminster, where I think there
are 10,000 electors; or suppose it be as in some
towns near Wales—for one of which I have the honour to serve—where the descendants of every burgess
claim a right to vote, and by consequence, they will
bring it in time almost to all the sons of Adam; for all
the sons and all the daughters' husbands, and all their
descendants claim a right to vote. Now, what a mis-
erable case must that officer be in when persons shall
come from east, west, north, and south, and say their
pedigree is so and so—for they are good at pedigrees
in those countries,—yet, what a condition is he in ?

[1] Parl. Hist., vi. 394.

He is bound to determine whether they have a vote
or not; and though he is no lawyer or herald, yet,
however, he is bound to give judgment one way or another at the peril of an action. And suppose but a hundred men shall bring their actions against the officer,
what man can stand a hundred actions though he be
in the right ? There are not only these difficulties in
the case, but there is revenge : and in popular elections, there are those heats and the voters engage with
that animosity, that the losing side next day will be
ready, perhaps, only for revenge, to send for a multitude of writs, and have the pleasure of ruining the
officer who was against them, though he was in the
right; for every one has a right to bring his action
whose vote was disallowed, though it should be found
at last that he had no right." [1]

It tended to the realisation of this vision, that on
the strength of the reversal by the Lords, not only
did Ashby take out execution, but five other men
claiming to be electors of Aylesbury brought actions
against the constable for rejecting their votes. These
five culprits were in their turn committed for breach
of privilege, each on a separate order or warrant setting forth in detail the offence committed. At this
point the Commons thought it necessary to address
the Throne against any counter-action through the
agency of her Majesty's courts of law, asserting "the
undoubted right and privilege of the Commons of
England in Parliament assembled to commit for
breach of privilege : and that the commitments of this
House are not examinable in any other court whatsoever." They could not especially be touched by

[1] Speech of Sir Thomas Powis, Parl. Hist., vi. 247, 248.

any " writ of error." At the same time they made
inquiry as to the truth of rumours that certain persons had been " concerned in soliciting, prosecuting,
or pleading" writs of *habeas corpus* or writs of error,
on behalf of the persons committed ; and having
reason, on the whole aspect of the affair, to be appre-
hensive " lest her Majesty should grant the writs of
error," they took a step that gave a touch of the
ludicrous to their side of the contest,—they ordered
the culprits "to be removed from Newgate and taken
into the custody of the sergeant-at-arms." [1]

The next step taken by the Commons was to smite
the legal advisers who were aiding and abetting in
the acts denounced as breach of privilege. A committee was appointed " to examine what persons have
been concerned in soliciting, prosecuting, or pleading
upon the writs of *habeas corpus* or writs of error, on
the part of the persons committed" for breach of
privilege. This brought into the contest "James
Montague, Esquire ; Nicholas Lechmere, Alexander
Denton, and Francis Page, counsellors at law ;
William Lee and John Harris, attorneys at law."
The sergeant-at-arms being required to account for
this new group of culprits, "he gave the House an
account accordingly ; that he had found Mr Denton
at his own chamber and had him in custody; but that

---

[1] Parl. Hist., vi. 385. A contemporary annalist scarcely extracts the
transaction from the condition of the ludicrous by noting " which order
was executed at midnight with such circumstances of severity and
terror as have been seldom exercised towards the greatest offenders."—
Annals of Queen Anne, p. 86. The annalist had, however, found this
passage in "the humble representation and address of the Right Hon.
the Lords spiritual and temporal in Parliament assembled, presented
to her Majesty the 14th day of March 1704," being a complaint against
the House of Commons.—See Parl. Hist., vi. 430.

he could not find the other persons." We are left to vague inferences as to their method of disappearance, in the terms of an order " by the Lords spiritual and temporal in Parliament assembled, that the said persons shall, and they have hereby, the protection and privilege of this House, in the advising, applying for, and prosecuting the said writs of error ; and that all keepers of prisons and jailors, and all sergeants-at-arms and other persons whatsoever be—and they are hereby, for or in respect of any of the cases aforesaid —strictly prohibited from arresting, imprisoning, or otherwise detaining or molesting or charging the said persons, or any or either of them, as they and every of them will answer the contrary to this House." It did not point towards moderate and tolerant councils, that the high executive officer of the Commons was thus contemptuously noticed among " all sergeants-at-arms and other persons." [1]

This is an occurrence of the 25th of February ; and on the 6th of March the sergeant-at-arms appears to inform the House how " that a person had this morning brought him a writ of *habeas corpus* under the Great Seal, for Mr Montague—in his custody by order of this House—to be brought, as he was informed, before the Lord Keeper of the Great Seal of England ; and he delivered the writ under the Seal in at the table." [2]

[1] Parl. Hist., vi. 386.

[2] This document in its barbarous Latin, contorted by official contractions, is in strange contrast with the expressive English of the debate and the parliamentary documents, reminding one of a rugged shapeless boulder on a glacier : " Anna Dei gratia Ang' Sco' Franc' et Hibern' Regina, Fidei Defensor, &c. Samuel Powel Ar' Servien ad arma attenden' Honorab' Dom' Commun' ejus Deputato et Deputatis salutem," &c.—Parl. Hist., vi. 389.

The instructions he received were—" That the ser-geant-at-arms attending this House do make no re-turn of, or yield any obedience to, the said writ of *habeas corpus;* and for such his refusal, that he have the protection of the House of Commons."[1]

Before the dispute had reached this point, a message passed to the Commons that " the Lords desire a present conference with the House in the Painted Chamber about some ancient fundamental liberties of the kingdom." They desired it, they said, " in order to a good understanding between the two Houses, which they will always endeavour to pre-serve. When either House of Parliament have ap-prehended the proceedings of the other to be liable to exception, the ancient parliamentary method has been to ask a conference, it being ever supposed that when the matters are fairly laid open and debated, that which may have been amiss will be rectified, or else the House that made the objections will be satisfied that their complaint was well grounded."[2]

But these conciliatory suggestions announced, as fundamental principles and in a very distinct form, those judicial claims of the House of Lords which the Commons resisted. And no one prepared with a full knowledge of the antecedents of the conference could expect it to work out a good understanding. In fact each of the Houses had acquired, and was yet ac-quiring, certain powers whether they were to be called prerogative or privilege, held by each as peculiarly its own, and jealousy to be protected from co - operation with or interference by the other. The appellate jurisdiction was the chief

---

[1] Parl. Hist.. vi. 402.　　　　[2] Ibid.. 387.

characteristic claim of the Peerage—the exclusive right of voting supplies was the counter-claim of the Commons. The items of the conference are not articulately preserved, but they are sufficiently clear in revealing irreconcilable claims and enmities. The first taunt of the Commons is occasioned by the first of the Lords' resolutions : " That neither House of Parliament hath any power, by any vote or declaration, to create to themselves any new privilege that is not warranted by the known laws and customs of Parliament." The commentary is : " This would effectually put an end to that en-croachment in judicature so lately assumed by your lordships and so often complained of by the Commons — we mean the hearing of appeals from courts of equity in your lordships' House. This would have hindered the bringing of original causes before your lordships ; and your unwarrantable pro-ceedings upon the petition of Thomas Lord Whar-ton," which the Commons characterised as a per-version of the power " heretofore exercised for the relief of the subject oppressed by the power of the great men of the realm " to a contrary purpose— the unjust aggrandisement of one of their own order.

And again, on the fifth resolution justifying the writs of error, among other bitter sayings are : " When it is considered how that usurpation in hearing of appeals from courts of equity, so easily traced though often denied and protested against, is still exercised, and almost every session of Par-liament extended, it is not to be wondered that, after the success your lordships have had in those great advances upon our constitution, you should now at once make an attempt upon the whole frame of it by drawing the choice of the Commons' representatives to your determination." And further, " The Commons cannot but see how your lordships are contriving by all methods to bring the determination of liberty and property into the bottomless and insatiable gulf of your lordships' judicature, which would swallow up both the prerogatives of the Crown and the rights and liberties of the people."[1]

And it is observable that the wrath of the Commons is under good government; for instead of incoherence there is supreme distinctness of utterance linking cause with effect when they come to their angriest climax.

" The bringing writs of *habeas corpus* upon the commitments of the Commons, and a writ of error thereupon before the Lords, would bring all the privileges of the Commons to be determined by the judges and afterwards by the Lords upon such writs of error.

" Nay, such writs of error upon every *habeas corpus* would bring the liberty of every commoner in England to the arbitrary disposition of the House of Lords.

" And if a writ of error cannot be denied in any case [this was repeatedly urged by the Lords apologetically—the writ was not of *grace* but of *right*], and the Lords alone are to judge whether the case be proper for a writ of error, then all the queen's revenues, all her prerogatives, and all the lives and liberties of the people of England will be in the

[1] Parl. Hist.. vi. 400.

hands of the Lords; for every felon, burglar, and traitor will be entitled to a writ of error before the Lords: and they will have even power over life and death.

"And by writs of error and appeals, as already exercised, they will have all our properties; by such newly invented actions they will have all our elections; and by such writs of *habeas corpus* and writs of error thereupon they will have all our privileges, liberties, and even lives at their determination: who determine by vote with their doors shut, and it is not certainly known who it is that hurts you. The novelty of those things, and the infinite consequences of them, is the greatest argument in law that they are not of right." [1]

There seemed to be some inclination in the Lords attending the conference to be courteous and complimentary, but it had a tinge of patronising grace that was perhaps slightly offensive, and it had little effect in soothing the wrath of the Commons, though they were told "that the Lords look upon the Commons to be a great part of the constitution, which cannot be preserved but by doing right to both Houses.

"That the constitution is the wonder of the world and the glory of the nation; it is founded upon liberty and property; and the House of Commons hath been a great fence and bulwark of liberty." [2]

The Lords, though they suggested the conference, did not find that it served their purpose. Those who represented them appear to have been somewhat

[1] Parl. Hist.. vi. 408.   [2] Ibid.. 402.

haughty and reserved.   They endeavoured to check
the Commons on the question of the aggrandisement
of the judicial powers of their House.   On reporting
back to their own House, the managers for the Commons conclude thus : " Your managers declared that
they had more to offer, and were ready to proceed
upon the subject-matter of the last conference in
such manner as they thought their duty to the Commons of England required, if their lordships thought
fit to hear them ; whereupon the Lords did rise and
break off the conference." [1]

The Lords then took a course not to be easily accounted for.   With bitter eloquence they registered
the items of their quarrel in a " Representation and
Address" to the queen, dated on the 14th of March.
It appears that difficulties had arisen in the matter of
the writs of error, for it was said that in two instances,
though the usual steps had been taken, the writs had
not passed.   They conclude their address by expressing a hope " that no importunity of the House of
Commons, nor any other consideration whatsoever,
may prevail with your Majesty to suffer a stop to be
put to the known course of justice, but that you will
be pleased to give effectual orders for the immediate
issuing of the writs of error."

Her Majesty made answer on the day of the reception of the address, and it was an answer so little to
the purpose that it must have been suggested by a
bold and subtle policy.   It was in these few words :
" My Lords, I should have granted the writs of
error desired in this address.   But finding an abso-

[1] Parl. Hist., vi. 420.

lute necessity of putting an immediate end to the session, I am sensible there could have been no further proceeding in that matter." [1]

If we test the merits of the parties to this great contest by the historical development of the constitution in the judicial remedies for correcting imperfections in elections, the leaning of approval would be towards the policy of the Lords. To bring elections under impartial law, and reserve them from the power of the party prevalent in the House has been a long and difficult process; and some of us are old enough to remember when, on the calling of the names on an election committee, there were cheers from the party that by the accident of the ballot was strongly represented in it. But one's sympathy in the discussion is apt to lie with the Commons. The rapid growth of the judicial powers of the Lords justly alarmed them, and it perhaps required more than usual sagacity to divine that, instead of serving the capricious selfishness and tyranny of an irresponsible aristocracy, the judicial powers would all pass into the hands of learned and industrious lawyers—that the arrangement would be of eminent service by recruiting the aristocratic branch of the Legislature with the powerful fresh blood of families that have gradually risen from the humbler ranks of society by capacity, integrity, and industry.

Two morsels of history not connected with each other save by continuity in time have in this chapter here been treated apart, with a view of keeping them out of the current of more conspicuous events.

[1] Parl. Hist.. vi. 435.

We have to enter on the hatreds and attachments that after many oscillations of hopes and anxieties culminated in the union of England and Scotland. While here one event follows another with a close sequence of cause and effect, another long historical drama, acted abroad, has to be brought before the reader in its successive steps of scarcely interrupted victory.

CHAPTER IV.

International Difficulties.

SINCE the union of the crowns, an incorporating
union of Scotland with England had become a traditional policy in both countries, and especially became
ripened into form and substance by debates and resolutions of the Parliament of England. It was bequeathed to both countries by King William under

conditions conferring on the bequest a mournful solemnity. On the 23d February in the year 1702, in a message to the Commons, he announced himself as "fully satisfied that nothing can more contribute to the present and future security and happiness of England and Scotland than a firm and entire union between them." Further, that he " would esteem it a peculiar felicity if during his reign some happy expedient for making both kingdoms one might take place." The message incidentally noted that he was " hindered by an unhappy accident from coming in person to his Parliament, and so could only signify to the Commons by message what he desired to have spoken to both Houses from the throne."[1] The " unhappy accident " occurring two days earlier was in fact his death-blow.

Whatever forces were at work for or against the Union, in the government and constitution of the two kingdoms, and the tempers and national prejudices of the people, had become familiar to both in a century of discussion. But ere the question came to a final and practical issue, new forces, arising with the growth of each nation during that century, were destined for predominance in the struggle. Before the civil war there had been disputes and difficulties between Englishmen and Scotsmen on questions of trade, especially wherever the Scots endeavoured to deal with the English colonies. These affairs arose rather out of frailties and imperfections in the law than from exclusive privileges and absolute prohibitions. Such as they were, all these difficulties were swept away for a time by the Protectorate Govern-

[1] Parl. Hist.. v. 1341.

ment. The exercise of many old constitutional and feudal powers were, especially in Scotland, then thwarted by the controlling hand of a military despotism. But trade was absolutely freed, and in all matters of commerce, navigation, and colonial enterprise, England, Scotland, and Ireland became one community.

The Navigation Acts had an instructive influence on the creation of the political forces that, by setting the two nations in antagonism, led to the complete union. The first Navigation Act was passed by the Protectorate Government in 1651. It was a blow dealt against Holland, and whatever economic reaction it had on Britain it was successful in its ostensible object of stopping the career of the States towards the dominion of the seas. The Dutch, by the force of their realised capital, acting on their facilities for shipbuilding, were engrossing the carrying trade of the sea : wherever there were commodities ready for exportation, and a community ready to purchase them as imports, Dutch vessels were at hand for their conveyance ; and it was vain for other communities to compete with them, for none could perform the service so effectively and cheaply. The policy of the Act was to exclude these carriers from the ports of England—unless the goods brought in cargo came from the place of their produce in Europe, they must be carried in English-built vessels, of which the commander with three-fourths of the crew were English subjects.

We may now believe that the natural enterprise of England would have raised it only the more rapidly to the commercial supremacy it was destined to attain without this invidious exclusion. But what we have here to note is, that Scotland was not excluded by the Act of the Protectorate. There was a complete union of the British Islands under one Government, and whatever advantages Englishmen believed themselves to derive from the exclusion, Scotsmen were entitled to arrogate to themselves. It was among the Englishman's denunciations of the Protectorate Government that it admitted the impoverished and sordid Scots to a participation in the sources of England's wealth.

Interpreted by the commercial creed of the age, the Navigation Act was a brilliant achievement, and though the work of the usurper it was speedily re-enacted by the Restoration Government. In its restoration it was shaken free of the defect that gave a share in its beneficence to Scotland. England and Scotland again stood separate and apart, and in the protective code of England, Scotland was as thoroughly a foreign country as France or Russia. In a remonstrance on the part of Scotland in the beginning of the year 1668, a claim of participation was stated in a shape to bring out distinctly the character of the exclusion, by pleading that "the same freedom may be allowed to such ships and vessels as do truly and without fraud belong only to the people of Scotland —whereof the master and three-fourth parts are Scotsmen or other his Majesty's subjects, and freighted only by his Majesty's subjects—as are allowed to his Majesty's subjects of Ireland, dominion of Wales, and town of Berwick-upon-Tweed." And further, "that it be declared that his Majesty's subjects of Scotland are not meant to be debarred by the clause debarring aliens or persons not born within the alle-

giance of our Sovereign Lord the King from exercising the trade or occupation of merchants or factors." [1]
But co-operation and harmonious action did not re-
spond to the tone of the commercial policy of the
age.   Retaliation was the keynote that raised the
energies of nations.   A feeble effort to effect a union
followed this remonstrance.   The active spirits began
to dream of exclusive schemes for Scotland in rivalry
with England.   The Dutch were an example to them.
Exclusion from English trade seemed only to concentrate their powers in doing for themselves.   Even
while the Protectorate exclusion pressed upon them
they were settling themselves at the Cape of Good
Hope, the resting-place for all the European States
ambitious of trade and dominion in the Indian seas ;
they were creeping with factories into Borneo and
other islands of the Eastern Archipelago, and had
audaciously planted themselves so far away in the
New World as Guiana.   Cut off from the English
sympathy and communion, they prospered so as to
rival if not to excel England as a trading and aggrandising community.

They might be excluded from the Thames, but if
the English patrician desired to select the decorations
of his dwelling from the splendours of the East and
the West he must go to muddy Amsterdam for them.
Even sullen Japan, shutting its door to the rest of
the world, admitted the Dutch trader to its great
mart of household finery.   Scotland likewise excluded
would do in like manner.   Even so the restless needy
man who sees his aggrandising neighbour heaping

[1] Bruce : Report on the events and circumstances which produced the
Union, Appx. ccl.

riches upon riches by bold enterprises that never fail in his hands, will follow in the wake of his speculative enterprises and make himself rich. But he forgets two absolute conditions of success. The one is, that capital must have accumulated, and either in the hands of the rich possessor or some ancestor, it has come in drop by drop in sordid gains, until it has become strong enough to rule the market. The other condition is, the capacity to handle so powerful and subtle an engine as capital. The Dutchman had achieved this accomplishment by practice in all the markets of the world. The Scot has shown since then that it is latent in his nature, but as yet he had neither realised capital for himself nor exemplified such capacity for handling it as might induce others to intrust it to his management.

Thus it befell that while the prohibitions and penalties of the Navigation Act were levelled against the prosperous Dutch—the rivals of England in trade and navigation—they struck and wounded the poor Scots, who might have expected brotherly treatment. A statement early in the year 1668, made by commissioners from Scotland meeting commissioners from England, going back to the time when there was no protective and exclusive Navigation Act, and passing on through the Navigation Act of the Protectorate to the Navigation Act of the Restoration, states the conditions with great clearness : " Whereas his Majestie's subjects of Scotland have enjoyed a free trade here in England, and in all the dominions and plantations belonging to the kingdom of England, more than fifty and six years without any considerable obstruction all that time ; yet since the twenty-fifth day of March, in the twelfth year of his Majesty's reign, by some Acts of Parliament here in England, the king's subjects of Scotland are thereby debarred from the privileges granted to all his Majesty's other subjects, seeing by those Acts the privileges are granted to such ships or vessels as do truly and without fraud belong only to the people of England or Ireland, dominion of Wales, or town of Berwick-upon-Tweed; and all other ships or vessels —without any exception—with all their goods and merchandises, are declared to be forfeited." [1]

There was an element of practical irony in this result of the effective struggle of the Scots to hold their independence. Ireland, the dominion of Wales, the town of Berwick-on-Tweed, were dependencies of the English Crown, subject to the authority of English legislation and participators in the privileges secured to the trade of England. Scotland was an independent state, and had to look to its own Legislature for sound laws and the redress of grievances. [2] It was in vain to plead, as the Scots did, that they and the English were under the allegiance of the

---

[1] Bruce : Report on the Union, App. ccxlix.

[2] The demand by Scotland of the privileges conferred on Ireland, is met thus : "The answer is most clear and obvious—viz., that Ireland is not only under one king with us, as Scotland, but belongs to, and is, an appendix of the Crown of England ; and laws made in the Parliament of England do bind them ; and no law can be enacted by the Parliament of Ireland but what passeth the Privy Council of England ; and orders of the Council of England and the Great Seal of England do take place in Ireland ; yea, the Treasurer and other great officers of State in England, have jurisdiction and superintendency in Ireland : by all which it is absolutely in our power when we grant privileges to them, to compel and keep them up to the restrictions and limitations of them ; all which is quite otherwise in relation to Scotland."—English Commissioners' Concessions, &c, 16th March 1678 : Bruce, cclxxiv.

same sovereign. In anything that touched their independence or nationality, the Scots would never admit that their sovereign could, because he was King of England, do what he could not have done had he been king only of Scotland. But they had better reasons to state for being included in the English privileges. A partnership in trade between England and Scotland would increase the wealth of both, and would strengthen the Crown by enlarging the customs duties; while the increase of shipping and seamen that would come of the united effort of the two nations, would increase the strength and security of the British empire. Of course, in the suggestions from Scotland there was no hint that the restrictions might well be relaxed—it was only just that Scotland should participate in the blessings they imparted. They desired that the privileges of the English colonial trade might be extended "to such ships and vessels as do truly and without fraud belong only to the people of Scotland, whereof the master and three-fourth parts are Scotsmen or other his Majesty's subjects, and freighted only by his Majesty's subjects;" and that vessels so navigated and freighted "may be declared to have liberty to bring into England the goods and commodities that are of foreign growth, production, or manufacture, under the same restrictions and limitations as are expressed for the ships of England."[1]

The discussion of the Scots claims of 1669 brought the whole question so far to a practical shape that commissioners were appointed on both sides to treat of a union. But the period of discord and gloom

[1] Bruce. ccli.

that settled for twenty years on the two kingdoms, and especially on Scotland, seems to have deadened the cheerful aspirations that seek their issue in trade and co-operative enterprises. The legislation of the period is exceptionally barren, even in the paternal legislation that professes to protect good and wholesome commerce, and to denounce all those efforts at selfish aggrandisement which are supposed to spread the seeds of commercial disease through the community at large.

The Revolution, with the influence social rather than political of the Dutch king and his followers, created a new spirit. The banker appeared beside the dealer. All kinds of coins, some of value difficult of adjustment, others debased or clipped, would double or triple the perplexities of the trader. Bills of exchange had been invented, but they depended not so much on their prompt conversion into bullion, as on the multitude of indorsers, all liable to the relief of the holder. Real property, such as land and houses, might be pledged for the paper money, and this might make it ultimately secure, but would not give it the flexibility of ready money. But Holland had solved the great problem, and the wondrous Bank of Amsterdam appeared to create out of nothing but the wisdom and cleverness of its creators a sufficiency of ready cash for all the wants of an affluent community.[1]

---

[1] The adepts who organised the Scots system of banking, carefully studied the mechanism of the Bank of Amsterdam. It is fortunate that a century ago, while it was still exceptionally effective as a national bank, and the Scots bankers were endeavouring to follow its instructive precedents, Adam Smith should have written an exposition of its peculiarities and merits. — See Wealth of Nations, book iv. chap. iii.

From the Revolution to the accession of Queen Anne, England was kept in restless agitation by speculative projects. Among these were the Bank of England, the Million Bank, two Land Banks, plantation projects in the colonies and great public companies for pearl-fishing, the Greenland and New-foundland fisheries, and many others. There were great organisations on the joint-stock system for sup-plying clothing, and the other common necessaries and amenities of life—as the Lustring Company, the various companies for linen and woollen manufac-tures, glass-blowing companies, and japanning com-panies. Many of these were ephemeral, but a few left their mark on history, as the two East India Companies, the old and the new, and the two African Companies. Lastly, the speculating spirit of the age gave existence to a new institution, which has had a vigorous life—the Stock Exchange of London.

It was natural that Scotland should be touched by the influences so forcibly prevalent in England, and perhaps equally natural that in the crowd of projects, an Act passed by the Scots Estates on the 25th of June 1695, called an " Act for a Company trading to Africa and the Indies," should be allowed to pass without much examination or criticism from those not immediately interested in the project. The legis-lation of the Scots Estates was ever more impulsive than that of the Parliament of England. The com-plete division into two Houses, and the many checks interrupting hasty or inconsiderate action, which had grown through the long struggle between prerogative and privilege in England, were scarcely known in Scotland ; and they were hardly missed, for it so hap-

pened that the Estates and the Crown generally acted
with so much harmony, as to leave it an open question
whether the Crown could reject a bill passed by the
Estates.   There was at the same time a local cause
deterring those not in the secret of the ultimate projects of the promoters of the measure from criticising
its nature, since the Estates were at the time all on
fire about "The Report of the Commission for in-
quiring into the Slaughter of the Glencoe men."

Yet the Act that passed thus quietly carried the
union of the kingdoms and went far in the securing of
the Hanover succession.   It cannot be said that there
never would have been a union of England and
Scotland but for this Act; but had there been a union
otherwise stimulated, it must have had a different
history from that now to be told.   And, indeed, when
the terms of the statute are interpreted by events
following on it, its importance and significance become powerfully visible, since it created in the new
company powers of declaring peace and war, upholding
navies and armies, founding colonies, and contracting
alliances.

The first step was to raise the necessary stock.
And here it was discovered that there was a fatal
weakness in the laws for keeping all the commerce of
England to her own people, and especially excluding
the participation of the Scots.   Englishmen could
hold stock in a Scots company, and however patriotism could collectively exclude Scots participation in
English profits, it was insufficient to restrain Englishmen separately from investing in a Scots adventure
promising to pay.

William Paterson, the soul and inspiration of the

scheme, was a London merchant deep in all the mysteries of the stock market. He recommended that the affair should receive its first impulse in that ardent atmosphere, instead of being first exposed to a lingering appreciation by the Scots, scant of cash, and unaccustomed to the bold adventures of England. He remarked that " when the Parliament gives a long day for money, that fund has hardly any success. The Bank of England had but six weeks' time from the opening of the books and that was finished in nine days. And in all subscriptions here it is always limited to a short day ; for if a thing go not on with the first heat, the raising of a fund seldom or never succeeds, the multitude being commonly led more by example than reason."

Under the auspices of ten English directors, the books were opened in London. The opening was in every way skilful both as to the seductive prospect and the limited opportunity for participation, and there was a rush for shares. Then the two demons of the market—the lust of gain and the dread of ruin —were raised and set to work. A later generation beheld wilder orgies in the South Sea and Mississippi schemes, but on this occasion even so barren a stage as poor Scotland afforded an exciting rehearsal of such scenes.

The capitalists of the English companies whose privileges were to be touched, arose in fury, and were successful in arousing sympathetic wrath in both Houses of Parliament. That solemn conclave, only exorcised into existence by conditions critical and weighty—a conference between the Lords and Commons, was dedicated to the emergency. And when the causes of wrath were set forth in detail, nothing could be more just and logical than their tenor. All the English companies possessed exclusive privileges, protected to them by stern and cruel laws ; and here started up a band of free-traders—of licensed smugglers—who were to outrage them all. Through the privileges granted to the Scots company, "a great part of the stock and shipping of this nation will be carried thither, and by this means Scotland be made a free port for all Indian commodities, and consequently those several places in Europe which were supplied from England, will be furnished from thence much cheaper ; " "and when once that nation shall have settled themselves in plantations in America, our commerce in tobacco, sugar, cotton, wool, skins, masts, &c., will be utterly lost, because the privileges of that nation, granted to them by this Act, are such that that kingdom must be the magazine for all those commodities, and the English plantations and the traffic there lost to us."[1]

Then came a demand for the impeachment of some of the statesmen who had counselled the Crown to the perpetration of this outrage, but all who could be charged with the guilty act were secure in Scotland, where nothing but a powerful invading force could touch them. In a short time the fury of the English capitalists burnt itself out. Those who had subscribed for stock took fright and courted obscurity. When the first instalment fell due none came forward to meet it and the shares were consequently forfeited. Thus the English privileged companies were not to

[1] Lords' Journals. 13th December 1695.

be invaded and ruined by rival capitalists at their own door.

The Scots were not in a humour to feel thwarted or disappointed by this result of their attempt on English capital. It is possible even to extract from their demeanour symptoms of exultation in the prospect of keeping the newly found treasure exclusively to themselves. But then arose the serious question —Could the nation produce the capital necessary for the mighty undertaking? Some efforts were made to get aid from abroad, but the national enthusiasm daily grew and strengthened, and it became clear that whatever funds existed would be available in the cause. It was a national cause, aided by an approving self-interest that had no doubt of the absolute certainty of the coming reward. The capital, as originally projected, was to be six hundred thousand pounds sterling, to be equally divided between the two kingdoms. Now that England had dropped off, the Scots bravely added a hundred thousand to their original allotment. That this slightly overdrew the pecuniary capacity of the country is shown by a small item only revealed to those who have examined the company's books. The last two thousand pounds subscribed to complete the round sum are fictitious. They were subscribed by a citizen of Edinburgh on a guarantee from the company at large.

And now came the dangerous delusion that a community are enriched because they are rapidly spending. Everything had a tone of prosperity. The country was, in gamblers' phrase, "flush of money," but nothing could less resemble the squandering of the gambler than the purpose to which it was applied. All the productive resources of the country were stimulated. Coal-mines, salt-mines, metallic ores, were worked up into saleable commodities. All kinds of linen, woollen, and leather goods were rapidly manufactured. The herring, cod, whale, and salmon fisheries expanded with the rising market. The building trade was even touched in the general stimulus, for the company began to build between Edinburgh and the Meadows stately chambers, bidding fair to become a national palace in the French style. Most significant, perhaps, of all this productiveness, was the creation of a fleet of vessels, equipped not only for the exportation of merchandise and emigrants, but for battle.

The first colony—the colonisation schemes were indefinite—was to rise in a spot selected by Paterson, who had made close acquaintance with it, and pronounced it to be the best adapted spot in all the world for giving effect to the ruling spirit of the new enterprise. That spirit was free trade. All the world was to be invited to buy and sell in the new territory of the Scots; and to suit the traders of all the world it was to be on the Isthmus of Panama—the neck of rocky land, looking so narrow on a terrestial globe, that by uniting the great northern and the great southern territories of America, just suffices to make the whole one continent. The spot selected, chiefly with an eye to its capacity of being well fortified, is too well known in the annals of national misfortune by the name of Darien.

Here then was established a real Scots colony, but

to what end ? By taking up its position where it did, it seemed to proclaim to the world at large,—Ye that want to buy the produce of European industry, come to us—we have abundance of commodities, useful and ornamental ; ye that want to sell the produce of your own distant lands, come to us—we have capital, and are prepared to buy.

But no one came for either purpose. Then it was found that the hardy Scotsman's constitution was not suited to endure a tropical climate, stimulating poisonous swamps, and dripping forests ; and for months the chief labour of the colonists was in burying their dead. In Scotland the harvest next after their departure was deficient. They seemed to have taken the heart and energy of the country with them, and those remaining at home longed to join their brethren in the happy regions of prosperity ; so that, ere anything was heard of the fate of the first colony, a second and a third had been sent out to increase its wants instead of supplying them.

Then they soon found themselves in the midst of enemies. In Spain there was a sick man, sick even unto death ; and when the hour of death came, it was as absolute as political cause and effect could be, that instantly all Europe would be at war for the disposal of his heritage. Was this a time for planting British subjects in the middle of the possessions of the Spaniards in their boasted Indies ? for though the colonists selected uninhabited ground, Darien was in the midst of Spanish communities, and the colonists had to fight for possession. Nor did they in their contests receive the courtesy due to national enemies. The career of the new-comers was identical with that of the several

groups of filibusters and pirates who infested the
Spanish main, and built fortified harbours for the
storage and defence of their plunder. There was no
official diplomatic staff to contradict this conclusion.
The ambassadors of King William to foreign courts
and the governors of the colonies were all Englishmen, with instincts and interests inimical to the new
colony. Of old, when the ancient league was in
full vigour, France stood by the Scots in difficulties
with the other Continental towns; but now all that
France could do for Scotland was to give hospitable
refuge to the king she had discarded. Scotsmen
had recently been conspicuous and powerful on the
European continent. It might be remembered how
the Scotsman Lockhart, whose wife was the niece
of the mighty Cromwell, was ambassador for the
Protectorate, and took Dunkirk out of the hands
both of France and Spain. Mackay's Scots Brigade lay conspicuous among the slain on the bloody
field of Steinkirk, where they were under the command of King William. But who would answer for
these Scots of Darien, who conducted themselves
after the fashion of the other pirates and buccaneers on the Spanish main? Nay, if the Spaniards
obtained minute information concerning the strangers,
it would lead to the knowledge that they were dis-
obedient servants who had offended their sovereign,
so far that he placed it on the record of Parliament
that, in permitting this expedition, he had been ill-
served in the Scots part of his dominions.

Starvation, disease, and vice were rapidly wasting
the colony, the account of their career that reached
their kinsfolk at home becoming sadder and sadder.

Yet before the exhausted remnant surrendered themselves to a powerful fleet, there was one gleam of brightness to penetrate the gloom that hung over Scotland. A Spanish army was approaching to crush Darien, when a small body of the colonists crossed the isthmus, attacked it with fury, and scattered it in wild rout. A medal was struck, representing Campbell of Finab, the glorious leader of the Scots, galloping on his war-steed across the battlefield; and the victory of Zubaccanti was solemnised by a riotous illumination in Edinburgh.

There was no redress for the inhospitality of the English representatives abroad to the suffering Scots adventurers, and the alternative was becoming daily more distinct, that the two nations were drifting into war, unless an incorporating union should save them. King William saw in this the only hope and remedy, and he influenced the House of Lords to take the first step in the direction of union. They passed a bill appointing commissioners for negotiation, and sent it to the Commons with a recommendation to their consideration as "a bill of great consequence." Any such effort by the one House to stimulate the other was, it seems, contrary to the etiquette between the Houses; and the Commons, taking huff, threw out the bill on the second reading. This might bring war with Scotland, but what was that to the humiliation of listening to a suggestion from the Lords? The king again raised the question; and thus we have come round to the period of our story where it appeared desirable to take this brief retrospect to assist in rendering the remainder intelligible.

On the 25th of August 1702, a commission was issued under Queen Anne's sign-manual, appointing, on the part of England, commissioners to treat on the terms of a union, with commissioners to be appointed for Scotland. When the work was begun, the demand of Scotland to be released from the restraints of the navigation laws and establish freedom of trade between the two kingdoms opened at once the great critical question where the whole issue lay. On the part of England it was early taken up as a plea conclusive on this claim, that participation in English trade was not so much a question of national polity as of personal vested interests and properties, which it would be confiscation to diminish. In the discussions of 1667 it was laid down, "That his Majesty's plantations in the East Indies, and several in the West Indies, belong to particular corporations of Englishmen ; that the rest in America were purchased and settled by the blood and estates of Englishmen—and there is no reason Scotland should reap the benefit thereof." [1]

On the 3d of December the Scots briefly put their claim for "such an union as entitles the subjects of both kingdoms to a mutual communication of trade privileges and advantages." On the part of the English commissioners this was accepted with a significant reservation, "though they allow the communication of trade and other privileges to be the necessary result of a complete union, yet in the method of proceeding they must first settle with your lordships the terms and conditions of this communication of trade and other privileges." [2]

[1] Bruce, ccclxxxv.   [2] Ibid., ccclxviii.

After some hesitating discussion the Scots put their claims in a shape not admitting doubt:—

1. "That there be a free trade between the two kingdoms, without any imposition or distinction.

2. "That both kingdoms be under the same regulations, and liable to equal impositions for exportation and importation, and that a book of rates be adjusted for both.

3. "That the subjects of both kingdoms, and their seamen and shipping, have equal freedom of trade and commerce to and from the plantations, and be under the same regulation.

4. "That the Acts of Navigation, and all other Acts in either kingdom, in so far as contrary to or inconsistent with any of the above-mentioned proposals, be rescinded."[1]

This was uttered on the 9th of December, and on the 16th the English commissioners met it with a specification of reservations and restrictions: "As to the first article, their lordships are of opinion that there be a free trade between the two kingdoms for the native commodities of the growth, product, and manufactures of the respective countries, with an exception to wool, sheep, and sheep-fells, and without any distinction or imposition other than equal duties upon the home consumption." This implied an exclusion on importation of foreign merchandise into England in Scots vessels, restricted the importation of Scots produce to the market for home consumption, and made important exceptions to the articles of home produce that might be imported.[2]

Here were clear demands, and refusal as clear.

[1] Bruce. ccclxx.   [2] Ibid., clxxi.

The question of the colonial trade was reserved in terms showing how tenaciously England might be expected to hold her advantages there : " As to the third article, their lordships say that the plantations are the property of Englishmen, and that this trade is of so great a consequence, and so beneficial, as not to be communicated as is proposed, till all other particulars which shall be thought necessary to this union be adjusted." And then, as if to render the impracticability of Scotsmen enjoying this trade, they are told that, with the exception of "salt fish" and some other commodities, "as the case now stands by law, no European goods can be carried to the English plantations but what have been first landed in England ; " "nor can the product of the plantations be carried to other parts of Europe till it has been first landed in England." [1]

At this point a sudden change appears to come over the spirit of the negotiations. Three days later —on the 19th of December—it is minuted that " The commissioners on both sides had a full conference upon the subject of the communication of trade in the foresaid proposals and answers, which was very amicable ; and their lordships for England agreed to all the proposals made by their lordships for Scotland." [2]

The results of this harmonious action stand embodied in articles adopted at a joint meeting on the 2d of January :—

" That there be a free trade between all the subjects of the Island of Great Britain, without any distinction, in the same manner as is now practised

---

[1] Bruce, cclxxiii.   [2] Defoe's Hist. of the Union, App. 740.

from one part of England to another ; and that the masters, mariners, and goods be under the same securities and penalties in the coasting trade.

"That both kingdoms be under the same regulations and prohibitions, and liable to equal impositions for exportation and importation ; and that a book of rates be adjusted for both.

"That the subjects of both kingdoms, and their seamen and shipping, have equal freedom of trade and commerce to and from the plantations, under such and the same regulations and restrictions as are and will be necessary for preserving the said trade to Great Britain." [1]

At a point where the negotiations appeared to be closing round so fortunate a conclusion, we have a glimpse into the inner thoughts of Secretary Tarbat, about the most active and able of the Scots statesmen of the day. He had been known as Sir George Mackenzie of Tarbat, and afterwards became known as Earl of Cromarty. As a man of letters he had written some godly books, and some others far removed from this qualification. He had a considerable share in that unscrupulous waywardness that came to its climax in the assembly of the west called "the Drunken Parliament." He was concerned in the "billeting" affair—an attempt to ostracise certain public men as doomed to perpetual incapacity for office. In applying for a general "remission," or prospective pardon for any sins that might be charged and proved against him, he uttered himself in words that might be a broad audacious jest, but might also be the impulse of a secret consciousness

[1] Bruce, ccclxxv.

of extreme danger : " I wish to have a very general remission sent me ; because I see faults fished for in others upon as great grounds. If it comes, let it contain treason, perduellion, and a general of all crimes ; though on all that is sacred I know not myself guilty, nor do I hear anything on this side Irish witnesses or evidence." Having passed through the sedate reign of King William, and reached the mature age of seventy-two, he might now be likened to the respectable observer of domestic responsibilities looking back to the sowing of his wild oats. So, in the trying oscillations of the Union contest, he steered his way with a firm hand. The letter now cited is addressed to Nottingham, and is dated on the 21st of December 1702 :—

" I am so much in love with the Union that if thereby I be pushed to press upon your time, I will hope for your pardon on account of the cause for which I am concerned. My lord, this treaty must either produce a very happy or a very unhappy conclusion ; and I must be afraid of the latter if an impossibility be proposed as a condition. This night at our meeting, wherein all did agree as to the terms of what concerned the burdens to be imposed on goods exported to foreign places, or imported from thence, and in what can concern the transport of merchandise from one part to another of Britain ; yet the very different articles, viz., of the taxes to be imposed upon consumpt at home, doth rise like a little cloud, which threatens a storm. I presume Scotland will go to the utmost reach of possibility for what may render Britain secure and happy ; but when 'impossibility' gives a stop on that side, the safety must be from the prudence of England." [1]

In the resolutions now reached, the chief desire of Scotland seemed to be achieved at last. There must be a secret history of this revulsion, for it stands forth like the proverbial inconsistencies in human action that precede insanity or sudden death. This resolution extinguished the treaty and the treaters. It was not a violent death. Its shape was, that the English commissioners dropped away from the meetings for bringing the affair to a conclusion; and though there was a professed attempt to remedy this desertion, nothing came of the attempt. [2]

Some conferences were held, where the burdens of English debt and the coexistence of the English and the Scots India Companies were discussed as secondary to the great question of freedom of trade, no longer an open question. On the 3d of February, by a queen's letter, the meetings of both commissions were adjourned to the 4th of October. [3] On the 3d of September, the Scots Estates resolved, on a review of the progress of the treaty, "That the commission of Parliament granted for the said treaty is terminate and extinct, and that there shall be no

[1] Mus. Brit. Addl. MSS., 29588, f. 379.

[2] "*Die veneris*, 22d January 1702-3.—There not being a quorum of the English, and the Scots being met in their own chamber in the Cockpit, the Marquis of Normanby and Earls of Pembroke and Nottingham came unto them from such of the English commissioners as were met in the council-chamber, to signify that they were so much ashamed of the frequent disappointments they had given them, that for preventing the like for the future, they had resolved amongst themselves to apply to her Majesty for a new commission under the Broad Seal, in which seven might be named a quorum."—Defoe, App. 744.

[3] Defoe, App. 750.

new commission for treating of an union betwixt the kingdoms of Scotland and England without consent of Parliament." [1]

So it appeared that Scotland's participation in the trading privileges of England was a proposal so preposterous that it sank under the weight of its own absurdity. Yet England, though rapidly becoming the greatest, was perhaps the least illiberal of the trading communities of the day. Monopoly and retaliation were the only trading doctrines and practices throughout Europe. Like many other evil qualities, they culminated among the Spaniards, who, as they believed themselves to have been, by the bounty of Providence, invested with the bulk of the sources of all wealth, held that they were all the more beholden by cruel laws and sanguinary deeds to keep it for themselves. It was considered as among the

---

[1] Scots Acts, xi. 101. The following announcement to Secretary Sir Charles Hedges, in the "Additional MSS." in the British Museum, may be counted as the last vestige of the negotiations under the commission of 1702 :—

"WHITEHALL, *Sept.* 30, 1703.

"SIR,—The Lords of the Comittee having mett this morning, took notice that on Monday next, the 4th of October, is the day to which the commission for the union of the two kingdoms is adjourned : and though their lordships, upon consideration of what *they heare* is past in Scotland, think it not necessary that the English commissioners should meet on that day, in regard there are no commissioners from Scotland in town to meet with them ; that the English commissioners have no power to act separately; and that the commission will on that day fall of course, *which their lordships do not think will be of any inconvenience,*—yet their lordships thought it their duty to submit the matter to her Majesty, what she will please to have done ; and their lordships desire you will receive her Majesty's pleasure herein, and let them know it.

"Having read this to my lords, their lordships commanded me to send it away to you, by a messenger, in regard the time for this meeting, or not, is so near at hand.—I am, with all respect, Sir, your most obedient humble servant.　　　　　　　　　　　　　　　RT. WARRE."

dangers of the Darien settlers that the Spanish, if strong enough to be victorious over them, would slay them all. Such was their practice towards the rash adventurers who pried into the secret sources of their commerce, and it was the climax of intrusion to be found prowling nigh their gold-fields. When vessels and their crews disappeared in the Spanish main, their fate was thus accounted for. And yet it was noticed at the time, that when the last remnants of the ruined colonists were seeking food and rest, they were more hospitably received by the Spaniards than by their own fellow-islanders. When we reach' the cause of this phenomenon, we may also find why the modern mechanic on pay-day contributes one shilling of his wages to a refuge for widows and orphans, and another to a fund for maiming, or, if need be, slaying, the fellow-workman who, to preserve his wife and children from starvation, has consented to work at the market value of his labour.[1]

[1] To steady men who went with the current opinions of the day, sentiments like the following must have sounded as malignantly as the anarchical announcements of the French revolutionists in the ears of the loyal old country gentlemen of England. In the first place, the newly discovered paradise of trade in Darien is announced:—

"The time and expense of navigation to China, Japan, the Spice Islands, and the far greatest part of the East Indies, will be lessened more than half, and the consumption of European commodities and manufactures will soon be more than doubled. Trade will increase trade, and money will beget money, and the trading world shall need no more to want work for their hands, but will rather want hands for their work. Thus the door of the seas, and key of the universe, with anything of a reasonable management, will of course enable its proprietors to give laws to both oceans, and to become arbitrators of the commercial world, without being liable to the fatigues, expenses, and dangers, in contracting the guilt and blood of Alexander and Cæsar."

And who are the chosen people that, to the exclusion of the rest of mankind, are to enjoy the paradise ?

"You may easily perceive that the nature of these discoveries are

The session of the Scots Estates in the summer
of 1703 was stormy. It was tossed by denunciations
against England, it was restless with anxieties on the
danger of putting all to the issues of war with so
great a power, and the whole was tainted by suspicions that the Ministers of the Crown for Scotland
were truckling to the great enemy. Some of the
explosive materials brought together, indeed, burst
forth before the battle had begun or the forces had
been paraded against each other. When the preliminary questions about doubtful elections and other
matters vital to the constitution of a formal Parliament had been decided, the record tells us how the
fiery Belhaven and Sir Alexander Ogilvie of Banff had
indulged in an outbreak so violent that they found it
prudent to throw themselves on the mercy of the
House, and in harmonious humility admit "unbe-
coming expressions and other undutiful behaviour ;
for which they are most heartily sorry and grieved.
Therefore they did in all humility acknowledge their
faults, and did crave pardon of her Majesty's Commissioner and the Estates of Parliament for the
offence committed by them, and did entreat that
their most humble submission might be received, and

such as not to be engrossed by any one nation or people to the exclusion of others ; nor can it be thus attempted without evident hazard
and ruin, as we see in the case of Spain and Portugal, who by their
prohibiting any other people to trade, or so much as to go to dwell in
the Indies, have not only lost that trade they were not able to maintain, but have depopulated and ruined their countries therewith ; so
that the Indies have rather conquered Spain and Portugal than they
have conquered the Indies."—Report by William Paterson, addressed
"To the Right Honourable the Court of Directors of the Indian and
African Company of Scotland."—Memoirs of Great Britain and Ireland, by Sir John Dalrymple, ii. 113.

they restored to their respective places in Parliament."
With certain verbose formalities, indicative of hesitation, the Estates resolved to "pardon and forgive the culprits, and restore them to their respective places in Parliament." [1]

From an account by one who, being present, thought the outbreak of sufficient importance to be told to the English Cabinet, it would appear that the two were rushing from the House to find a more suitable spot for the practical conclusion of their quarrel, when, being interrupted by a closed door, and coming together on the parliamentary side of the impediment, they fell to kicking each other there.

" Immediately after the election was determined, Belhaven and Sir Alexander Ogilvie went out together with design to have fought. But after they had passed the place where we sit, and had come the length of the door, and the same not being so readily opened to them, they did again fall in passion, and Belhaven struck Sir Alexander Ogilvie with his foot, and Sir Alexander struck him again in his own defence. This occasioned a great deal of noise; and many of the members, particularly the Duke of Hamilton, thought Belhaven had been insulted, and so did express himself very passionately, as did several others; but none of us who were in our seats could see what happened.

" After this I went home, and did expect to see no person, it being so late. But his Grace my Lord Duke of Hamilton and his two brothers came to my house, and proposed that, seeing this scuffle had happened betwixt my Lord Belhaven, who is a

[1] Act. Parl. Scot.. ix. 65.

Hamilton, and Sir Alexander Ogilvie, who is of my name, and my relation—that therefore we might interpose betwixt them and settle any difference they had." [1]

The intervention was immediately successful, so far as the two perpetrators of the scuffle were concerned. But there seemed to arise a competition among others of a more pretentious character. First, "The Earl of Errol, as Lord High Constable, pretends to have the jurisdiction of all riots committed during the sitting of the Parliament, as well within as without the Parliament House—so notwithstanding of the reconciliation, he put sentries upon them." Then the Crown was insulted in the person of the Lord High Commissioner, and there was a threat of trial for high treason. This aroused the Estates to claim the privilege of suffering or repelling the insult, and they determined, by "a great plurality," "that no member could be accused of what was said or done within the House but by order and appointment of Parliament." High treason or not, the affair gravitated into an admission that Parliament was the party injured or insulted, and submission and assurances of penitence were accepted by Parliament. So the culprits appeared at the bar, when the judgment, as here cited from the record, was pronounced. It was reported in the following words by Chancellor Seafield to Godolphin : "His Grace and the Estates were highly displeased because of the misdemeanour they had committed, and that in law they might have been punished ; but upon hearing of their petition, in which they do humbly crave his Grace and the

[1] Mus. Brit. Addl. MSS.. 2055. f. 364-368.

Estates' pardon, they were now brought to the bar that they might again have the opportunity of making their acknowledgments; and accordingly they both did so in the humblest manner." [1]

The queen's message at the opening of the session had called attention to the necessity of a parliamentary settlement of the Crown; and the hint was taken, though in a sense significantly opposite to the meaning of the invitation. The first actual storm came when the Lord Marchmont, having secured attention by announcing that he had in his hand an overture or bill for the settlement of the succession, came, in the course of his reading, to the words "Princess Sophia." The fury of the meeting seemed to be too intense to let the members understand the sense in which the name was used—the very use of that name in a meeting of the Scots Estates was an indecorum and an insult. We have seen by what process of analysis the English Parliament reached that name; and had the Scots followed the same process—the exhaustion of the descendants of King James until a Protestant line was reached—it must have been with the same result. But the result of such a logical process had been reached, and had been employed so insultingly against Scotland that, since logical exhaustion had been set as an example, Scotland was prepared to reach a conclusion of her own more briefly and absolutely; and this was done by excluding from the succession to the crown of Scotland the person who should succeed to the crown of England. To this end was passed the "Act for the Security of the Kingdom," containing a provision that on the

[1] Seafield to Godolphin, Mus. Brit. Addl. MSS., 28055, f. 364.

death of the queen the Estates should meet to appoint a successor to the crown—a Protestant—from among the descendants of the old line of Scottish sovereigns, with a special provision that the person chosen to succeed to the crown of England should be excluded from the selection, unless " there be such conditions of government settled and enacted as may secure the honour and sovereignty of this crown and kingdom,—the freedom, frequency, and power of Parliaments—the religion, freedom, and trade of the nation,—from English or any foreign influence."

The Commissioner frankly informed the angry House that he would not give the royal assent to this Act by the touch of the sceptre. Then was debated the question whether that touch was necessary to making an Act of the Estates the law of the land— whether it was more than a courteous acknowledgment of approval and acceptance of a law duly adopted by the Estates. Further perilous matter was struck out in that hot debate, and an opportunity was given to Fletcher of Saltoun to ventilate—to use an expressive neology—his republican proclivities, and embody them in a statute of " limitations." The object of these was to secure the country against regal power being exercised within it by any one who should become, at any time after the departure of Queen Anne, sovereign of England. To this end the assent of an elected president of the Parliament was to supersede the touch of the sceptre, and the patronage of office and the command of the army were to be vested in the Estates.[1] When the Commissioner

[1] We find a collector of intelligence on the Continent, named Cockburn, who appears to have been in the service of Nottingham,

tried to soothe the irritation by persuasions and
assurances of healing measures, he was asked if he
had secured the approval of my Lord Treasurer of
England to what he promised. This touched a point
to make Felix tremble, as the letters cited in these
pages will amply show. Had certain dingy scraps of
paper now sleeping on the shelves of the Manuscript
Department of the British Museum been intercepted
on their way southward, the quarrel might have
drifted to formidable if not tragic results.[1]

writing to him on the 3d of October thus : " The proceedings of the
Scots Parliament are largely set forth in our Dutch courants, and the
overtures of Mr Fletcher of Saltoun are written at length. These
things are matter of admiration to some, and of laughter to others. If
your lordship knew the man—I mean Mr Fletcher—you would not be
surprised at his extravagances ; he is enheaded, as the French phrase is,
with the notions of a republic, and has an inveterate pique at all
sovereignty."—MS. Mus. Brit., 89, f. 79.

See ' Lettres historiques contenant ce qui se passe de plus important
en Europe' (attributed to Jean Dumont)—vol. xxiv.—'à la Haye, chez
Adrian Moetjens :' 1703. This contemporary history, the precedent of
the annual registers and other periodical chronicles of later times, gives
ample testimony to the interest created abroad by the Scots Parliament
of 1703. To France it seemed to open the question of separation from
the interests of England, and a possible restoration of the " Ancient
League " between France and Scotland. Some one had supplied a full
and tolerably accurate account of this stormy session for the Lettres,
as—" Le Parlement d'Ecosse est toujours fort occupé. On y a lû
plusieurs differents Projets d'Actes pour regler la succession à la Couronne." " Ce qui en a retardé jusqu'ici la conclusion c'est que l'on a
presenté de jour en jour des articles pour y être inserés, et que cela
demande une longue discussion. Le Lord Salton en presenta douze
le 18 Juin, tous concernant la limitation du successeur qui devra être
choisi après la mort de sa Majesté."—Pp. 202, 203. The " Lettres "
were rendered by translations in London, and thus the English people
received the news of their neighbours in Scotland.

[1] The following morsels, addressed by the Earl of Leven, are suggestive when interpreted with the letters cited in the text :—

" I was obliged to make use of a borrowed hand the last two letters
I sent to you, because I understood that some were very busy upon the
inquiry if I kept correspondence with any in England, and would have
been glad to have got a letter under my hand to any English minister ;

The passages following, from letters by Atholl, Lord Privy Seal, to Godolphin, if they had not interest in themselves, would have it as testimony to the clandestine communications between the queen's ministers in Scotland and the English Cabinet.

"HOLYROOD HOUSE, *July* 10, 1703.

"We have all concurred—I mean the queen's servants—to keep the limitations out of the Act of Security, which we have done with a great deal of difficulty, and in which I am sure I have done all I could, both by myself and friends that are of the cavalier party, without whose assistance they had certainly been voted before this time, particularly the Act lodging the power of declaring peace or war in the Parliament after her Majesty's decease without heirs. As this appears the most necessary, so it is the first is pressed ; but none can answer but others may be insisted on."[1]

On the 1st of September (1703), Atholl writes to Godolphin, desiring to be informed of the fate of the Act of Security—is the queen to give it the royal assent, or is she not ?

"You may imagine, since there was so much zeal

but now that the Parliament is at an end, that danger is over."—Mus. Brit. Addl. MSS., 28055, f. 56. Some things, indeed, were not to be trusted to paper, and must await the opportunity of a private interview.

"I did wish rather than beg to have seen your lordship ere now. I had reasons for it not so fit for paper. But for the little assistance I have given and must give to what I think is intended—or should be intended—here, I shall regret my stay the less. However, I am presumptuous enough to assert that my designs were and are unaltered and unalterable in endeavouring to serve the queen, the monarchy, and Britain faithfully—and with all the endeavours possible for an old man and an old loyalist."—Ibid., f. 2.

[1] Mus. Brit. Addl. MSS.. 28055. f. 40.

and heat in the Parliament to get this Act, it will be a very great disappointment if it should not be passed. It may make the Ministry here have no interest either to carry the supply in this Parliament or in any other. But, on the other hand, if the queen does consent to it, this session I doubt not will conclude immediately by giving supplies for the army. But without the Act be passed, or assurances that it will, we find that they will not enter on the supplies, but I am afraid will enter on new Acts that will be more and more uneasy. Therefore I am sure it is the queen's interest to put a conclusion as soon as possible, either by allowing the Act to be passed—or if her Majesty is persuaded it may prejudice her affairs more elsewhere than advance them here, then that it is fit her pleasure be known as soon as possible, that we may be adjourned." [1]

Revelations of the personal feelings or opinions of royalty as to critical political conditions are rare. Hence the following morsel, addressed by Queen Anne to her faithful friend and servant Godolphin, may have some interest, though it reveals little. It is dated from Windsor on the 14th of June.

To those who are acquainted with the gossip of the period, the self-consciousness that in this letter anticipates an accusation of obstinacy may be curious and interesting. Until the great contest with Duchess Sarah who made the charge of obstinacy, it would be difficult to find any period in history so absolutely free of vestiges of such an interruptive element. We

[1] Ibid., 54. A few days later we find Tarbat writing in like tone to Nottingham on the same critical question of the completion of the Act of Security.

see the empire passing onward to its mighty destinies
with a calm unimpeded flow unexampled in its previous history.   If we desire to see what obstinacy in
the sovereign is capable of accomplishing, we have
but to look back to the reign of Charles I.   And
when the great contest came with Duchess Sarah
on the one side and Abigail Hill on the other, we
shall find that it was on a question of ecclesiastical
patronage affecting its highest range — the Bench
of Bishops.   The existing but endangered Ministry
would have it a political, but the queen made it a
religious question; and it was an instance of that
impulse, whether we call it zeal or fanaticism, that
strove to bend everything to its service.

"Though you tell me you intend to be here either
to-morrow night or Saturday morning, I cannot help
venting my thoughts upon the Scotch affairs : and in
the first place I think these people use me very hardly
in opposing Lord Forfar being of the Treasury ; and
I should be very glad to know your opinion whether
upon this refusal I might not write to the Commissioner to let him know, if he does not think it for the
service that Lord Forfar should have the post I recommended him to, I would let him have some other that
may be equivalent to it; and that I do expect he should
comply with this one desire of mine, in return of all
the compliances I have made to him.   This may dis-
please his Grace's touchy temper, but I can't see it
can do any prejudice to my service ; and in my poor
opinion such usage should be resented.   As to the
Duke of Queensberry, though he is none of my
choice, I own it goes mightily against me — it
grates my soul — to take a man into my service

that has not only betrayed me, but tricked me several times,—one that has been obnoxious to his own countrymen these many years, and one that I can never be convinced can be of any use. But after all this, since my friends may be censured, and that it may be said if I had not been obstinate everything would have gone well, I will do myself the violence these unreasonable Scotsmen desire; and indeed it is an inexpressible one. The draft of the letter and instructions, as you propose, will certainly be much better than those that are come out of Scotland; but I am entirely of your opinion, that no method will succeed. My heart was so full that it was impossible for me to forbear easing it a little, and therefore I hope you will excuse this trouble." [1]

In harmony with these expressions of the royal mind, we find Godolphin, in a letter to his colleague Nottingham, saying, "I find the queen is not at all easy at the accounts she has from time to time received of her affairs in Scotland. She has commanded me this morning to desire that your lordship would, against the next coming hither, consider what directions and instructions may be proper to be sent to

[1] Mus. Brit., *ut supra*. The Lord Forfar here referred to is Archibald Douglas, Earl of Forfar. He held none of the high offices or other conspicuous political positions that secure to a man a place in the history of his country, but "he was made a Privy Councillor of King William, and appointed one of the commissioners for executing the office of Keeper of the Privy Seal. He was also of the Privy Council to Queen Anne, and was by her Majesty constituted one of the Commissioners of the Treasury, which he held till the dissolution of that Court in consequence of the Treaty of Union, which he supported in Parliament, dividing with Ministers on every question."—Douglas's Peerage of Scotland, i. 597.

her commissioner there, before she begins her journey to the Bath."[1]

He has, in the passage that follows, to open his colleague's eyes to an alarming incident in the situation. The queen had sent instructions for the suppression or rejection of the Act of Security, and they arrived too late—an accident not to be regretted, since they would have proved futile.

"Since I troubled you yesterday I have had letters from Scotland, by which I find the Act of Security was passed the House before the queen's orders came for her servants to endeavour the laying of it aside; and my letters say that if the order had come sooner, they should not have had strength to do it. They seem now to persuade themselves they shall have the cess they desire, but not without that condition of passing this Act; and I find the Duke of Queensberry himself, as well as all the others, inclining to wish the queen would pass both together, because he says that without it neither the troops nor the civil Government can be supported, but all must fall to pieces and give way to the power of the opposite party there; since, without a new one be granted, the prsent cess will not be paid."[2]

Three days later the matter comes so home to these statesmen, as responsible for the peace and safety of England, that they find it necessary to act, and begin by a meeting of the Cabinet.

"Bath, 23d *August* 1703.—As to the affairs of Scotland, her Majesty doth also agree with you that the difficulty will be great either to pass the Acts

[1] Mus. Brit. Addl. MSS., 29589, f. 82.
[2] 20th Aug. 1703.—Mus. Brit. Addl. MSS., 29589, f. 96.

desired by that kingdom, or to be without a provision for the support of the civil and military government there, the want of which must probably bring that country into great confusion, and give opportunity of advantage to the factious and opposite party. But since it is necessary that some resolution of her Majesty should speedily be sent to Scotland, and that the matter is of so much consequence to England as well as Scotland, as not to be determined without the opinion of the lords of the Cabinet Council, the queen commands me to tell your lordship that she desires you would acquaint those lords who are with you at London with the matters of fact which have passed there, and the consequences of them one way and the other, and transmit to her Majesty the result of their thoughts; upon the receipt of which her Majesty intends to call together those lords who are here, in order to guide her in such a resolution as they shall think most proper, to be sent to Scotland upon due consideration of the whole matter; in which for the fuller information of your lordship, and those lords whom you shall summon upon this occasion, the queen has commanded me to send you the two last letters she has received from the Duke of Queensberry and my Lord Tarbatt; and I beg leave to add one more from my Lord Privy Seal to myself,—desiring the favour of your lordship that you would not forget to return me these letters again, because they should also be considered by the lords of the Cabinet Council who are here.

" It is observable enough that the queen's servants in Scotland, who agree in nothing else, do yet all agree it would be for her Majesty's service in that kingdom to pass these Acts, since they relate only to what may happen after her Majesty's reign; and in the meantime there may be opportunities of retrieving in another session of Parliament the inconveniences which would otherwise happen; but my Lord Privy Seal's letter says very plainly, that in case this should bring a difficulty upon her Majesty's affairs in England, he would use all his endeavours with those he could influence to quiet the minds of the people of Scotland."[1]

Throughout what appears in historical narrative as the wild work of an excited multitude, a thorough practical spirit governed the legislation of this Parliament. The disposal of the armed power of the nation must not be left to chance, or be placed absolutely in the hands of any one having power to assume the title of sovereign. Accordingly, through much hot debate, there passed by majority an " Act anent peace and war," the material provision being, that on the death of the queen, if childless, "no person being king or queen of Scotland and England shall have the sole power of making war with any prince, potentate, or state whatsoever without consent of Parliament; and that no declaration of war without consent foresaid shall be binding on the subjects of this kingdom."[2]

If this Act, as supplementary to the Act of Security, carried defiance on its face, another Act, that seemed to carry in its terms an innocent and eminently genial character, was discovered by the Opposition to contain hidden elements of danger.

---

[1] Mus. Brit. Addl. MSS. 29589, f. 107.   [2] Act. Parl. Scot., xi. 107.

Its tendency was to make wine abundant and cheap, declaring "That it shall be lawful, from and after the date hereof, to import into this kingdom all sorts of wine and other foreign liquors, any former Act or statute on the contrary notwithstanding." The Act passed after a vain protestation by a minority, pleading "that this Act allowing the importation of French wine and brandy ought not to pass, as being dishonourable to her Majesty, inconsistent with the grand alliance wherein she is engaged, and prejudicial to the honour, safety, interest, and trade of this kingdom."[1]

A curious little personal affair, communicated to Godolphin by some member of the Estates, who did not sign his letter, is further exemplification of the fiery particles scattered in that assembly. It brings together the names of two men who were then the antithesis of each other as eminent and obscure, but whose position was afterwards signally reversed—Edward Chamerland or Chamberlayne and John Law. Chamberlayne was an "authority" on matters of finance, trade, and currency; and he was solemnly consulted by the statesmen of the day as an adept in these matters, though, as it often is with those who profess to enrich nations, he seems to have been steeped in poverty; and in the proceedings of the Estates his projects for enriching others alternate with interpositions to protect him from his creditors.[2]

---

[1] Act. Parl. Scot., xi. 102-112.

[2] "Chamberlain, Hugh, M.D., memorial relating to land credit, presented by him remitted to a committee;" "read, and ordered to be printed;" "an overture by him for the better employment of the poor to be considered;" "warrant granted to him to cite his creditors with a view to a protection."—Index to Scots Acts.

Many less defensible projects than his land credit scheme had charms for those smitten by the speculative frenzy of the day. Its founder could always preach with truth that its security was absolute. He had not, however, reached the inner truth discovered and revealed by the French at the heavy cost of the ruin of their assignats, that not being convertible at sight it was a security unfit for the protection of a currency. The " one Mr Law," who will be recognised as the owner of a name destined to ring over all Europe, was then a young gentleman—pleasant, gay, and dissipated. But what gives importance to their names here is the testimony to the inflammability of the assembled Estates, in the paltry nature of the dispute about them that set two statesmen to mortal conflict. This was, in the words of Godolphin's correspondent, " occasioned by a proposal of one Mr Law, whom Fletcher was for confronting with Dr Chamberlain in full Parliament, there to reason and debate the matter, so as that the House might be the better satisfied which of their proposals was the most practicable and advantageous. This the Earl of Roxburgh thought very unfair—to oblige a gentleman to come to the bar without he himself was willing to appear in so public a manner, especially since he had not dedicated his book to the Estates of Parliament, nor so much as put his name to it ; and therefore his lordship said that Mr Law, or any other gentleman who had employed his time and thoughts for the good of his country, ought to be treated with good manners." These words roused the fiery soul of Fletcher, who pushed the application until he was told,—that if he took it to himself he might. "Upon which Fletcher stood up and said, 'I take it as I ought.'" This justified the commissioner in ordering both under arrest. However, they found their way, with seconds, to the sands at Leith—the accustomed spot for the adjustment of such affairs. Roxburgh's second objected to swords, on account of an injury or weakness that disqualified him from fair fencing; but Fletcher produced a pair of pistols, "desiring very *cavalièrement* his lordship to take his choice." At this critical moment the affair was interrupted by a party of the Horse Guards.[1]

When the Scots Parliament reassembled in July 1704, the Act of Security was repassed without debate as a thing settled by the Estates. It was followed by provisions for calling out the wapenshaws or meetings of militia, and for a general arming of the nation. A supply was also passed, and it was significant in not being passed before, but after, the Act of Security: this was a precaution imitated from the tacking devices of the English Commons, of which we have seen examples. It might be conjectured from the action of England at this juncture, that the sage Godolphin did not regret the formidable measures of Scotland, in some hope that the dread of war might frighten the great trading interests of England into compliance with the free trade demands of Scotland. The tone of the alternative presented tended to this effect: "Doubtless if you let these starving Scots compete with you in a free trade, every pound made by them will be a pound lost to you. But if you do not yield there will be war, and

[1] Brit. Mus. Addl. MSS. 28055. f. 248. 249.

that will damage your trade more than competition. It cannot be helped : the sacrifice of free trade must be made."

Meanwhile England took a step that was at once the most dignified and safe for her own national interests, and the least offensive to the Scots, however formidable it might be. The policy that seemed to keep out of sight the existence of Scotland as an independent State, capable of making war or peace with any other State, England included, was dropped, and in return for the threat by Scotland, active preparations were made for war on the side of England. The whole question was discussed in a solemn sitting of the Lords — the queen present. An address to her desired the fortifying of Newcastle and Tynemouth, and the repairing of the works at Carlisle and Hull ; further, that an army of regular troops be marched to the Border, and that the militia in the four northern counties be embodied. It was enacted that, with the exception of Scots naturalised and permanently resident within the dominions of the Crown of England, or enrolled in the fleet or army, no native of Scotland "shall be capable to inherit any lands, tenements, and hereditaments within this kingdom of England, or the dominions thereunto belonging, or enjoy any benefit or advantage of a natural-born subject of England ; but every such person shall be from thenceforth adjudged and taken as an alien, born out of the allegiance of the Queen of England, until such time as the succession to the crown of Scotland be declared and settled by an Act of Parliament in Scotland in the same manner as the succession to the crown of England is now settled by Act of Parliament in England, in case of her Majesty's decease without issue of her body." [1] Here were threats—and they were threats that proved effective for their end,—but they were the threats not of a master but of a bargainer, leaving to the other party acceptance or rejection. England said virtually, "We have chosen our line of succession : if you see fit to select the same, we are ready to unite with you as one empire ; if you do otherwise, we remain separate independent sovereignties, at peace or war as it may be."

Then followed restrictions and prohibitions for fully completing the disruption, if so it was to be ; but what suffused a healing balm throughout this formidable statute was, that at the commencement, as introductory to its hostile and penal clauses, stood a plenary authority to the queen to appoint commissioners to treat with such commissioners as might be appointed on the authority of the Parliament of Scotland to meet them for the adjustment of a treaty of union between the two kingdoms.

If in the minds of those chiefly responsible for the adjustment of this Act there arose any vista of doubts or difficulties, fed from religious antagonism, they led to a conclusion in the same spirit. There was no word or hint as to religion in Scotland ; but the final clause secured England, by enacting "That the commissioners to be named in pursuance of this Act shall not, by virtue of such commission, treat of or concerning any alteration of the liturgy, rites, ceremonies,

[1] 3 & 4 Anne, ch. 7, "An Act for the effectual securing the kingdom of England from the apparent dangers that may arise from several Acts lately passed in the Parliament of Scotland."

discipline, or government of the Church, as by law established within this realm." [1]

In the Scots Parliament there was much talking, and some wild things were said by Fletcher and others, but there was nothing that could be called a debate. The only party who had critical issues to put to debate and division were the Jacobites. But action on their part was a question of life and death, and no opportunity came for their interposing, with the faintest chance of safety. They ventured, indeed, on a critical division, but it was rather because it would bring to their numbers, on that division, the Fletcher party, than because the policy they proposed was congenial to Jacobitism; and, in fact, Fletcher was the champion of their cause. The question was opened on the appointment of the commissioners to meet those appointed by England—should they be named by the queen or by the Estates? The majority felt their power, and would give no quarter. The business was hurried through with the impatience of people who have their opportunity and may lose it. The nomination by the queen was carried by a majority of 40; and on the 1st of September, close to midnight, the Act for a treaty with England passed. In response to the concluding clause of the English Act, a condition was carefully prepared and adopted with deliberate consideration: "That the commissioners shall not treat of or concerning any alteration of the worship, discipline, or government of the Church of this kingdom, as now by law established."

We have now come to the end of the Parliamentary contest that happily ripened into the conclusion

[1] 3 & 4 Anne. ch. 7. s. 11.

that a union of the two kingdoms was a thing that
must be, and created the machinery that was to
adjust it.   Between this point, however, and the
final adjustment, the two kingdoms were perplexed
and troubled by incidents, some of them violent and
tragical, and all pointing to the sad conclusion that
war between the two nations might still break in
upon the blessed prospect that had been opened.
Before dealing with these difficulties and their solution, let us turn to a war elsewhere, where English
and Scots fought side by side with such success as
to destroy at its source that element of peril to the
two countries that was the most imminent of all, an
invasion by King Louis in the cause of the house of
Stewart.

CHAPTER V.

The War in the Netherlands and Germany.

THE two great divisions of Spain were united into
one monarchy by the marriage of Isabella of Castile
with Ferdinand of Aragon. By previous successions
the house of Aragon had acquired Majorca, Sardinia,
Naples, and Sicily. Their only surviving child was
a daughter,—the mother of two emperors and four
queens,—but known in history as "Jane the mad;"
she, by her marriage with Philip of Austria, carried
the succession to all these realms to their son, the
Emperor Charles V., who added his possessions in

the Netherlands, and the duchy of Milan, to the rapidly - accumulated dominions. To the House, endowed with dominions so vast among the ancient States of Europe, there arose a vision of boundless empire beyond the Atlantic; and all of America then known to exist, with all that should afterwards be discovered, was claimed in the sovereignty of " the Indies," completing the chain of dominion on which " the sun never set."

The traditions of the revival of an Empire of the World—of a unity in the civil government of mankind, such as Rome had bequeathed in the popedom —was then a lively image in the eyes of ambitious sovereigns; and he who was master of so many realms seemed on the way to achieve it. Its natural consummation seemed to be defeated and postponed when the imperial rank was severed from the throne of Spain and the Indies—the one falling to the brother of Charles V., the other to his son Philip II. of Spain. During the reign of Philip's great-grandson, Charles II., there had arisen a rival Power that might, in the end, dispute the Empire of the World. At the end of the seventeenth century, Louis XIV. had reached the climax of his aggressive career, and turned the apprehension of statesmen from the Spanish to the French empire, when a succession of events raised the alarming question, What if the King of France should acquire the vast empire ruled by the sovereign of Spain and the Indies ?

It became clear that Charles II., King of Spain, was to die childless. On whom, then, would the succession to his vast dominions fall ? Two princesses of Spain, daughters of Philip IV., and therefore sisters

of King Charles, were married.   The husband of the
elder, Maria Theresa, was Louis XIV. of France.
Their eldest son, the Dauphin of France, was accordingly, under the rules of pure hereditary succession,
admitting female descent when there was no male
representative equally near, the heir to the possessions of the King of Spain.   The younger daughter,
Margaret Theresa, was married to the Emperor Leopold.   They had one daughter, who became the wife
of Maximilian Emanuel, Elector of Bavaria : their
son, yet a child, Joseph Ferdinand, Electoral Prince
of Bavaria, was hence the second in the order of succession.   At the same time his grandfather, the emperor, stood third in order, his mother having been a
sister of Philip IV. of Spain, and the aunt of King
Charles and his two married sisters.

There might be special customs or laws applicable
to some of the territories held by the King of Spain
excepting them from the direct line of succession.
Milan, for instance, was claimed as a fief of the
empire, lapsing to the emperor on the death of the
King of Spain.   But among the priests and civilians
clustering round the despotic Courts it was becoming
a prevalent doctrine that the rule of succession by
primogeniture should prevail over all others as the
law of God.   Hitherto but imperfectly known and
obeyed, it was, on close examination, seen to be a
beneficent law, telling all men how to act, and showing them the way to keep absolutely clear of all mistakes and all disputes.   Whether it were limited to
the male descendants alone, as in France, or successively exhausted the several male branches and
then passed into the female, the precise position of

every descendant in the line of succession was known
as absolutely as the celestial phenomena of the rota-
tion of the moon and of the earth. It was a period
when discoveries in the fixed laws of nature were
coming forth in rapid succession, surprising mankind with their beautiful simplicity and the absolute-
ness of their precision; and here was one of these
laws given to man for the preservation of peace and
loyalty, could he but see and obey it. The mighty
calamities that had shaken England for sixty years
were the punishment preadjusted by the Deity to
follow any outrage or neglect of these beneficent
laws; just as calamities follow when the laws of the
physical forces of nature are outraged. King Louis
himself had paid homage to this law, in so far that,
while it was his manifest interest to conciliate the
powerful monarch who reigned in England under the
Revolution Settlement, he solemnly acknowledged as
king of the British dominions the son of the exiled
James II. immediately on the father's death.

At the Treaty of the Pyrenees, where the marriage
of King Louis with the Spanish princess was adopted,
there were clauses abjuring, on both parts, any claim
by the offspring of the marriage to any of the possessions of the Crown of Spain, and in strong terms
declaring any such right of succession to be a thing
impossible.[1] Louis himself came under not only a
solemn obligation, but an oath sanctioned by invo-
cations and denunciations the most sacred that the

---

[1] " Les enfans et descendans, que Dieu nous donnera de ce mariage,
soyons et demeurions inhabiles et incapables, et absolument exclus du
droit et espoir de succéder à aucun des Royaumes, États, et Seigneuries,
dont se composé cette couronne et monarchie d'Espagne."—Dumont,
Corps universel diplomatique, vol. vi. part ii. p. 288.

Church could find, that he would be faithful to these conditions, and do everything in his power to make them effectual. But this treaty was now forty years old, and the aspect of things had changed. If the laws of God bestowed rights on any of his descendants, was it in his power prospectively to cut them off? Then, as to the obligations of the promise and the sanctions of the oath—these were things transacted with the Church, and the Pope was a party to them. The Church could relieve him from his obligations : they were like the securities impledged with a creditor, who can discharge the debt and renounce the pledges. Rome would do what was required. Louis XIV. was not the most submissive son of the Church, but he was its most valuable champion. He was remorseless in the extirpation of heresy, and all his projects of aggrandisement made common cause with the expansion of the spiritual supremacy of Rome. At such a juncture the nature, and especially the value, of the Spanish inheritance were eagerly examined and discussed. It could not but be that the land possessed of all the known gold-districts in the New World, and receiving successive galleons laden with ingots, must be the richest of all nations. Yet Spain was about the most impoverished of European States ; for the gold was not permitted to be used for its legitimate purpose as a medium of commerce—its exportation was prohibited. The servants of a Duke of Albuquerque were starving, and his creditors unpaid ; but what the outside world saw was, that he had forty silver ladders to mount up to the sideboards where his plate was piled in hundredweights. The country of which such things were said, dazzled the eyes of statesmen so that they could not see its real poverty and misery.

But would the richness of the new possession be available to assure and strengthen the old? There were misgivings in the very greatness of such an acquisition. Its size and weight might overbalance the old possessions of the house of Aragon, and lead to results that could not be with certainty counted on as propitious. Misgivings on this point were fostered by the political aspect of Spain. Those who represented its nationality were not afraid of coming under the dominions of a Bourbon, or any other stranger, so long as the dominions of the Crown of Spain kept together under their existing constitution. Of this constitution the proud kingdom of Old Castile was the centre—the other territories that, one after the other, clustered round it being counted as subordinate provinces or colonial possessions. Whatever other part of the world came under the same sovereignty would be looked on with the same eye. There could be no more community of spirit between the governing powers of France and Spain than between the fresh glories of Versailles and the sombre gloom of the Escurial; and Spain would count the difference between the two as expressed in her own superiority. Of all the proud aristocracies of Europe, the hidalgos of Spain were the proudest. If the brilliant courtiers of the Tuileries looked down on them as sombre provincials, retaining obsolete etiquettes and costumes, the hidalgos would reverse the order of the estimate, largely enhancing the difference in their own favour.

From such considerations the sage advisers of King Louis seem to have persuaded him that it would be the wiser course in the meantime to be content, or profess to be content, with the outlying possessions of the King of Spain—possessions that France might some day enclose within an expanding frontier—and leave Spain to be otherwise disposed of, always provided it did not fall to the Empire: that would be the rise of a rival Power to a distinct superiority over the power of France.   Our sole real testimony to the influence of such considerations is the renowned Partition Treaty, negotiated at King William's Dutch palace of Loo, and concluded at the Hague, on the 11th of October 1698, by the representatives of France, England, and Holland.   By a complicated phraseology of obligatory assurances, the royal family of France abandoned all claim to the crown of Spain, on condition that the Dauphin was insured Naples and Sicily, with some small islands off the Italian coast, the principality of Piombino, to which the celebrated island of Elba belonged, and the Marquisate of Finale — a small territory, but strongly fortified, that might prove valuable to France as an entrance to Savoy and Piedmont.   To these were added an extension of frontier on the side of the Pyrenees equivalent to the old province of Guipuscoa.   Milan was to be given to the Archduke Charles, the second son of the emperor.   These territories being so distributed, the electoral prince—the second, as we have seen, in the hereditary order of succession — was to have what remained, — the kingdom of Spain, including the Spanish Netherlands and "the Indies." [1]   Events crowding on each other immedi-

[1] See the treaty at length—Dumont, 'Corps universel diplomatique,' vii. 442.   This—"the first Partition Treaty"—has been severely

ately after the treaty, proclaimed its futility. Before the end of the year 1699, the electoral prince died. Had the succession been left to the rule of hereditary descent, this would have had no immediate effect; but it made waste-paper of the Partition Treaty. At the same time, it rendered more emphatic and distinct the supreme claims of the Dauphin. These, it is true, were not weakened by the existence of the electoral prince. As the son of the elder sister of King Charles, the Dauphin was his heir; and as the

handled, both in history and political controversy, as a prospective dismemberment and distribution of an empire by those who had no occasion, either through right or duty, to dispose of it. There is this, however, to be said for the treaty, that it did not break up a compact nationality, or bring to an end relations between a paternal Government and confiding subjects. It could not be an obvious calamity to the Neapolitans and the Sicilians that they were no longer to be the subjects of a sovereign who was King of Spain and lived in the Escurial. On the question of interference, the family that stood in order of succession as heirs to the whole, could come forward with a good grace to abandon the greater part—" parce que sa majesté catholique n'aiant point d'enfans, et la succession venant a manquer, cela causeroit infailliblement une nuvelle guerre si le Roi T. C. vouloit soutenir ses prétensions, ou celles du Dauphin, à toute la succession d'Espagne." The great source of misgiving about the treaty lay in the question, What did King Louis mean by it? Was it possible to believe him to be sincere? If he had secured to himself the Spanish Netherlands—the next prospective stage in the progress of French aggrandisement—it would have been more easy to believe in his sincerity. No doubt King William would not have agreed to this. But that still leaves it a mystery that King Louis should have bound himself to abandon a possession so desirable—a possession he seemed never to lose any other opportunity but this of bringing within his grasp. In the debates in the English Parliament when the treaty was discovered, charges of perfidy and treachery were distinctly made against King Louis. But the main object of Parliament was to censure King William for transacting this great affair in secret. It was in the royal prerogative, no doubt, to make treaties; but if Parliament were not consulted beforehand on their tenor, it was the duty of the sovereign immediately to tell Parliament what he had done: and members seemed to feel that it mitigated the disagreeable duty of censuring their own king to cast heavier charges against the other.

son of the younger sister, the electoral prince was not his heir. But both were nephews of the King of Spain; and when the person who was next to the Dauphin was a cousin of King Charles, the disqualification of the second in order during the life of the first was more emphatic and distinct.

The politic brains of the chief European statesmen were now at work in devising a new Partition Treaty, and it was all but completed. There was, however, a conclave in the Escurial who thought they might find stronger words to conjure with if they could lay before the world the deathbed injunction of one who never was endowed with the faculties, bodily and mental, common to mankind at large, and who retained but a remnant of his meagre allotment of vitality. They were successful in giving practical shape to the suggestion. The French interest prevailed in that conclave by securing an unscrupulous priest, who led its councils. The British Government took no further concern in the hidden work of the conclave than in the feeling of a becoming and natural curiosity to know results. A story has been often and picturesquely told of machinations dealing with the dead in the great burial-vault of the Escurial, and summoning the aid of diabolical agencies.[1]

Charles II. of Spain died on the 1st November 1700. It was immediately announced that a month before his death he had signed a will disposing of his empire to one of the royal family of France. King

[1] See Coxe, 'History of the House of Austria,' chap. lxvii.; Dunlop, 'Memoirs of Spain during the Reigns of Philip IV. and Charles II.;' and the conclusion of Macaulay's History.

Louis had but one son. He, the Dauphin, already spoken of as heir to the Spanish dominions according to the rule of hereditary descent, had three sons. The eldest of these was heir to the crown of France. The second—the Duke of Anjou—was named in the will as King of Spain. This he in the end became, founding the Bourbon dynasty of Spain ; and therefore it is unnecessary here to follow the long testamentary document signed by King Charles through its intricate provisions in case of the Duke of Anjou's death and other contingencies.[1]

This was a divergence from the divine right of hereditary succession, but it was a divergence in a legitimate direction—the direction not of delegating the power of sovereigns to their people, but of continuing it in the persons of sovereigns. King Louis accepted the bequest in a solemn instrument signed, sealed, and registered by the Parliament of Paris. In this document he took occasion, through his " pleine puissance et autorité royale," to alter an important provision of the will. The choice of the second son had been made, that the heritage might not fall to the King of France, and the complex provisions of the will were directed to meet any future contingency that might settle the two crowns on one head. All this King Louis swept away by a declaration that the new King of Spain and his offspring should lose no claim that any of them might inherit to the crown of France.[2]

---

[1] See the document at length, Dumont, v. 485. A translation of it was printed in London in a pamphlet of the day.

[2] " Lettres patentes de Louis XIV., Roi de France et de Navarre, pour conserver à Philippe, Duc d'Anjou, son petit-fils, et tout ses descendans mâles, les droits entiers de leur naissance, et particulièrement celui de

The Dutch had made themselves a sort of centre of equipoise in the balance of the greater European States. Their small republic was kept in existence because its extinction would forebode danger to greater Powers. The chief fortified towns of the Spanish Netherlands were said to be a barrier of protection to the United Provinces ; and that they might practically be what they were called, it was the duty and the privilege of the provinces to furnish a certain contingent to their garrisons. These " barrier fortresses " were Luxemburg, Namur, Charleroy, Mons, Ath, Nieuport, and Oudenarde. King Louis with great dexterity drew out these Dutch troops and replaced them with Frenchmen : he was not to let the king, his grandson, be dependent on foreigners—on foreigners of an offen-

pouvoir succéder a leur tour a la couronne de France, nonobstant leur elevation a celle d'Espagne," &c.—Dumont, vii. 494.

King Louis had an accomplished and diligent representative at the bedside of the sick man—the Duc de Harcourt, Maréchal of France, who arrived at his post in 1698, and held close correspondence with his master until the end. In the chateau of Harcourt, in Normandy, were the muniments of an ancient house, and it was supposed that the correspondence between the king and his representative might be among them. In the thick of the Revolution, however, a bonfire was made of the family *chartrier*. It is now known that Madame de Harcourt had thrown a quantity of valuable papers into a wardrobe, piling over them uninviting morsels of clothing ; but she left the chateau and never returned, either to search for what she had hidden or reveal the secret. It was in a search throughout the castle for materials for a history of Normandy that the correspondence was recently discovered, and it will be found in ' Avenement des Bourbons au Trône d'Espagne, correspondence inédite du Marquis d'Harcourt, Ambassadeur de France, au près des Rois Charles II. et Philippe V., tirés des archives du Chateau d'Harcourt et des Archives du Ministère des Affairs Étrangérs, publiée avec un introduction, par C. Hippeau :' Paris, 1875 : 2 vols. The reader of this book who expects to find in it full revelations of the subtle, unscrupulous, and successful diplomacy of King Louis will not be disappointed.

sive kind—while he had in France a superabundance
of unemployed soldiers.[1] There was a terrible significance in this act. It was feared that Louis would
take possession of these Dutchmen as prisoners of
war. But war had not yet been proclaimed. The
kidnapping would be too flagrant even for King
Louis, and with a greedy reluctance he let them go.

On the 16th of September 1701, the exiled King
James II. of England and VII. of Scotland died at
St Germains. The event would have been of little
moment but for another that immediately followed
it. King Louis publicly acknowledged his son as
his successor in the kingdom he had lost. There was
a curious haste in the act, but it was performed with
accessories of solemn state calculated to draw the
eyes of all the world to the ceremonial. Thus there
appeared at Versailles and St Germains a new king
of the British empire, appointing officers of State and
granting patents of nobility. It was a thing done
not only without ministerial approval, but in defiance
of all entreaty and remonstrance by the ministers of
the French Crown—one of the deeds of passionate
insult and defiance such as self-willed and tyrannical
natures are liable to when they are lashing themselves
into the humour for a quarrel. The official people
did their best to neutralise its effects. It was the mere
kindly impulse of a generous nature—it meant no-

[1] The best account that I have seen of this achievement is in the
'Mémoires militaires relatifs à la succession d'Espagne sous Louis
XIV. Extraits de la correspondance de la cour et des généraux par le
Lieutenant-Général de Vault, directeur du dépôt de la guerre, mort in
1790.' 1834-50. This book, which will hereafter be cited briefly as
'Mémoires militaires,' is in the "Collection de Documents inédits sur
l'Histoire de France," published by the French Government under
the direction of Guizot.

thing that could affect diplomatic relations. But it was a thing done that could not be undone. The English ambassador was withdrawn from Paris without the ceremony of leave-taking, and the French ambassador was hastily dismissed from London.

When these sinister events had their climax in the death of King William, it was as if a guardian angel had departed. The protector of the British constitution, the champion of Protestantism in Europe, were lost together. It was in the decrees of fate, however, that a mightier spirit was to arise in one more affluently endowed with the powers and the accomplishments fitted to meet the perils of the time than William of Nassau, great warrior and great statesman though he was. When we look back upon the stormy and perilous crisis from a serene distance, we can feel satisfaction in the dispensation of events that let no one supersede Marlborough in the work for which nature had endowed him—work sublimely described by one nearly as supreme in letters as the object of his panegyric was in arms, "to ride the whirlwind and direct the storm." How absolutely King William while he lived would have taken the direction of the war was shown by this, that only with difficulty was it kept out of the hands of Prince George of Denmark. He was compensated with the office of Lord High Admiral—a sagacious choice between the two, since the handling of a fleet, even to the extent of mismanagement, required an amount of technical skill far beyond his attainments and his capacity.

It is worthy of remembrance that the powers imparted to Marlborough to represent England both in diplomacy and war in the coming crisis, were conferred by King William, and were his last great act of statesmanship before his death. It has been suggested that as Marlborough was known to have supreme influence with the princess who was likely soon to be queen, foreign Powers would rely on his capacity to fulfil the obligations he accepted, and would all the more readily listen to the conditions demanded by him. But we may also be assured that King William would have made no such selection had he not believed Marlborough to be preeminently qualified for his mighty task.

As the fruit of his diplomatic skill and industry, the Government of Queen Anne inherited the Grand Alliance, completed on the 7th of June 1701. It professed to bind in perpetual and inviolable friendship and co-operation the Emperor, Great Britain, and the United Provinces. Other Powers attached themselves to it as a fundamental organisation for all. It superseded separate diplomacy with such Powers. They were free to accede to it, or cast their lot with its enemies, but it could not be qualified or amended to suit their inclinations. There was a powerful simplicity in this principle conducive to rapidity and decision throughout the momentous train of events inaugurated by it. The preamble, or statement of the conditions demanding such an alliance were,—that the inheritance to the dominions of the King of Spain belonged in right to the house of Austria; that France claimed and was taking possession of them; that thus the French and Spanish dominions would come to be virtually one empire, and that the Power thus created would be so formid-

able that it would become supreme in Europe.[1]   There
were other dangers to the trade of Britain and the
existence of the United Provinces ; but the ultimate
aim of the Grand Alliance was expressed in this brief
and comprehensive form.[2]

When the bursting of some great storm is imminent,
the eyes of men search out the spot where its first
blow is to be dealt—the spot where it may be seen by
the merely curious, and may be averted or mitigated
by those more closely interested.   In this instance
the spot was small, but the gathering of the forces
pointed to it with indubitable distinctness ; it was
the small town of Nymeguen, on the eastern frontier
of the United Provinces, generally, for brevity's sake,
called Holland.

The possession of Nymeguen came of the craving
of watery Holland to have one foot on the firm
ground.   Nature had made the rest of the country a
morass of sedge, sand, and mud.   People who were
prepared to buy freedom at any price fled to the in-
hospitable shelter of these wilds ; and as the people
who loved freedom were also industrious and frugal,
the wilderness began to smile under their industry,
and after centuries became the richest soil in Europe.
It was not only thus an object of cupidity to robber
Powers, but it was traversed by roads and canals,
available to those who had possession.   And this
availability was not merely from place to place in
Holland, but through Holland towards France on the

[1] " Qu'enfin les François et les Espagnols, étant ainsi unis devien-
droiens en peu de tems si formidables qu'ils pourroiens aisément sou-
mettre toute l'Europe à leur obéirs et empire."

[2] See it in French, 'Actes mémoires et autres pièces authentiques
concernant la paix d'Utrecht,' i. 1 *et seq.*   In Latin, Dumont, viii. 91.

one hand, and Germany on the other. This, if it was a cause of danger to Holland, was also a source of strength if adroitly managed ; and hence it was that the small group of republics had so much to say along with the great Powers in all disturbances and readjustments of the map of Europe.

Thus Holland was a desirable acquisition for France to make; and in the political school of King Louis and his worshippers, it was in the hands of a very odious people,—a kingless people, living in civilisation and acquiring wealth—a practical outrage on the divine right of sovereigns. There must be some source of quarrel more palpable than this spirit to justify the annexation of Holland, and such a source was ready at hand. The Dutch were rebels against the sovereignty that now by divine right belonged to the grandson of King Louis. It is true that half a century had passed since the independence of the Provinces had been confirmed by all Europe in the peace of Westphalia. But rebellion and sacrilege remain the same in character, however successful the wicked perpetrators may have been for a time : the hour of retribution had come at last.

Within its wall the town of Nymeguen, with its winding steep streets, stands much as it did when the eyes of Europe were upon it. Outside, its mighty fortifications have been crumbling into unsightly hillocks of sand and turf, save where portions of them have been made available in the construction of railway lines and harbour works. The great river Waal—carrying with it the larger portion of the Rhine to the sea—washes the town ; but though the Waal is the natural boundary of this part of Holland,

Nymeguen has its back to the river, and stands outside facing the enemy with its fortresses. This position gave Nymeguen the mastery of all the branches
of the Rhine. The only other branch lying between
Holland and Germany turns off a few miles eastward,
and is naturally under the protection of Nymeguen,
which was thus the entrance-gate not only to Holland, but to the German bank of the Rhine. The
events of later wars give accumulated proof of the
momentous significance of such local conditions. In
the words of the statesmen of the time, the critical
nature of the situation was expressed in the words,
"Nymeguen on the Rhine boundary." Those who were
not hearty in the cause spoke of the narrow selfishness
of the Dutch in driving Europe into war for so small a
matter. Holland, too, was fundamentally strong. Like
some amphibious animals, she could get under water
for a time ; her pastures had been flooded in the hour
of imminent peril, and the resource might be sought
again. But the drenching would be a dire loss both
of possessions and people. Was it fair that Germany
should be saved by this sacrifice ? Would Britain
stand by and see, in stolid indifference, so pitiful a
calamity to a friend and neighbour ? But there were
considerations that sharply touched a powerful party
in England with something more palpable than the
prospective predominance of France upsetting the
balance of the European Powers. It was at the time
when theories of the vast contributions made to the
wealth of the world by monopolies and exclusive
trading privileges were at their climax. The more
amply a community was furnished with this source
of wealth the richer it became. But it was not in

the nature of the commodity that two communities could partake in its wealth-producing resources. The gain of one was ever measured by the loss to the other. If any State became rich, some other State had become so much the poorer to provide the fund whence the riches of its neighbour had been increased. It is true that there were treaties of commerce by which some nation admitted another as " a favoured nation " to certain assigned trading privileges. But these admittances were distinct pecuniary sacrifices to the exigencies of politics. No nation conceded them willingly, and the man who spoke of them as advantages to both parties would have been counted a maniac. It was simply the policy of imparting a share in the precious privilege to a friend, lest, becoming an enemy, he might seize the whole. If the London capitalist could not well see it to be his duty to sacrifice some of his money to stop the house of Bourbon in its march to universal empire, his tenderest susceptibilities were touched when he was told how that universality of dominion included the exclusive command over the trade of the world. The process had already begun by which England was to be excluded from this and that market. In the first place, the Spanish market was lost ; and Portugal had agreed by treaty to share in the policy of Spain under her Bourbon king. The command of the entrance to the Mediterranean— Gibraltar—secured the trade of all that seaboard, by guarding Sicily, Naples, and the other Italian possessions of the Austrian kings of Spain, for the Bourbons. It was more alarming than even all this that the Indies—the Spanish American colonies, with all their boundless prospects of enlarging inhabitancy and commerce—were to be closed to the trading vessels of England. The Spanish Netherlands were lost to English enterprise. The blight was to work its way through Holland, and might pass into Germany and Scandinavia. The great trading interests of England had been roused into a paroxysm of fear and wrath by the Scots projects of an Indian and African company, with a settlement at Darien; but what was the puny competition of this poor relation when measured with the vast combination of forces that now threatened to crush out of life the trade of England?

Nymeguen was the entrance-gate to Holland, and all that could be reached by passing through Holland. When the fortifications outside, commanding all the approaches available to an enemy, were fully equipped and manned, the gate was closed. But there was no garrison in the fortresses, and they were so divested of equipment that there was said not to be a gun mounted on the vast works. In the spirit of economy it appeared that the Dutch Government had trusted to the Barrier Forts as a sufficient protection. But when these forts, with a suddenness more like the wave of a Prospero's wand than even the most rapid operations of diplomacy or war, passed from the hands of protectors into the hands of enemies, the gate was open. All now depended on adroitness and nimbleness in attack or rescue when both parties had shaken free of the trammels of the expiring peace.

As the armies assembled on both sides were hovering on the frontier territories between the Maas and the Rhine, watching each other, and meeting in the casual affairs that generally begin great wars, it became known to the Earl of Athlone, commanding a force of British and allied troops near Cleve, that on the 10th of June Marshal Boufflers was to cross his front, drive it back with a superior force, and make a dash at Nymeguen. The estimates of the time are, that Athlone's force was from thirty to thirty-five thousand strong, and the French force numerically stronger by a third. There were casual encounters on the way, and in these Athlone's troops were the chief sufferers. Their tactic became a retreat, but it was a retreat towards Nymeguen, with no considerable enemy in the way. It was one of the instances of scarcely merited good fortune. Nymeguen was saved, and the allied force found shelter in its fortresses not only from their immediate assailants, but from a stronger enemy, who were said to be not half an hour's march behind them.

From Lord Cutts, whose name is of frequent occurrence in the details of Marlborough's wars, we have this account of his own part in the relief of Nymeguen : "By the several accounts we had of sudden march, their design seemed to be to get between us and Nymeguen, by which means they would have cut off our provisions, ammunition, and forage ; and being very much superior to us in numbers, as well horse as foot, this town with several others would have been at their mercy."

" When our troops were got under the cannon of the town, which began now to play upon the enemy, the queen's forces under my command, who had the honour to close the whole retreat, returned likewise

in good order ; and the troops of the French household coming very near me towards the last, and
seeming to dispose themselves for an attack, the
Prince of Wirtemberg was pleased to join me in
person at the head of a body of horse, and to give
me his assistance until the very last." [1]

Had the race come to another conclusion, a strength
more critical in its command over the great issues than
almost any other in Europe, would have changed hands
without a blow, without being subject to the deterio-
ration that a fortress must suffer from a siege, and
without the exhaustion which a besieging army
must pay as the price of success.[2]   The Dutch saw

[1] A Relation of the Retreat of the Allies' Army, under the command
of the Earl of Athlone, from their camp at Clarembeck to Nymeguen,
June the 11th, N.S., 1702, addressed to Lord Nottingham.—Addl. MSS.
B.M., 29588, f. 59.

[2] Du Bosc, Military History, i. 101 *et seq.*   There is an account of
this affair by one who professed to have taken part in it.   He says :
" By daylight we were within a league of Nymeguen, at which time
the enemy's horse began to appear on both sides of us.   This made
us mend our pace, and they pushed forward to try if they could get
between us and the town.   Some of their dragoons came so near
as to make a push at the Dutch foot, which put them in some disorder.
But the next regiments to them facing about, fired upon them, and
made them scour back.   At length we arrived safe within the
outworks of Nymeguen ; " and yet, but for aid of an uncommon kind,
there would have been no safety in these unequipped outworks.   The
citizens, seeing the crisis, made a desperate effort to get guns and muni-
tion under difficulties, suspected by the writer to have been caused
by treachery.   " Nor could the burghers obtain the keys of the stores,
but were obliged to break them open, to draw the cannon up to the
ramparts, and to bring the powder and ball on their backs.   When
this was done they fired with fury on the enemy and made them retire
immediately ; otherwise, as their foot was just come up, it was believed
they would have attacked us in those noble advanced works, which
had been made there during the short interval of the last peace by
the famous engineer Cohorn."—Memoirs of the most remarkable Military Transactions from the year 1683 to 1718, &c., by Captain Robert
Parker, pp. 76, 77.   There is an account of the affair in the ' Mém. du
M. de Berwick ' (1778), i. 179 *et seq.*

what they had escaped in the sackings and foragings
of the French within the fruitful district of Cleve,
to which their marauding was restrained by the
Waal and the Rhine. It was estimated that Boufflers
gleaned in that district twenty thousand head of
cattle and half a million of crowns.

Before resuming the chronological order of events
the opportunity may here be taken to offer a statement
of the situation—of the nature and the position towards each other, diplomatical and military, of the
opposing forces. In the middle of March in the year
1702, the anxious States-General were cheered by
learning from the British resident that his queen had
determined "to despatch the Earl of Marlborough
over to Holland, with the character of her Majesty's
Ambassador Extraordinary and Plenipotentiary, to give
the States-General assurance of her steadfast resolution to adhere to all the treaties of alliance that have
been entered into, and to pursue all the measures
that have been concerted between his Majesty the
Emperor and the States for carrying on the common
cause."[1] On the 4th of August, proclamation was
made at St James's Palace Gate, Chancery Lane, and
the Royal Exchange, of war against the King of
France, "who had taken and still keeps possession
of a great part of the Spanish dominions, exercising
an absolute authority over all the monarchy, having
seized Milan and the Spanish low countries by his
armies, and made himself master of Cadiz, of the
entrance into the Mediterranean, and of the ports
into the Spanish West Indies, by his fleets, every-

[1] Mr Vernon to George Stepney.—Letters relative to the Reign of
William III., edited by G. P. R. James, iii. 193.

where designing to invade the liberties of Europe, and to obstruct the freedom of navigation and commerce."[1]

King Louis made a final effort to secure the Dutch. The change in their position, when they no longer counted the king of the British empire as the head of their State, seemed to offer an opportunity; and from the position of the Dutch lying between France and Northern Europe, their concurrence would have been an acquisition of great value.   He addressed their High Mightinesses the States-General in a tone of friendly patronage, shading off into occasional menace. They had shown an ungrateful unconsciousness of the favours he had conferred on them.   But the past would be forgiven if there were amendment in the future.   They had heretofore been under restraint— they were now free to choose their course, and recover the place they had forfeited in his countenance and friendship.   Let them make their choice—quiet and liberty under his august protection, or war and ruin.   This was one among the many insolences that seemed to do as much for the subsequent humiliation of the proud king as his reverses in the field.   The Estates answered him in proud defiance.   They pushed home the dubious references to a state of coercion, accepting them as referring to the loss of their illustrious chief who was King of Great Britain.   His memory was fresh, not as an oppressor who had thwarted the national aspirations, but as a friend who had fostered and given power and shape to them; and it was utterly to mistake the nature of their constitution to doubt that they had ever been

[1] Annals. i. 29.

less free than they had been when visited by their great calamity. They were invited to send a representative to the Court of France. They thought this a needless ceremony—all questions must now abide the issues of war.

In the distribution of the forces, Britain was to provide 40,000 men in the meantime, and prospective reinforcements—these were to serve against France. There was a separate vote for troops to be sent to Portugal, and 40,000 men were voted for the navy. The Empire—that is to say, the combined German States—engaged to furnish 120,000 men.[1]

Brandenburg, now merging into Prussia, was in a peculiar position. The elector was endeavouring, according to the old expression, to "close his crown" or become a king. Before the Reformation the See of Rome arrogated the function of distinguishing the

---

[1] These were partitioned according to sovereignties :—

	Horse.	Foot.
The circle of the Rhine,	1,800	8,121
„ „ of Upper Saxony,	3,963	8,121
„ „ of Austria,	7,563	16,521
„ „ of Burgundy,	3,963	8,121
„ „ of Franconia,	2,940	5,703
„ „ of Bavaria,	2,400	4,479
„ „ of Swabia,	3,963	8,121
„ „ of the Upper Rhine,	1,473	8,559
„ „ of Westphalia,	3,963	8,121
„ „ of Lower Saxony,	3,963	8,121
	35,991	83,988

119,979
—Annals, i. 120.

So it was adjusted by the Imperial Diet; but in all German affairs of the kind there is the action and reaction of the collective empire and the several "circles" to be estimated. Bavaria of course contributed nothing to this contingent, and sent to the French side a far larger force than the Diet claimed for the Empire. The Imperial contingent is usually estimated in round numbers at 100,000.

potentates who were kings from those who were not, by the ceremonial of anointing at the coronation and making an anointed king. The house of Brandenburg was Protestant, and could not claim this sanction, whatever other it might seek. The power of settling such questions of dignity was claimed by the Empire and the Diet; but practically it came to be gradually adjusted by the pressure of diplomacy, furthered by something like general acclamation. Elector Frederick had set the crown on his own head in the church of Königsburg, but it remained to be seen what that bold assumption was worth. It was certain that without a heavy bribe France, and the Powers influenced by France, would not acknowledge the transaction. Frederick could perhaps remember how, some twenty-four years earlier, in the days of his father the Great Elector, the ambassador of King Louis, by special instruction, refused to meet in conference the ambassador of that elector. The Grand Monarque would not concede that the Kur-Fürsten or electors were entitled to commission ambassadors. They were themselves scarcely the equals of the *haute noblesse* of France who would have to meet their servants. If the elector had anything to say to the King of France, let him attend at Court with the other suitors. This came from no reckless impulse of haughty insolence. It rested on a deep and dangerous policy, pointing to the acquisition of territory. If the electors had no sovereignties, they had no place in European diplomacy, and might be the more easily pillaged. In the intricate feudalities that still infested the political organisation of Europe, the acute French lawyers found for their master seign-

orial rights touching the territories or the titles of
dignity enjoyed by the electors. Whatever feudal
prerogative the house of Bourbon claimed must be
supreme. To claim sovereignty in competition with
the crown of France was rank mutiny; and from the
elector who afforded an excuse for charging him
with this feudal crime, King Louis might take whatever he felt he had the power to take. Hence he
was sometimes a more dangerous neighbour in time
of peace than in time of war.[1]

It was in this way that France got possession of
the greater portion of those territories in Alsace and
Lorraine which have now been gained back to Germany, and acknowledge the supreme authority of the
descendant of Prince Frederick. It might be long
ere the disintegrating process could reach the banks
of the Spree: but the pleasant territory of Cleve was
near; the Barrier Forts, all in the hands of France,
were at hand; and had Nymeguen been taken, the
road would have been cleared for the acquisition of
a territory that would have given France, following
on the acquisition of Strasburg, a second hold on the
Rhine.[2]

[1] "En voyant cette puissance qui s'étendait ainsi de tous côtés, et qui
acquérait pendant la paix, plus que dix rois prédécesseurs de Louis
XIV. n'avaient acquis par leurs guerres, les alarmes de l'Europe re-
commencèrent."—Voltaire, Siècle de Louis XIV., ch. 14.

[2] The rapid extension during the seventeenth century of the territories ruled by the house of Valois seems to have excited among the
French, traditions of something like universal empire. The more they
gained, the more they professed to have lost of what had in ancient
times been theirs. To the Germans, Kaiser Karl was a shadowy tradition not easily appropriated; but the French domesticate the Carolus
Magnus of the Chronicles into their own Charlemagne, whose throne
was in Lutetia—now known as Paris—whence he ruled all the civilised
world. Any one who has a curiosity about the literature of these tra-

Considerations as to these sources of danger to the smaller States on the one hand, and on the other the practicability of embodying a force sufficient for their protection, and possibly for the punishment of the great aggressor, were engrossing the thoughts of European statesmen, when the Elector of Brandenburg challenged them to commit themselves by acknowledging him as king. If there were difficulties with others, Marlborough, who wanted the troops and influence of the claimant of monarchy, had no hesitation how to act. Hence the new king's eyes were gladdened by a letter addressed to him with the august title of "Sire," by one who was "de sa Majesté le très-humble et très-obeissant serviteur."[1]

This prompt cordiality secured to the cause a firm

ditions may gratify it by reading a volume of 789 pages, with the title, "La Recherche des droicts du Roy et de la couronne de France, sur les Royaumes, Duchez, Comtez, Villes, et Pays occupez par les Princes estrangers appartenans aux Rois tres-chrestiens, par conquestes, successions, achapts, donations, et autres titres legitimes. Ensemble de leurs droicts sur l'Empire, et des debuoirs et hommages deubs a leur couronne par divers princes etrangers. Par M. Jacques de Cassan, Counseiller du Roy et son Premier Advocat au Siege Presidial de Beziers." Much of the lore brought to light by M. Cassan will create only astonishment and ridicule in the present day ; but the book went through several editions, and excited much bitter controversy, chiefly between Frenchmen and Germans.

[1] Such is the first morsel in the extremely valuable contribution to historical literature called 'The Letters and Dispatches of John Churchill, Duke of Marlborough, from 1702 to 1712, edited by General the Right Honourable Sir George Murray'—in five volumes: 1847. With many other pleasant things the writer says : "Je suis très persuadé qu'il n'y a aucun moyen dont je puisse me servir avec plus de succès pour faire ma cour auprès de la Reine ma maitresse, qu'en cherchant des occasions d'affermir et de cultiver l'amitié entre elle et votre Majesté pour le bien de la cause commune ; je prie votre Majestè aussi très-humblement de vouloir bien croire qu'il n'y a personne qui soit avec plus d'attachement et de dévotion. Sire, de votre Majesté le très-humble et très-obeissant serviteur."

and powerful friend. Next to the Imperial Diet the vote of England on such a claim as his was the most powerful of sanctions, and it came from a sovereign who wanted no man's land, and would not seize the first opportunity for quarrel and aggression. King William saw the reflection of his own wisdom in the hapless fate of his brother Kur-Fürst of Bavaria. The Prussian contingent to the army of the allies was to commence with 5000 men, and it expanded by degrees to 20,000.

It became a momentous question of Home policy how Britain was to provide the great force she had promised to her allies. The old feudal institutions, merged into the commission of array, and the militia, provided no resources to meet such a drain; and, in fact, the forces so embodied could only be employed in defence of the kingdom. The country was prosperous and work was abundant. That prosperity called loud for protection from the hostile Power that was to close the avenues of trade, but it enhanced the price at which the services of the soldier could be bought. The country would neither submit to a general conscription nor to the kidnapping feats by which despotic Powers supplemented the supplies of the conscription. Such practices were criminal in the eye of the law, and there was no power in England above the law to sanction them. And yet there were many thousands of men who were a burden and a scandal to the community rather than a benefit. These, though bad citizens, were the stuff that the best soldiers in the ranks are made of. The question was, how to get possession of them in proper form of law.

In King William's wars, those who set themselves
to the task of recruiting the army had been wont to
search out the victims of society who were so miser-
able that foreign service might improve, and could
not deteriorate, their condition.   The arbitrary laws
for the recovery of debt gave to the creditor a power
over his debtor vying with, and often far exceeding,
the inflictive power possessed by a despotic Government.   Early in the statute-book of Queen Anne's
reign there is "An Act for the discharge out of prison
of such insolvent debtors as shall serve, or procure a
person to serve, in her Majesty's fleet or army." [1]   All
projects of the kind required in England to be carefully provided with sufficient powers to break through
the technical trammels of the common law.   A previous Act, for certain reasons, "did not answer the
intent for which it was made: wherefore to supply the
defects which did obstruct the good ends and purposes
of the said Act, be it enacted," &c.   So separating
from other prisoners the mere pecuniary debtors,
to whose relief the Act is limited, it drew out any
debtor so poor as to be unable to maintain himself in
prison without being burdensome to relations or the
parish.   The creditor could only resist the liberation
and enlistment by providing a maintenance "not exceeding fourpence per day, which shall be paid to the
prisoner himself, and not to the jailer, keeper, or any
other person for him." [2]   There is, in this simple clause,
a sad significance; for the tyranny let loose by the
law of debtor and creditor was seized and held fast
by a machinery of rapacious and cruel "vested interests."   Among these were the officers of the law,

[1] 2 & 3 Anne. c. 16.   [2] 2 & 3 Anne. c. 16.

and the jailers or keepers of the prisons; and subsequent inquiries showed that people were buried in loathsome dungeons for years after the just claims of creditors had been discharged—were detained in prison, in fact, so long as there was any chance that affection or humanity could extract money from any relation or friend of the sufferer. It was in further protection against this class of harpies that "all persons discharged by virtue of this Act are and shall be freed and discharged from all chamber-rent and other fees to jailers and their respective officers, and all securities given by such poor prisoners, or others bound with them, to any jailers, or to any other person in trust for them, are hereby discharged and made void." The recruiting officer having thus been admitted within the prison-gate, it was thought that the emergency might justify an enlargement of his privilege of selection among the inmates of that gloomy home. Why not give the recruiting officer the run of its criminal inmates? They were the curse and terror of the country at home—let their powers of destructiveness be turned upon the enemy. It is the calamity of themselves, and of all who have concern with them, that they cannot govern their wild natures: put them in the hands of the drill-sergeant—he will bring them into order, and the power of military discipline will keep them in it. Sometimes, at that period, the poor gentleman had to become a common soldier; and it was felt that an admixture of the felon class, however small, must blot a profession that, down to the humblest in its ranks, ought to be inspired by a sense of honour. But the emergency was imperative; and it must be granted that there was more reluctance in Queen Anne's reign than even a century later to admit this element within the British army.[1]

Here again we are admitted into some secrets, and find how the cumbrous apparatus raised by common law and statute law for the protection of the subject from arbitrary power may give opportunity for cruelties and tyrannies, such as the agents of arbitrary power might be ashamed to inflict. The letter of the law dictated penalties and punishments which the administrators of the law dared not, in the face of humanity and justice, inflict. Some "fiction of law," or other subtle subterfuge, was found to save appearances — as in the long notorious practice of pleading " benefit of clergy " where sentence of death was recorded. But these complex devices gave power and opportunity to cunning, unscrupulous men ; and all outlets in the direction of mercy and justice were blocked by operations which inferred official services, and for the official services fees, which in process of time, became " vested interests."

It required, as we have seen, an Act of Parliament to take debtors out of the hands of the creditors, their lawful owners ; but the prerogative of mercy was sufficient to put the criminal at the disposal of

[1] " The exact number of this class admitted during the Peninsular war is not easily traceable. Three regiments—one of military distinction —were then formed, and others were recruited. A return of the number of these regiments was moved for in 1812 ; but the motion was opposed by the Ministers and negatived by the House of Commons. During the Crimean war a suggestion was made by an experienced member of the House of Commons, that some of the labour of the siege should be borne by convicts under enlistment ; but circumstances had so changed that it was not entertained."—The Military Forces of the Crown : their Administration and Government, by Charles M. Clode, ii. 14.

the military force by attaching the condition of service to the pardon. Yet a clause in the first Mutiny Act of Queen Anne's reign lucidly explains the nature of impeding interests which the Crown could not sweep away. "Whereas several persons convicted or attainted of capital felonies and offences are thought fit to be reprieved from execution in order to obtain their pardon upon condition of being transported beyond seas, or as persons fit to serve her Majesty in her army or navy, and oftentimes lie in prison for a long time in expectation of the passing such pardon under the Great Seal, and the pleading and allowing thereof in due form of law, to the great charge and burden of the county where they have been so convicted." [1]

There still remained in the regions of social degradation a richer stratum of material for drill than even the debtor or the criminal. There was that terrible and abundant monster the vagrant, gregariously assailed in numberless statutes as "idle and disorderly persons, rogues and vagabonds, incorrigible rogues," and the like. It seems an anomaly that the most industrious country in the world should ever be wailing over the idleness so deeply rooted in its social conditions. But the vagrant classes were a necessary secondary effect of industry, growing upon its primary effect — the increase of wealth. Every community will have a percentage of the idle and the worthless within it; and the temptations afforded by the wealth and luxury of England were so seductively attractive to those who live on other people's wealth, that, as her own people did not supply suffi-

[1] 1 Anne. c. 16. s. 43.

cient numbers to prey on the available riches, they were recruited by bands of dusky strangers who crossed all Europe to reach the happy hunting-ground.

The warfare between these subtle pests and the clumsy statute and common law was ceaseless and brutalising; for the exasperated citizen of respectability and substance was provoked beyond endurance, and would stick at no cruelty if it would rid him of the nuisance. Yet all must be done according to law; there must be no arbitrary despotism under the name of a paternal Government, ruling society by an administrative police. Hence the mighty load of vagrance statute-law. It was, in a great measure, a contest with an invisible enemy; for the fundamental crime of the vagrant was idleness: and how could a man be punished for the act of doing nothing? Then came into existence the almost illogical offence of " an act of vagrancy." It had some substantiality in it when it dealt with " every person pretending or professing to tell fortunes, or using any subtle craft, means, or device, by palmistry or otherwise, to deceive and impose." But when it came to " loitering " for questionable purposes, to sleeping in the open air, to not " giving a good account " of one's self, or to " having no visible means of subsistence," it was felt that the criminal law was treading upon precarious ground. It was after the war had begun, and, as it were, with decorous reluctance, that it was determined to make a conscript of the vagrant; and certain justices of the peace were empowered " to raise and levy such able-bodied men as have not any lawful calling or employment, or visible means for their maintenance and livelihood, to serve as soldiers."[1] The inducements for gathering in this fresh harvest, of course gave new activity to the recruiting department; but the law was careful to guard against the actual enforcement of the Act falling into military hands. The regular officers of the army were excluded from acting as justices for the enrolment, and the Mutiny Act and Articles of War were to be read over to the recruit before he was sworn and enrolled.[2]

It has been remarked that great fires or other destructive calamities in cities have the Asmodeus faculty of revealing domestic interiors, and exposing social conditions unsuspected and astounding. In some respects the sudden call upon the country to provide for a great war has a like effect, through the invasion of households, the ruthless inquiries into the resources of the citizen, and the demand for the ser-

---

[1] 2 & 3 Anne, c. 19 ; and see Clode, Military Forces of the Crown.

[2] We may count the following as a lively caricature of possible abuses in the working of this arrangement :—

"*Scale.* Here, you, constable—the next. Set up that black-faced fellow ; he has a gunpowder look. What can you say against this man, constable ?

Const. Nothing but that he is a very honest man.

Balance. What are you, friend ?

Nut. A collier. I work in the coal-pits.

Scruple. Lookee, gentlemen, this fellow has a trade ; and the Act of Parliament here expresses that we are to impress no man that has any visible means of a livelihood.

Kite. May it please your worships, this man has no visible means of a livelihood ; for he works underground.

Plume. Well said, Kite ; besides, the army wants miners.

Balance. Right ; and had we an order of Government for't, we could raise you in this and the neighbouring county of Stafford five hundred colliers that would run you underground like moles, and do more service in a siege than all the miners in the army."—The Recruiting Officer, by George Farquhar, Act v.

vices of all the men of health and sinew that can
be spared. There happened to be in the midst of all
the hurry and confusion a looker-on endowed with
acute observation, brilliant wit, and a lively sense of
the ludicrous. It was in the year 1705 that George
Farquhar gave the world his play of ' The Recruiting
Officer,' and left a legacy of riotous mirth to generations of his countrymen. " Sergeant Kite " was no absolute creation of the imagination, but a realisation
of a figure too well known from that day to this as a
minister of good and evil, the causer of certain joys
and exaltations, but of a much larger fund of sorrows
—the typical "recruiting sergeant." He is unscrupulous and genial, " a fellow of infinite humour."
He is a mighty orator of the pot-house order—a great
historian of brilliant and successful ideal warriors.
His own potency and heroism are exemplified in the
mightiness of his potations; for he is gifted with
almost superhuman powers, for drawing forth all
strengthening, rousing, and exhilarating influences
from his liquor, without permitting it to steal away
his brains.[1]

---

[1] The felicity of Farquhar's characters is not in invention, but in the
slight touch of exaggeration that converts a rather questionable reality
into a picturesquely monstrous iniquity. We have seen one specimen
of his manner; here is another, arising out of the birth of an infant
whose entry into the world is embarrassing to the recruiting department :—

" *Plume.* Kite, you must father the child.

Kite. And so her friends will oblige me to marry the mother ?

Plume. If they should, we'll take her with us. She can wash, you
know, and make a bed upon occasion.

.   .   .   .

Plume. Kite, is the child a boy or a girl ?

Kite. A chopping boy.

Plume. Then set the mother down in your list, and the boy in mine.

If in such and other shapes the recruiting organisation of Britain was tainted with scandals freely exposed by an open press, we may safely believe that there were deeper blots in the shape of injustices and cruelties in the machinations by which those who were to be our allies raised their forces. If in some measure the traps and subterfuges of the recruiting ser-

Enter him a granadier by the name of Francis Kite absent upon furlow. I'll allow you a man's pay for his subsistence," &c.

If such an incident never occurred, the practice of the day made it possible. The army estimates and accounts were adjusted to the cost of supporting certain rank and file, and when there was some call for emergency or humanity, it was met by a fictitious rating on the actual force—as, for instance :

"WHITEHALL, *September* 28, 1711.

"Her Majesty having been pleased to grant Titton Minshull, a child, a commission of ensign in Brigadier Stanwix's Regiment of Foot, in order for the support of his mother and family, in consequence of the loss of his father and uncle, who died in the service ; and has likewise given him a furlough to be absent from his duty until further order."—Clode : Military Forces, i. 610.

Three years after the beginning of the war, an attempt was made to check abuses naturally following on this clumsy arrangement. By a Royal Order, "Her Majesty, finding it very prejudicial to the service to have commissions given to children and others unfit to do duty with their regiments, is pleased to declare that for the future no person who is not of age sufficient to serve shall be admitted into any of her Majesty's troops, except the children of officers who have been slain or suffered extremely in the service, in which case the merits of the father may make it reasonable to show that mark of royal favour to the son." There are to be but two such commissions for each regiment, and when a regiment is ordered on foreign service its boys are to exchange with adult officers in other regiments. This practice had so tenacious an existence that old people of the present day remember it as exemplified by stories about colonels in nurseries. In the book where the document cited in this note is to be found, it is said, "That this system was known to, if not approved by, Parliament, is endorsed by the 1st and 2d rules relating to half-pay, enacted 4 Geo. I. c. 5, sect. 18, and it continued in practice until the late Duke of York assumed the command of the army, when not only did he refuse to make such appointments, but superseded many officers who were children or boys at school."—Clode : Military Forces, ii. 91.

vice were demoralising to the embodied force, we may believe that both in physical and moral condition they were far above the companions they were to meet in Flanders and Germany. In fact, the conditions that went to make recruiting difficult in the British empire — and especially in England — enhanced the value of British troops when they could be got. The country was flourishing. Work was abundant and well paid ; and the soldiers who could be by any means, fair or foul, drawn forth from such a community, were capable of great exertion and the long endurance of fatigue. With such an army in his hands—with his kinsman Godolphin at the helm of the Treasury, amply supplying all its needs and punctually paying the subsidies to allies needy and greedy—Marlborough went forth with the materials in his hand for guiding and commanding the greatest game that had been played in Europe since the days of Charlemagne.

And he was the man made for the occasion. The commander of an army, if he be a thorough soldier, has great weight in the council as well as in the field ; but it is generally the weight of his sword, the necessity of keeping him in the spirit and humour to do his field duty effectually; and to secure this, many a point is yielded to the abrupt, surly soldier who knows nothing but command and obedience. But Marlborough was as supreme at the calm council-table as in the storm of battle. Dealing with his many-ranked illustrious groups of monarchs, lesser royalties, and august statesmen, he exemplified on a grand scale what it falls to common people's lot often to see exemplified on a little scale. This is, when in some select vestry or sub-committee of councilmen, the one clever man of the little cluster appears to hear every one, to agree with every one, and in the end, with the unanimous consent and common applause of all, transacts the business on hand precisely in his own way.

Unlike most men of great firmness and self-reliance, Marlborough courted counsel and discussion. He could conduct it with absolute calmness and courtesy. On his own clear views of what was to be done it had no effect, but it gained him coadjutors; for he was, like Wolsey, fair-spoken and persuasive. His patience was inexhaustible. He was cautious, but his caution had its corrective in an unmatched promptitude of vision. He thus never committed a rash act, and he never missed an opportunity for striking an effective blow. His fertility in resources made him less amenable to disappointment when his favourite scheme was thwarted, than men of smaller resources, whose mind contains but one scheme at a time, and that being forbidden, are destitute of other resource, and helpless. To him, if one way were closed there was ever another opening. He felt secure in himself,—be the conditions that were to be wrought with what they might, he would bring out of them results which no other man could effect.

It would be difficult to name another man whose communications ranged through so many strata of social grade as his. They passed through the whole world of Europe, from the emperor, who was still by courtesy the chief of kings, through various grades of royalty into still more numerous grades of nobility,

till they reached the riff-raff brought out of the dregs
of the various nations by the recruiter or the crimp.
Having had the arduous duty of thus addressing men
far above himself in rank, and of addressing in
remonstrance, in rebuke, sometimes in menace, he
knew and practised the maxim that a strict observ-
ance of etiquette in communication with superiors is
the way to save the inferior man's self-respect and
true position from invasion by the higher power. The
sovereign is addressed with the simple and emphatic
" Sire." For Serene Highnesses and Electoral Highnesses there is the Monseigneur. The great partner
in his glories, Prince Eugene, being a prince by courtesy only, and neither a sovereign nor the son of
a sovereign, is " Monsieur" simply, but the courtesy of the conclusion is " de votre Altesse le très-
humble et très-obeissant servateur." With none
is he more punctilious than with their " High
Mightinesses" the States-General. In his long lec-
tures to them he brings in at stated intervals the
" Hauts et Puissants Seigneurs; " with these words
he must have filled a surface equal to some quires
of paper, for he was the most diligent and minute of
correspondents.

It would not be easy to determine whether Marlborough was acquainted with either High or Low
Dutch. These languages might have been of occasional use to him, but they were a small matter to
one who was master of the language of diplomacy.
It would not suffice to say that he spoke and wrote
French like a native. He wielded it with the subtle
completeness of polish only to be attained by those
natives whose felicity it was to cluster round the re-

ception-chambers of Versailles.[1] It was in the reign of Louis XIV. that the language of his Court finally established a claim to be the language of diplomacy for Europe, superseding alike the Latin common to all, and the exchange between communities of articles in which each spoke in its own vernacular. It is not easy to dispute the charge of those who maintain that Marlborough was not master of English, and spelt it badly; for it was then for conversational purposes imperfectly developed, and the spelling in the correspondence of all classes was eclectic. But Marlborough's skill in the language of diplomacy was so complete as to be one of the great powers at his command for political purposes.

When the various parties to the alliance, their contingencies, and subsidies, had all been settled, there remained the most difficult problem of all— the command of the united force. There was the difficulty, as we have seen, that if a royal personage were available, he must naturally take the command in virtue of his rank; and there was at hand Prince George of Denmark, the queen's husband. It was believed that what really settled his exclusion was the consciousness in those who were most punctilious on the question of etiquette, that if there were anything more than nominal in his rank, he might expose his incapacity. Then there were other royalties available, if rank were to decide the momentous question. There was the Archduke

---

[1] It is perhaps right to say that Marlborough's command of the French language is not undisputed. In a thick quarto volume, called 'Protestant Exiles from France,' by the Rev. David C. A. Agnew, he comes forth as a thorough blockhead in this as in other shapes.

Charles, conspicuous in our story as "the King of Spain." There was the Elector of Hanover and the Duke of Zell. Greater than all was the newly-created King of Prussia. The Dutch, to whom the question of the command was an affair of life and death, kept their eye steadily on the commander of the English force, as the man fittest for the supremacy; and when it came to the question whether they would serve under Marlborough, they decided that they would. They made it a condition, however, that they should be represented by "field deputies" in attendance on the army, who should be entitled to withhold the troops of the States-General from any particular service. Here was a body of civilians who had to be consulted on great military operations. The deputies did interfere, as we shall see; and there is little doubt that they baffled more than one brilliant project. Before the French army required the co-operation of the Bavarians, there were many invidious comparisons between the army of one language and one discipline, united by a common enthusiasm, inspired by victory after victory and conquest after conquest, on the one side, and, on the other, an ill-assorted gathering of men speaking all European tongues, under a commander who, if he should even frame some great project in which his unconformable masses might be directed by a common movement, was liable to see it tripped up by a conclave of merchants and money-lenders.

But there is much to be said in vindication of the Dutch statesmen, who have come down to us well abused for timidity, presumption, obstinacy, and the like. For them the enemy was at the gate, and everything in the world at stake on the great issues. Then even the brilliant genius of the man set over them was some apology for hesitation. Marlborough's projects went far beyond the comprehension of the greatest commanders of his day, and naturally they were still further beyond the comprehension of the field deputies. There was, for this, compensation in the very boldness and versatility of his genius, since no commander, when baffled in one project, could so readily find another.

The British and Dutch being thus at one as to the command in chief, made a centre to which the other forces acting in the north of Europe required to gravitate, not merely for co-operation in the general undertaking, but for safety. Marlborough's dealing with the petty sovereignties owning these outlying contingents remains as a brilliant specimen of the firm and the conciliatory in the management of men. He is invariably courteous. Tendering advice or even objection is a favour. If he has to press hard, his tone is supplicatory rather than imperious, and there are no bounds to the merit and the distinction he is prepared to concede to those who will give their invaluable co-operation to his next great project.[1] Under all, too, it is generally made evident to the potentate so appealed to that co-operation in

[1] Frederick of Prussia, who had to thank Marlborough for the prompt acknowledgment of his sovereignty, had presently to hear " de l'entière satisfaction et plaisir que la reine ma maîtresse a eu en apprenant le zèle et l'empressement avec lequel votre Majesté épousait les intérêts de la cause commune, non seulement en augmentant le nombre de ses troupes dans l'Empire, mais aussi par ses négociations particulières avec M. l'Electeur de Bavière, dans lesquelles, si elle pouvait réussir, elle éterniserait son nom et mériterait avec justice le glorieux titre De Libérateur de l'Empire."—Marlb. Despatches, i. 235.

the project, audacious though it may appear, is the safer policy.

Nymeguen, but a short time ago abiding in desertion and danger, with a few despairing but brave burgesses endeavouring to drag some old cannon to the dismantled barriers, was now equipped with everything, both in material and men, that a great fortress should have in time of war. Around it, on both sides of the Waal, lay the gathering-ground of an army so great that it could not well disperse without leaving its mark in the recasting of the map of Europe. All the tribes and languages of Europe were there represented. Predominant were the languages of the great Northern States, High and Low Dutch, and English. There were other varieties of the Teutonic group of tongues—Danish, Norwegian, Swedish, and Lowland Scots. There were Croats, Bohemians, and Hungarians from the Empire, and Celts from Scotland, Ireland, and Biscay. There was a sprinkling of Italian and Spanish—nay, even of French from the Netherlands and the western slopes of the Alps.

The district was well fitted for the organising of the army. With access to all the world, and close to abundant supplies, it had stretches of waste ground where troops could encamp and march without injury to inhabitants and property. Northward and westward were the richest provinces of the States; but on the other side, the waste, beginning with a few gentle undulations, spread itself into a vast arid plain for miles, bounded only by the horizon—perfectly flat, and perfectly fruitless but for a thin covering of short heather. The river Maas, co-operating with this waste district, made a strong frontier, and a virtually neutral ground between the Dutch and Prussian States. The waste, a hard dry cake of drift, has no fructifying organic elements save what have been laid down upon it by the hand of man ; and even the industrious Dutch have not been tempted to convert this desert into a smiling garden.

This district, where the High and Low Dutch met each other, was a common centre and radiating-point whence both the water-transit and the great roads of Western Europe radiated. Nymeguen is, as we have seen, washed by the Waal, carrying the bulk of the waters of the Rhine into the sea, and opening the way to all its upper regions. Successive tributary streams on the right bank—the Lippe, the Lenne, the Lahn, the Nahe, the Main, the Neckar—gave openings into Central Germany. More momentous, however, and more suggestive to the presiding genius over all, were the Moselle and the Saar, penetrating to the heart of France. Another river—the Maas or the Meuse—less an affluent of the Rhine than a river discharging itself through the same channel into the ocean, had water - communication with Nymeguen through the Waal, and was, as we shall find, the companion of the army in many of its earlier operations.

Where these abundant water-tracks were not navigable by sailing-vessels, their banks generally afforded towing-paths for horses. The waters reaching the sea in flat Holland, descend from vast regions of mountain-ground ; but the prevailing character of their banks is the perfectly flat, hard plain, formed by the diluvial deposits of the river, supplied from mountain-chains. These plains afforded at that period not only towing-paths, but the best roads in Western Europe. Their flatness and dryness made admirable ground for the marching of troops. This was a quality often not so valuable to the inhabitant of the district as to the unwelcome stranger. Hence came another feature in the world spread around the new army—the abundance and vastness of the fortresses laid down here and there on the borders of the rivers. Some of these were, of necessity, on the diluvial plain; but others, like the citadel and Chartreuse at Liege, and Ehrenbreitstein on the Rhine, were on heights. The diluvial plain on the margin of the stream was generally bounded by a chain of hills; and when, as it sometimes was found, a spur or branch of such a chain crossed the plain and dipped into the water, opportunities came for playing critical games in tactic and strategy.

The war had already begun in some small affairs. The greatest of these was the siege by a German detachment of Kaiserswerth, a small fortified town on the Rhine, some four miles further down than Dusseldorf, and on the opposite or right bank of that river. It belonged to the Elector of Cologne, who, as an ally of France, had given it over to a French garrison. On the 15th of June 1702, Kaiserswerth surrendered, and Marlborough drew the 8000 Germans from the siege to his army at Nymeguen, where they arrived on the 6th of July. There were now in all 60,000 men under the command of Marlborough, and the momentous question arose how they were to be employed. Councils of war were held, with little more definite object, as it would appear, than to enable the commander fully to understand the men whom he must co-operate with while he controlled them. The enemy were some eight miles to the eastward, strongly posted between Gennep and Goch, on the small river Niers, an affluent of the Maas. By opening sluices of reserved waters they made their position still stronger than it was by nature, and they had three bridges enabling them to cross to the country westward of the Maas, if that were necessary. It would have only been in harmony with the later years of his career had Marlborough instantly attacked them where they stood ; but in the words of his secretary, he " would gladly venture a battle with the French if they were to be come at on reasonable terms, but it would be too great a hazard to attack them as they are now posted."[1] Then it would be a vain hope to expect the consent of the Dutch deputies to a hazard that might bring a victorious enemy again before their gate.[2]

The final resolution was to invest and take the fortified towns on the Maas, one after the other,— let Boufflers, the French commander, if he thought fit, come forth and fight a battle in their defence. But Marlborough had even here to feel the difficulties of a chief who has several subordinates in command,

[1] Despatches, i. 7.

[2] "I am ashamed to write from this camp, for we ought to have marched from hence three or four days ago," Marlborough says to Godolphin, dating on the 13th of July from Duckenburg, about five miles southward of Nymeguen ; " but the fears the Dutch had for Nymeguen and the Rhine, created such difficulties when we were to take a resolution, that we were forced to send to the Hague ; and the States would not come to any resolution, but have made it more difficult by leaving it to the general officers, at the same time recommending in the first place the safety of the Rhine and Nymeguen."—Coxe, i. 171.

each at the head of a body of his own countrymen. The difficulty in this instance was with the Elector of Hanover—that ally who, as the adopted heir of the British throne, lay under the weightiest obligations to fight heartily in the great contest. Nor was it assuring that the difficulty arose not from any reluctance at the Electoral Court, but from pedantic scruples of military etiquette. As this was the first occasion when Marlborough had to make it felt as well as known that he was a commander-in-chief, he addressed Bothmar, the Hanoverian agent or ambassador, with a touch of courteous decision, productive of immediate remedy.[1]

When the Hanoverian and Prussian contingents joined him he felt himself in sufficient force for all contingencies, and on the 26th of July he crossed the Maas.

It was his determination to begin the contest with the siege of Venlo, the strongest of the line of fortified towns on the Maas. In crossing that river, however, he had gone away both from Venlo and the enemy. They were both on the north side of the river, and

---

[1] This is a fair specimen of Marlborough's style when, deeply in earnest, he lets the earnestness be visible through the polish of his politeness : " M. le Lieutenant-Général Somerfeldt viens d'arriver, et m'a extrêmement surpris et même mortifié en m'apprenant qu'il ne pouvait agir avec ses troupes sans vos ordres, ce qui est de telle conséquence que si je pouvais me dispenser d'ici je serais parti dès cette nuit pour la Haye, afin de vous prier de les dépêcher sans le moindre retardement. Vous savez, monsieur, combien cela importe à la cause commune ou nous sommes tous engagés, et à laquelle je sais que vous êtes en particulier si bien intentionné. C'est pourquoi j'ose vous conjurer, monsieur, de ne perdre pas un moment de temps à nous renvoyer le courrier avec les ordres nécessaires pour la marche de vos troupes ; cela est d'autant plus pressant que nous faisons état de marcher avec l'armée dimanche prochain. J'attendrai le retour du courrier avec la dernière impatience, et serai toujours très-sincèrement," &c.—Despatches, i. 5, 6.

he marched in the opposite direction towards Hamont. It was the policy of Marlborough that when he went to Venlo he should not find it in the centre of the French army, so as to fight an enemy in a strongly fortified camp. It was, on the other hand, the necessary policy of the French commander to hang about Marlborough's army, and be at hand wherever it should strike a blow. It was now marching southwards towards the richest and least fortified districts of the Spanish Netherlands, and Boufflers must follow; hence he too had to cross the Maas.[1] If he could be drawn far enough southward, Marlborough was to get between him and the Maas. In these shiftings both had to cross the great flat heath of Dutch Brabant, an excellent battle-ground for those who desired to fight; and Marlborough remarked, "If they would venture anything this summer it ought to be this day; for our work is upon an open heath, and we are weaker by sixteen regiments of foot than we shall be three days hence." [2] The expected addition to the army duly arrived; and he felt all the assurance of one who, having practically tested the sufficiency of his force for keeping off his enemy, finds it becoming in his hands stronger than ever. He had the satisfaction to see a long and not very well protected train of his baggage-waggons pass unmolested before the eye of the enemy.

The letters passing between King Louis on the one side, and his commanders Boufflers and Catinat, are preserved, and they are found to be historically in-

[1] " S'ils eussent voulu, ils n'avaient qu'à quitter leurs enterprises sur la Gueldre, et marcher droit à Bruxelles, Louvain, et Malines—en un mot, prendre tout le Brabant."—Mém. du Maréchal de Berwick, i. 195.

[2] To Godolphin.—Coxe, i. 175.

structive on the Grand Monarch's method of warfare. His grandson, the Duke of Burgundy, then twenty years old, is on the spot, and is nominally the commander-in-chief of all the forces. But the king himself is the real commander, giving not only opinions and criticisms, but instructions. It was true that Marlborough had never commanded an army, but he was known to be endowed with a high military genius, and his coming, as the realisation of the fact that the resources of Britain were thrown into the contest, awakened the French generals to the heavy responsibilities of a critical war. They were cautious and defensive; but their master, habituated to unfailing success, was impatient and imperious. Landau is doomed unless speedy and ample relief be sent. But Catinat mumbles his difficulties about supplying the relief, impressed with the feeling that so doing he may fatally weaken the army. The loss of Landau is to be lamented, but the defeat of the army commanded by the Royal Duke would be a more terrible calamity.

The troubled generals endeavour to find a propitious refuge in bursts of eloquence—in the wondrous warlike genius budding and blooming in the young prince intrusted to their care—and are dryly reminded that it is not in harmony with the glory of that prince that he should be the commander of an unsuccessful force.[1]   It was altogether a hard lot for

---

[1] "Il ne conviendrait pas à la dignité du Duc de Bourgogne, qui partira mardi prochain pour aller commander son armée, de se trouver à la tête d'un corps qui serait trop faible pour rien entreprendre ou pour tenir contre celle de mes ennemis."—Mémoires Militaires, ii. 16.

Here is a passage selected for its brevity from the reports of Boufflers to the king: "Ce qui ne se peut assez louer et admirer, c'est l'extrême

Catinat, with Marlborough silently strengthening himself, dead to all efforts by irritation, or teasing, as soldiers sometimes call it, into premature action, and watchfully abiding the time when his opportunity would come.

It was a contingency of the glory the commanders were bound to derive from the presence of the prince, that the effective fighting march that supplied a garrison to Nymeguen was represented as a disastrous flight before a conquering host, commanded by the king's grandson. The temptation to give the affair this tenor was great, and it could be effected without any false statement, and by the ingenious use of expletives.[1]

désir que Monseigneur le Duc de Bourgogne a fait paraître de voir, d'agir, et se porter partout : la sagesse et le sangfroid, l'air libre et naturel qu'il conserve, sa gaieté, sa hardiesse, son coup-d'œil et son bon esprit : en un mot, il met au jour toutes les bonnes qualités et vertus qui font un grande homme, qui peuvent fair assurer qu'il sera un jour très-grand et bon général et très-digne petit-fils de votre Majesté."—Mémoires Militaires, ii. 531, 532. King Louis did his part in the claim of military genius, as one of the divine rights of royalty. In ordering a *Te Deum* for the capture of Brisac, he tells the Archbishop of Paris—" Ce siège a été fait par mon petit-fils le Duc de Bourgogne, qui dans cette expédition a marqué toute la fermeté, l'intelligence et l'application, qu'on auroit pû désirer dans un Capitaine experimenté."—Lettres Historiques, xxiv. 438.

[1] " Monseigneur le Duc de Bourgogne ordonna que l'on suivit l'armée ennemie avec un peu plus de vivacité, ce qui fut exécuté ; en sorte qu'elle fut poussée et plusieurs troupes furent culbutées jusque sur les glacis de Nimègue, avec beaucoup d'audace et de valeur de la part des troupes de votre Majesté. . . . Je ne crois pas qu'il y ait d'example qu'un armée entière ait été poussée jusque sur la contrescarpe et les pallissades d'une place, et qu'el y ait été ensuite attaquée et harcelée de manière a être forcée de se jeter dans les chemins couverts et dans les fossés, ne pouvant plus tenir dehors contre le mousqueterie et le canon de l'armée opposée."—Boufflers to Louis XIV., Mém. Milit., ii. 530. Taken in this shape, there would be little in the arrival of the British force to give serious uneasiness to King Louis.

It seemed at one time that in spite of the field deputies, and all other obstructions, the two hosts must converge into a battle—there was actual cannonading and some sharp affairs between outposts. But the enemy broke up their camp and marched towards Beverloo, whether in retreat or because they thought protection urgent in that region. " I could not," says Marlborough on the occasion, " believe the French were so strong as we now know they are ; for my Lord Carr, one of my aides-de-camp, was taken, so that he marched with them the day they retreated, and the Duke of Berwick showed him the whole army. He counted 72 battalions and 109 squadrons, but he says that our battalions are much stronger than theirs." [1] And now the Dutch field deputies were made uneasy by the too active character of their cautiousness. There were ominous murmurs among the troops, and a dangerous spirit, taking the anomalous shape of a mutinous feeling in favour of their great commander. It was the talk even in the enemy's camp that they were not an army free to strike—that they were there only to watch over the safety of the Dutch traders, not to fight battles. It was one redeeming effect of this spirit that the troops became ardent and impatient for action, just as the way to Venlo was opened.

On the 5th of September the investment of Venlo was completed, but heavy siege-guns had yet to be

[1] To Godolphin.—Coxe, i. 180. The Duke of Berwick, who, it will be remembered, was Marlborough's nephew, after showing for several tactical reasons that Boufflers could not safely make the attack, says,— " Outre que les ennemis avoiens vingt bataillons de plus que nous, et que chacun de leurs bataillons avaient au moins cent hommes de plus que les nôtres."—Mém., i. 196.

waited for. The cuttings and embankments of the
siege approaches were directed by Cohorn, the celebrated Dutch engineer. A veteran in the practice of
the code of attack and defence invented by himself,
the pedantic precision of his motions fretted Marlborough, whose inventive genius and ardent nature
sought original and rapid operations. He seemed to
feel that with the Dutch deputies, thus backed by
Dutch science, there was a heavy impedimental
burden in store for him; but Cohorn was near the
close of his career. He hung but a few months on
his active coadjutor, and died in 1704.

Venlo stood over against Nymeguen, as the chief
fortress protecting the Spanish Netherlands from
aggression on the side of Holland and Germany.
Like Nymeguen, the old strength of the fortresses in
which the town was nestled is attested at this day
by the long stretches of grassy hillocks on both sides
of the Maas. The town itself being on the north
side of the Maas, the remains on the south side are
those of the detached fort of St Michael. Here the
fiery Lord Cutts was in command of the besieging
party. He desired that the covered-way should, if
possible, be cleared, to save the working-parties from
assault, and hinted to those told off for the duty, that
if the enemy seemed to retire readily they might try
an assault. The troops, as impatient as their commander, jumped into the covered-way, ran with the
garrison through it, and finding some planks laid for
the convenience of the garrison across the moat,
climbed up the counterscarp by the aid of long grass.
It was an effectual surprise, and the garrison surrendered. The assailing party lost only 27 men in this

first achievement of the war.[1] The assailants now
held a post whence they could cannonade the town.
It happened that on the 23d of September news came
of the capitulation of Landau, besieged by the imperialists. This event called for a congratulatory discharge
of great guns, and their roar so confounded the citizens
as testimony to a furious cannonading, that they
demanded a capitulation. The garrison had to yield,
and were permitted to march forth with the honours
of war through a breach made by the assailants.[2]

The fortified town of Roermond was the next to
be attacked. It is some twenty miles further up the

---

[1] One of the assailing party thus describes the critical part of the
affair : " The enemy gave us one scattering fire only, and away they
ran. We jumped into the covered-way and ran after them. They
made to a ravelin which covered the curtain of the fort, in which were
a captain and sixty men. We, seeing them get into the ravelin, pursued
them, got in with them, and soon put most of them to the sword.
They that escaped us fled over a small wooden bridge, exposed to the
fire of the great and small shot of the body of the fort. However, we
got over the *fausse braye*, where we had nothing for it but to take the
fort or die." The author notes two acts of carelessness on the part
of the garrison combining to afford to the assailants their opportunity. The one was in those who retreated not carrying the loose
planks with them, when " we would all have fallen into the moat,
which was ten feet deep in water ; " and again, " Had the governor
kept the grass by which we climbed close mowed, as he ought to have
done, what must have been our fate ?"—Parker : Military Transactions, 84-87.

[2] Coxe, i. 185. We have from Lord Cutts this brief characteristic
account of his own share in this success. It is addressed to Secretary
Nottingham, who greedily welcomed every morsel of well-authenti-
cated information from the theatre of the war :—

" My action at Fort St Michael I will say no more of than only that
it was my own contrivance and execution, commanding that attack in
chief. It was successful, and produced good and quick effects, by
occasioning the speedy surrender of Venlo, and making way for farther
successes ; and it met with general approbation, for the world has made
more noise of it than it deserves. I had the honour to command brave
men ; I had the fortune to take my measures right ; and God blessed
me with success."—Mus. Brit. Addl. MSS.. 25. f. 383.

Maas than Venlo; and its defences being much narrower, Marlborough chafed at its being tolerated as an impediment, and he found when it was invested that "Mr Cohorn is more nice than wise. He is losing time there, as he did before Venlo, and will not begin till he has everything ready to a tittle, though half the preparations might do the business." [1] Roermond was, however, speedily taken, along with Stevensweert, a town less important but more heavily fortified. There were still a few fortresses on the lower Maas at the command of the enemy; but instead of wasting time on them, Marlborough bethought him of a bolder stroke, which, if successful, would bring every post in the lower Maas into his hands. He heard that Boufflers was marching eastward to cover and protect Liege, and resolved to be there before him. When Boufflers came within sight of his intended camping-ground, he saw Marlborough's besieging force there, and that he was just in sufficient time to save himself from destruction by retiring.

Though two great fortresses overhung Liege, owing to their height and distance the town below was considered as unfortified, and Marlborough's force was received by the citizens. The nearly complete circle of hills around Liege afforded strong ground for fortresses; but unless the whole was covered with works, it also afforded good positions for assailants. A cannonade was then opened on the citadel, and a practicable breach was beaten out of the body of the fort. By Marlborough's own account, "after the French were beaten out of the counterscarp, our men attacked the breach, and after a resistance of

[1] Coxe. i. 188.

half an hour they carried it. The governor was taken in the breach by an English lieutenant, which shows that the queen's subjects were the first upon the breach."[1] The other great hill-fort overlooking Liege, known as the Chartreuse, capitulated without standing an attack. So came the line of strong places on the Maas all into the hands of the allies. Maastricht, between Liege and Venlo, did not require to be taken. Under a stipulation in the treaty of Nymeguen it was occupied by a Dutch garrison, and was under a sort of hybrid government by the States - General and the Episcopate of Liege. As the ancient capital of Brabant, it had grown to be the largest and richest of all the towns on the lower Maas. Isolated as it was, for all that it was also strongly fortified, it must have been lost to the States had the fortune of the war been reversed. Thus Marlborough completed the design of sweeping the enemy from the Maas.[2]

These successive achievements did not gratify the vulgar with the sanguinary lustre of so many contested battles in the field. They lacked the tragic interest of the long catalogues of casualties, devoured by eyes dimmed with the conflict of fears and hopes —the houses of mourning hiding themselves amidst the saturnalia of frantic mobs. But very few such battles were so momentous as military achievements. They were terribly humiliating to the mighty heart of France. They were an insult to the great King Louis such as the blood of countless thousands could not wipe out. They were worse than battles

[1] Coxe, i. 190.

[2] "Il n'y a rien qui nous serait de plus grand utilité que de nettoyer la Meuse," 31st Aug.—Despatches, i. 28.

lost. Each strength taken was a blow on the face —a blow that could neither be warded off nor returned. It made the punishment all the more significant that these blows seemed to be dealt in substantial punishment of the impalpable insult cast at the British people by the disowning of their chosen king. And by whom were the insulting blows dealt? By the paltry Dutch boors who inhabited the ditches near the dominions of the Grand Monarque, under the guidance and protection of the people who had degraded themselves by driving their king from his throne.

It made the insult all the deeper that a son of France had deigned to wear the laurels that were to be reaped by the French host. We have seen that though the work of commander was done by Boufflers, the Duke of Burgundy, the king's eldest grandson, presided over the army in all the state of a commander - in - chief. It scarcely redeemed the vaunting folly of this arrangement that the prince went home whenever it became clear that Venlo was to fall. That it touched the royal house, made the insult all the more keenly felt throughout all France. We have seen in later times so different a spirit among the people of that country, that we can scarcely realise the extent to which the monarch was at that time justified in his arrogance by the abject worship of his people. The nation had down to its lowest dregs been stirred with delirious joy when it was trumpeted forth that sons of France had partaken of the victory of Steenkirk.

To those at home capable of measuring their significance, the achievements on the banks of the Maas were significant vindications of sanguine prognostications. We had a general who, go where he would and do what he might, could be neither hindered nor touched by the mighty monarch who had heretofore been the great bully of Europe. Let our general be intrusted with a sufficient number of British troops, sufficiently supplied, and the future of Europe was secure. One consideration only cast its shadow on the future. It was certain that King Louis would not bear his humiliation with passive resignation. His resources were still vast, and Britain must be prepared for a tough contest. Already it was realising itself to Marlborough that the war would only be ended by striking at the heart of France in the seizure of Paris. So far the British and the Dutch had stood by each other to good purpose. They had strong bonds of union in common dangers and common objects. But the fact that these latter were common to both, was apt to cause rivalry and discord. We have seen how powerfully the dangers of the trade of England, threatened with annihilation by the insolent policy of King Louis, had stimulated the Parliament and the Government to enter on the mighty struggle. But the Dutch were driven by trade influences still more absorbing. There is no reason to suppose that they abjured the economic creed of the day, which rated the gain of every community as something lost by some other community. But their peculiar position forced them, more than any other State, from the restraining and cramping influence of this doctrine. They had, in comparison with other districts containing a less amount of population and wealth, few commodities to sell. Their staple wealth was in their shipping; and this enabled them to find profit in the trading transactions of others, whether these were conducted on sound canons of trading economy or not. It was hence their tendency to engross the carrying trade of the world.

But this meant something beyond the humble duty of conveying merchandise from place to place; it meant the nursing and creating a great sea Power. The community that had shipping for the carriage of all the merchandise in the world would, if permitted a free development, become the first maritime Power in the world. This had become more distinct since the departure of the feudal system, with its military retainers, had separated the soldier from the citizen, so that the army could only be supplied by a peculiar class drilled to the duties of the soldier. Every able seaman in the merchant service had little to add to his accomplishments to make him a sea-warrior. Indeed, the sailor was in general drilled to all but the little that remained for applying his skill to craft larger than the kind he had been accustomed to; for all vessels frequenting the open seas were armed, and indeed a large portion of them followed the desperately warlike trade of piracy.

These distinctions bring us to another of a still broader character, between land and sea. It is not only possible, but of continual occurrence, that two Powers may be equally supreme and hostile to each other; but there cannot be two Powers hostile to each other equally supreme at sea: a law of political dynamics requires that, in the end, one shall crush the other. The Czar of Russia and the King of

France might be sworn enemies, and supreme in power each at his own end of the Continent; but Britain and Holland could not be at enmity with each other and each supreme over a portion of the ocean—they both commanded in an element where they must meet and fight out the quarrel to the end. This was a condition strengthened by the progress of nautical science. The further a ship could sail, the wider became the region where one flag must be supreme. With their galleys, that could live only in the Mediterranean, the Venetians might be supreme there, so long as the rigged vessel of the Northern seas had not found its way through the Strait. The command of the ocean seemed at one time destined for Denmark. Then came the Dutch, more enterprising and closer to the centre of Europe. So far had they gone on the path of empire, that they, and they alone, among the nations of the world, could boast that the booming of their cannon had frightened the citizens of London. The Dutch were, however, but a small community, soon reaching their utmost development, and their progress was outstripped by the wider expansive resources of the British empire. Then came the English Navigation Act, cutting off the favourite carrying trade of Holland from all the commerce of Britain and her dependencies. Recent experiences in economic science have taught us that this measure could not have fostered the real aggrandisement of England. But if it crippled England, it crushed Holland. According to the economics of the day, that fact alone proved that it was a source of prosperity to England.

Meanwhile, out of the trading rivalries of the two

countries, there arose matter of grave dissatisfaction in the Dutch method of taking the quarrel with France. The trading propensity seemed to overcome the patriotic, and the trade between the Provinces and France remained open. It was very tempting; for Dutch vessels could glide along the coast to the neighbouring French coast, and the access by land was short and easy. It would require some powerful influence to make the Dutchman abandon a trade he had set his affections on. With him, indeed, trade was rather a passion, and an object of ardent ambition, than the sombre drudgery seeking its reward in a comfortable competence. He had a subtle instinct for discovering and pursuing hidden ducts of trade imperceptible to the vulgar dealer of other lands. Difficulties and dangers only fed his ardour in the pursuit.[1] It is but fair to remember that a high spirit of honour accompanied all this ardour. It was the Dutchman's sense of chivalry to stand to his bargain, both in the

---

[1] Voltaire happily notices some instances where the Dutchman's lust of trade overcame the worthier influences : " Ce qui avançait encore la chute des Hollandais, c'est que le Marquis de Louvois avait acheter chez eux—par le Comte de Benthim secrètement gagné—une grande partie des munitions qui allaient servir à les détruire, et avait ainsi degarné beaucoup leurs magasins. Il n'est point du tout étonnant que des marchands eussent vendu ces provisions avant la declaration de la guerre, eux qui en vendait touts les jours à leurs ennemis pendant les plus vives campagnes. On sait qu'un négociant de ce pays avait autrefois repondu au Prince Maurice qui le reprimandait sur un négoce, ' Monseigneur, si on pouvait par mer faire quelque commerce avantageuse avec l'Enfer, je hasarderai d'y aller bruler mes poiles.' "—Siècle de Louis XIV., chap. x. It is from such incidents that a story found its way into the old English collections of anecdotes. There is a fight between an English vessel and a Dutch. The English captain, finding his powder running short, trusts so far to the spirit of trade animating his enemy as to send a flag of truce offering to purchase certain kegs of powder. The powder is sold and paid for, and the fight is resumed.

letter and the spirit, though it should bring ruin
with it, and ways could be found for escaping that
ruin. But he chafed under all restrictions in bargain-
making; and the national enemy who should come
to him with a remunerative transaction in hand was
not to be counted his personal enemy.

With the English, on the other hand, the spirit of
trade saw only the smiting of the enemy. His trade
was to be crippled—if possible, to be extinguished—
be the cost to England what it might. It was certain that ere long the two trading policies would jostle
against each other. The opportunity came in winter,
when the States, depressed and frightened, appealed
to Britain for further aid.

This appeal suggested to the Commons an odd
source of relief. That headstrong madcap, Charles
XII. of Sweden, was wasting a treasury of warlike
energy in quarrels with his Slavonic neighbours, instead of throwing himself into the cause of freedom
and Protestantism in the great European crisis. If
he could be brought to reason and peace with his
present opponents, there would be a force of 12,000
Swedes and 6000 Saxons to fight in the good cause.[1]

The Dutch admitted that the consummation of such
a scheme would be a great gain to the good cause;
but meanwhile ruin might seize themselves. The project was circuitous, and its success doubtful, while
their peril was imminent and certain. They appealed
to the cruel wrongs they had suffered, in words few
and simple, but sufficient to arouse the recollections
of a tale that had filled Europe with compassion and
horror. Their tyrant enemy had sworn to take

[1] Commons Journals. Dec. 4. 1702.

Amsterdam. They had opened the sluices, let in the waters, and defied him to do his worst. Partaking in the fury of their baffled master, the French troops, wherever they could set foot on Holland, flung off the restraints of civilised warfare, and visited the hapless spots with such ruin as if the whole calamities that an ordinary war could have spread over the whole territory were concentrated on them in punishment for their saving of the rest. In testimony of these horrors was the remembrance of two fair cities, Swammerdam and Bodegreve, blotted in blood and fire out of the map of Europe. An illustrious Frenchman of a later generation mused over the fiendish ferocity of the French soldier of that period as a phenomenon not easily to be explained, and could mention as a natural result, that in his own day, to inculcate a hatred of the French was part of the education of children in the United Provinces.[1]

Then, in letting in the sea, they had found a costly protector. The desperate alternative could not be achieved without peril and loss to human life. Dwelling-houses and farm-steadings were ruined and drifted away. The bright green pastures of the polders were wet and smeared with sludge and sand. The cost of the war was heavy on the State. And now it was to be renewed in more formidable shape than ever. King Louis was more infuriated than

---

[1] "Il est étonnant que le soldat Français soit si barbare, étant commandé par ce prodigieux nombre d'officiers, qui ont avec justice la réputation d'être aussi humaine que courageux. Ce pillage laissa une impression si profonde que plus de quarante ans après j'ai vu les livres Hollandais, dans lesquels on apprenait à lire aux enfans, retracer cette aventure, et inspirer la haine contre les Français à des generations nouvelles."—Voltaire: Siècle de Louis XIV., chap. xi.

depressed by his losses.   That the paltry trading
commonwealth should find the means of thwarting
him was a humiliation not to be endured.   The
States, in their appeal to the British Government,
said they knew that King Louis was preparing to
renew the war with an overwhelming force.   In his
thirst for vengeance, he was less the ambitious com-
batant weighing his resources as adapted to success,
than the fiend who shall annihilate his enemy
though both perish together.   He would drag forth
from among his subjects the last man able to carry
a fusil ere the States should boast that they had
defied him.

The piteous appeal of the Dutch—the full knowledge of all they had endured—the chivalrous instinct
to back up those who had been thrown in the front
of the great contest,—all throbbed to the heart of the
British people.   There stood some technical parliamentary difficulties in the way of immediate relief.
The supplies and their appropriation, with the establishment of the forces, had been voted.   A prorogation
would be necessary to open the business again, and
against a prorogation there were weighty reasons.
The blood of the nation, however, was up to the
fighting point.   The Commons promised co-operation
with the executive, and the executive knew that it
could rely on the fulfilment of the promise.   The
opportunity, however, was not allowed to pass without a reference to—indeed an effective extinction of
—those little trading tricks to which our unfortunate
partners were addicted.   The Commons "assured her
Majesty of their co-operation in any measure for increasing the forces which are to act in conjunction

with the forces of the States-General," with this distinct condition, "your Commons do further crave leave humbly to beseech your Majesty that you will be pleased to insist upon it with the States-General, that there be an immediate stop of all posts, and all letters, bills, and all other correspondence, trade, and commerce with France and Spain; which your Commons are humbly of opinion is so absolutely necessary for carrying on the just and necessary war wherein your Majesty is engaged, to the interrupting the trade of your enemies, and reducing them to the greatest straits, that your Commons do humbly desire that England may not be charged with the pay of such additional troops, but from the day when such stop shall be made by the States-General."[1]

When Parliament reassembled in November, besides continuing the maintenance of the 40,000 men voted for the previous session, there was a vote for 10,000 "augmentation troops" to join the army in the Low Countries, along with a vote of 8000 men to be sent to Portugal for service in the branch of the war arising in the Spanish peninsula. The Commons were assured on the occasion by a message from the Throne that the delinquencies of the Dutch dealers in trading with the enemy would be suppressed.

[1] Commons Journals. 7th January 1703.

CHAPTER VI.

𝕿𝖍𝖊 𝖂𝖆𝖗.

(*Continued.*)

MARLBOROUGH had in the meantime returned to
England, shifting his labours in the great cause from
the field to the court and the council board. In
setting out on his journey homewards, an adventure
befell him trifling in itself, yet of such a nature that
a slight turn in its incidents might have stopped his
career and made the history of Europe other than it
became. He was dropping down the Maas with but
a small escort. Darkness came on when he was a few
miles below Shoermann. Descending the stream no

towage was required, but somehow the tow-rope
got loose and was caught by a body of the enemy
going along the bank. They pulled the barge to the
shore and took possession of its inmates. Some
Dutchmen of importance among them, civilians apparently, had passes—Marlborough had none; but an
attendant, as it is said, thrust an old pass of some
kind into his hand, and it satisfied the captors, who
left him and his Dutch companions, removing the
effective men of their guard. The party seem to
have been crimps securing men for the service of
the enemy. Whatever they were they were easily
satisfied, and they seemed to think the fine gentlemen
who talked French fluently would not make a valuable acquisition. If the Dutch had not up to this
moment shown any enthusiastic appreciation of the
achievements of their champion, they redeemed themselves from the charge of indifference when the rumour sped that he was lost to them. At first came
apprehensions and lamentations, then heroic projects
for snatching him out of the enemies' camp, and lastly,
a vehement and sincere outburst of joy when in all
his majestic serenity he reappeared at the Hague.[1]

On his return to London he received what in this
country is always deemed the highest of all the distinctions open to the soldier—an address of thanks
for his services from each House of Parliament. He
was created Marquis of Blandford and Duke of
Marlborough.[2] When the services he had performed,
substantial as they were, are estimated along with his
later achievements, his elevation to the highest rank

[1] Coxe i., 192, 193.
[2] 14th Dec. 1702. Nicolas's Synopsis of the Peerage.

obtainable in his own country might look like the reward not of accomplished but of anticipated service. It was the policy of the Government, however, to strengthen his hand for the exercise of his high command, by giving him whatever could be bestowed in rank on a subject of the British Crown, and to cherish his authority in an army where persons who claimed the attributes of royalty had to obey him. But for all that he was conscious he had achieved, and all that a grateful nation conferred on him, it was his doom to return to his duties a stricken man. His only son, called by courtesy the Marquis of Blandford, a fine boy in his seventeenth year, died. Long afterwards, when it was clear that Marlborough was to die without leaving a son to inherit his honours, the national sympathy with the man so illustrious and so bereaved was shown in an arrangement that his honours should be borne while there were descendants of his daughters—that so long as any male descendant of any one of these existed, there should always be a duke of Marlborough to grace the peerage. This national homage was technically completed when an Act of Parliament settled all his honours on his daughters and their heirs-male. The boy died on the 20th of February 1703. No one, not even an enemy, doubted the intensity of the father's grief and sufferings; but his weighty duties called him off so swiftly after his bereavement, that, on the 17th of March, he was at the Hague arranging the future of the war.

It was now no longer to be a vapid local effort to secure the frontier of Holland from an invasion doing mischief that might never be retrieved. The Dutch States and Northern Germany were safe in

the meantime, though the States must be prepared
for a hard contest with King Louis whenever he
found himself so clear of work elsewhere that he
could throw the bulk of his power upon them. But
the general quarrel had now so deepened and broad-
ened as to divide all Europe into two camps, in one
or other of which every state must take its part,
or prepare itself to face the dangers and difficulties of those who have no friends to stand by them
in the hour of need. The rallying-cries concentrating
the two forces were on the one side the integrity of
the imperial system—the old "Holy Roman Empire;"
on the other, France and the claims of the Bourbon
family on all the dominions that had been ruled by
the last king of Spain of the Austrian race. And to
those who rallied round the Empire, their cause was
far more than the preservation of an old decayed
system, forming an ideal unity among the European
Powers. It was because France was a power aggressive on the Empire, that the Empire itself became
anything worth defending. The Bourbons, if strong
enough, would take possession of the imperial organisation with all that it could give them to make them
supreme in Europe. Hence it was that communities
like the United Provinces and the Northern German
States having little concern with the imperial system—
no more, perhaps, than that a few of their towns enjoyed the title and privilege of free imperial cities
—stood by the cause of the Empire with such zeal
as if they were defending their own native land from
aggression.

A careless reader of the events of the war might
take the impression that France stood alone on one

side, and that the greater part of Europe was combined
against her on the other.   When there is a battle it
brings up the King of France's army on the one side
—the army of the Allies on the other.   But the
French commander of the king's armies was supplied from a far broader area of the Continent out
of France than the area whence Marlborough drew
the contingents of Powers in alliance with Britain.
There were the great possessions of the Crown of
Spain in Italy and the Italian islands : if the inhabitants of these territories did not furnish many
men to the French forces in the north, yet they
supplied material for a separate conflict with Prince
Eugene and the Imperialists.   There were close at
hand and ever dangerous the towns of the Spanish
Netherlands, and if their inhabitants were not likely
to take part with France and Spain, a large body of
Spanish soldiers were dispersed among their fortresses
co-operating with the French.   There was Spain itself.
Perhaps few Spaniards joined the French army in
the north, but the Spanish people and the Court were
with the claims of the Bourbons, and there was a
separate war in Spain calling off forces that might
have enhanced the army of the Allies in the north.
There were French also, no doubt, employed in Spain,
but they were few in number in a country where the
people were for the cause of France, and thus the
balance of the weakening influence of the separate
war in Spain was against the Allies.   Portugal, too,
was at the beginning of the war attached to France,
though it was antagonistic to the traditions of that
country to fight side by side with its larger and
dangerous neighbour—the two acted in European

politics a part like that of England and Scotland. Early in the war Portugal assumed its old position, throwing its lot into that of the Allies.

All that belonged to or could be influenced by Spain naturally gravitated to the cause of the French king. The more dubious and exciting elements in the composition of the opposing forces, were in the part to be taken in each instance by the outlying minor states, chiefly German. There was a strong feeling that France must gain the ultimate victory in the great contest. Whatever, therefore, conscientious principle, or a sense of nationality, or political friendships might whisper, safety and ultimate supremacy called to the smaller Power to rally round the banner of the Grand Monarque. To doubt that he must triumph in any great European contest was almost deemed a mark of imperfect understanding or defective intellect. It has happened more than once in the course of history that France has been elevated to this position of the prospectively unconquerable — that the delusion has been scattered by a stern Nemesis, and that none have suffered more in its dispersal than those who held the firmest faith in it. They are the victims of a dynamic law in war and politics, bringing it to pass that great warlike communities, when they are also aggressive and dangerous, create an opposite balance of warlike power and spirit which may in the end outweigh their own.

The largest of these states was Bavaria—an electorate of the Empire, covering a space from Donauworth on the Danube up to the watershed of the Alps, where it marched with Italy and the Austrian Tyrol. To have Bavaria with France was virtually to divide the Imperial force, if it were counted that the Empire and Germany were one. The Elector of Bavaria had done signal service to King Louis. He was governor for Spain of the Spanish Netherlands, and it was he who in this capacity had the chief merit in the adroit displacement of the Dutch contingents in the garrisons of the Barrier towns. Whatever might be his capacity in the more illustrious schools of war and statesmanship, he accomplished this transmigration with signal skill. We do not hear of a casualty or a blow struck in the affair, and there is something almost ludicrous in the silent dexterity of the manœuvre by which the Dutch found that they were shut out of the forts, and that French soldiers held their posts.[1] In the French State correspondence of the time the Elector of Bavaria is called "Monsieur de Bavière," and he is treated with all the respect due to an officer high in the service of the King of France's grandson. As the partisan of France he would retain his office of governor, with the prospect of other prizes falling to him who should be an important contributor to the success of a conquering cause. The other side of

---

[1] The following passage from the "Lettre de S. A. Electorale à chaque gouverneur des places des Pays-Bas où il doit entrer des troupes de France" may have interest as a precedent in the practice of treachery : "Je vous écris celle-ci pour vous avertir que, dans la nuit du 5 ou 6 de février, une heure ou environ avant le jour, doit entrer dans votre place un détachement de troupes françaises, que vous recevrez et ferez loger de la manière accoutumée. Prenez vos precautions pour que les officiers des troupes hollandaises qui composent votre garnison ne se puissent apercevoir de cette disposition, qu'après que les dites troupes françaises seront entrées ; et pour leur ôter toute la méfiance que cette nouveauté leur pourrait causer, vous appellerez aussitôt le commandant des dites troupes hollandaises, à qui vous direz qu'il ne doit pas s'alarmer de voir des François dans votre place ; qu'ils n'y viennent comme eux qu'en qualité de troupes auxiliaires."—Mém. Militaires, i. 433.

course offered him inducements, but these were insufficient to draw him from the service where in fact
he officially found himself.   There were other claims
on him appealing to duty and loyalty.   He was an
Elector of the Holy Roman Empire, and now he was
virtually at war with that Empire—he was becoming a deserter and a rebel.   The Imperial law was
fulminated against him.   This was a process issued
from the civil side of the Imperial system, in a sort
of rivalry with the interdict and excommunication of
the ecclesiastical side.   It cursed him against whom
it was sent forth, and called him by many hard
names.   He had no longer a seat in the Diet or any
place in the Imperial system.   He and his race were
divested of all they possessed, land and goods.   He
was to be impoverished and destitute, and no true
German was to assist or comfort him in his destitu-
tion.   All this would go for little if the cause he
adopted should be triumphant, especially if it were
his fortune to give substantial assistance in the
triumph.   But if he were to be a partner of France in
misfortune, or even in any dubious success, the law
of the Empire pointed significantly to the fact that
Bavaria, a part of Germany, was fighting against the
cause of the German people—against the great Fatherland.   And this stigma gave bitterness to the fall
of this unfortunate dealer in subtle politics, of whom
we shall hear more presently.

But there was another consideration weighing
heavily on the counsels of the minor Governments
that had to ponder on the attractions of the French
interest.   The great King Louis acknowledged no
equality with his allies.   He studiously taught them

their place as subordinates. If war and conquest
brought the absorption of conquered states into the
French dominion, co-operation and friendship with
France only pointed to the same end. And now a
new strong protecting power had come into the
field. Britain had contributed a weight of military strength totally unanticipated to the coming
struggle. Britain had great resources for the protection of those who secured her favour, and Britain
coveted no man's land—at least on the continent
of Europe.

King Louis was met by this influence when he
least expected it. The states ruled by Victor Amadeus Duke of Savoy he treated almost as a province
of France. He had admitted the house of Savoy to
mighty privileges and distinctions. If King Louis
imagined that he had some hold on Bavaria, in his
eldest son the Dauphin having married a Bavarian
princess, the house of Savoy was attached to him by
a double tie of a like kind, since the Dauphin's son
had married a daughter of Victor Amadeus, and
another daughter had recently been married to the
grandson of King Louis, who was known in Britain
as the Duke of Anjou, and competitor for the crown
of Spain, while in French phraseology he was King
of Spain, and his wife, a princess of the house of
Savoy, was Queen of Spain. The house of Savoy,
however, had, as we shall see, to tell against these
genealogical influences, a stronger connection of the
same kind with the succession to the British empire.
Then its relations with France had come to a rather
too close embrace. In geographical position and the
language of a large portion of the people the states

governed by the Duke of Savoy seemed naturally to fit into France as a dependency.

The house of Savoy was one of the gradually rising Powers. The Duke looked to his chances as the ally of Britain. He saw that Marlborough had a strong hand for Britain in the Netherlands, and he had as a champion at hand Marlborough's companion in arms Prince Eugene. It is among the developments in events worth noting, that Britain's hearty co-operation in the contest for the safety of Holland and the integrity of the Empire, brought out against the aggressive progress of King Louis two contradictory forces of aggrandisement: the one in the last Margrave of Brandenburg and first King of Prussia, whose descendant has restored the Empire of Charlemagne; the other in that Duke of Savoy, whose descendant has become King of Italy.

The position of Savoy in the map of Europe, and its physical geography as a strong mountain district, were of a kind to give it great political and military power in co-operation with France. But these very qualities also tended to the conclusion that this effectiveness would be enhanced if both were under one supreme sovereignty, and of course that sovereignty must be in the house of Bourbon. It might be supposed that the kinship of Victor Amadeus with the house of Bourbon would have in some measure saved him from the rapacity of King Louis. But rapacity was not the most dangerous shape taken by the capacity of the French Crown for the absorption of minor Powers. Its paternal friendliness for weak neighbours was a more effective aggrandiser. Many small sovereignties had been acquired by the younger sons

of the French kings.   Others were related to the
Crown of France by tangled genealogical connec-
tions arising from intermarriages.   All these small
principalities, if they were not far distant from Paris,
were treated as in some measure dependent on the
French Crown.   The immediate lords of such territories had for centuries been known in the annals of
France as the " Sieurs des Fleurs de Lis," and as a class
of men who were not independent sovereigns, and were
yet something more than subjects even of the highest
rank ; they were often politically troublesome.   King
Louis had shown rather abruptly a disposition to
treat his kinsman the Duke of Savoy as one of these.
In the war of ten years earlier the King sent orders
to the Duke to send troops to Flanders, and demanded for strategic purposes possession of Turin,
his capital.   This roused resistance, and King Louis
found that he might finally lose the aid of one able
to be very useful as a friend if he persisted in coerc-
ing him as a vassal.   The Duke's dominions were,
in the hands of an enemy to France, a strong barrier
in the way of aggression in the direction of Italy—in
the hands of a friend they were the gates between
Italy and France, to be opened on the side of the
friend and closed on that of the enemy.   If the Duke
were powerful enough to hold his own in his stronghold, it would be his safer policy to defy France; and
the friendship of the Empire, bringing with it the
championship of Marlborough and Eugene, seemed to
give him that strength.   But if he retained any lingering doubts about the prudence of what he had
done, they must have been at once dispersed when
he received a brief letter from King Louis comment-

ing on his choice. In his passion the King revealed
his ulterior designs, by treating the Duke not as a
sovereign entitled to make and unmake alliances with
other sovereigns, but as a vassal who had mutinied
against his lord. His burst of wrath was like the
snarl of the beast of prey who, close on his victim,
sees it escape.[1]

Another consideration, more connected with prospective political chances than with the immediate
war policy of the period, may have had its influence
in turning the Duke to the British alliance. If from
the succession to the English crown the offspring
of James II. were simply excluded, the house of Victor Amadeus was next in succession to that crown,
his wife being a granddaughter of Charles I. through
her mother, Henrietta-Maria, married to the Duke
of Orleans. It is true that Britain had shown a
strong determination not to permit a member of a
Popish house to ascend the throne. There was an
Act of Parliament passing over the house of Savoy
and seeking an heir in the Electress of Hanover,
descended from a sister of Charles I. But this was
an act of statesmanship so utterly at variance with
all Continental ideas of monarchical prerogative,
that it was scarcely believed in as an adjustment
capable of reaching practical effect. It was remembered, too, that when the intricate question of the
regulation of the succession was one still open to dis-

---

[1] "*Septembre* 1703. Monsieur, puisque la religion, l'honneur, l'in-
térêt, l'alliance et votre propre signature ne sont rien entre nous, j'en-
voie mon cousin le Duc de Vendôme à la tête de mes armées pour
vous expliquer mes intentions. Il ne vous donnera que vingt-quatre
heures pour vous determiner. Louis." — Œuvres de Louis XIV.,
vi. 135.

cussion, there was actually a party with a preference for the house of Savoy. Whatever policy in Britain has reached the position of avowal by an actual party who may venture to speak their mind is apt to retain after defeat a strong vitality. The succession of the race of Victor Amadeus to the crown of Great Britain was a future not utterly desperate. All these things considered, the Duke of Savoy heartily cast his lot with the fortunes of the Allies.

The contest that was now to derive new life and vigour, came to be known as the war of the Spanish Succession. It was thus a kind of quarrel that could not rest in a mere negative shape of antipathy to a Bourbon prince — there must be two sides of the quarrel in the shape of two heirs to the throne of Spain. France had accepted the succession for the grandson of King Louis, as bequeathed to him by the King of Spain. It was not until September 1703 that the Archduke Charles, the younger son of the Emperor Leopold, was proclaimed King of Spain at Vienna, and accepted in that capacity by the Allies in general. He was ever afterwards in the correspondence of the Allies called "The King of Spain," or "His Catholic Majesty."

It was necessary in the meantime to find a cause that could be named in the diplomatic and military correspondence. The real cause was to stop the aggression and break the existing power of the house of Bourbon. It was not perhaps considered becoming that the war should get its name from such a motive, and be called, for instance, the coalition against France. The object more usually named was the protection of the Empire, or the safety of the Empire.

But these were hardly names to conjure with, had not great achievements adorned the cause of the Allies, whatever it might be called, with a lustre of glory. It was but vaguely known beyond the boundaries of the electoral circles that there still existed the Holy Roman Empire, arrogating some sort of civil allegiance over the civilised world, as the Bishop of Rome claimed ecclesiastical allegiance. Given the conclusion that it was worth fighting for, the other elements of the motive, the Empire's feebleness and state of danger, were beyond question. The possessor and official guardian of its honours, the house of Austria, was also enfeebled, for it had suffered from many trying shocks. About half a century before the time we have reached, Busbec, a Fleming, who represented the Empire as ambassador at the Porte, beheld with alarm the splendidly equipped and thoroughly disciplined janizaries, and was unable to see where they could be opposed should they be effectively commanded in a march westward over Europe. Such presages seemed to be fulfilled when the news swept over frightened Europe that three hundred thousand Turks were gathered around Vienna, like hungry wolves around a mountain village. The crisis passed over, and with strangely slight fighting. The great army was gone. It had fallen to pieces and dispersed without efficient military cause for the blessed effect.

But as with the survivor of some awful catastrophe that threatens instant death and leaves but a slight hurt, the nerves of the community were shattered. There were still contests with the Turks, and they were conducted with a tremulous uneasiness unknown to the soldier confident in himself and in his cause.

The Turks gave their aid to a harassing war in Hungary—a war that rebuked Austria as the champion of the humiliation of France, since it assailed the aggrandising policy of the house of Austria, and demanded the restoration of old national institutions. On the other hand, when in the new war Bavarian troops penetrated into the Tyrol, the peasantry rose to protect themselves in the paternal rule of Austria : they manned the passes, as they have done in later times, and tossed fragments of their mountains down upon the invading host, driving them back into their own country.

In such episodes of war there is something of refreshing contrast with the gloomy uniformity of the greater part of the warfare of that day. If there were not mighty achievements filling the ear of fame, there was patriotism, adherence to ancient local usage, or some vitality other than that of the battalions inspired by the crimp, the drill-sergeant, and the paymaster. Since the map of Europe had been thoroughly recast by the Treaty of Westphalia the art of war had reached a sort of perfection that brought it almost into the category of the exact sciences. There were certain things, and no other, that it behoved an accomplished commander to do. It was sometimes said that a commander divined with precise accuracy what his adversary was doing, because he knew what he himself would do under the same conditions — of course the compliment inferred in such a divination was superlative.[1] No soldier of the day would have

---

[1] " Montécuculi était seul digne d'être opposé à Turenne. Tous deux avaient réduit la guerre en art. Ils passerent quatre mois à se suivre, à s'observer, dans des marches et dans des campemens, plus estimés

acknowledged such a motive; but in the courtesies of
war there was creeping in among military men, under
the guise of a mutual respect, a principle of live and
let live. Victory was no doubt a great thing, but
a true soldier would rather see absolute destruction
alight somewhere else than on the army of the enemy.
The exploits of Prince Eugene on the Adige and along
the Italian passes of the Alps justly earned the title
of brilliant, because he sometimes made a vehement
and effective attack on superior forces, and accomplished adventurous marches through difficult passes
to pounce unexpectedly on the Bavarians. But the
most brilliant of all his achievements in this portion
of the war was the battle of Luzara, of the result of
which it is told by the great master of epigrammatic
irony, that it called forth the *Te Deum* of triumph
simultaneously in Vienna and in Paris.

That such events afforded opportunity for the occasional pointing of an epigram could not divest them
of their tragic character as bloody contests productive of wasted slaughter. But surely we may enjoy
the farce after the tragedy when we are told how, on
the ground to be some months later made immortal
by the battle of Blenheim, a French and a German
force meeting face to face fled from each other in
mutual panic.[1]

que des victoires par les officiers Allemands et Français. L'un et l'autre
jugeait de ce que son adversaire allait tenter, par les démarches que lui-
même eût voulu faire à sa place, et ils ne se tromperent jamais."—Voltaire : Siècle, ch. xii.

[1] "Après la première charge on vit encore un effet de ce que peut
la fortune dans les combats. L'armée ennemie et la Française, saisies
d'une terreure panique, prirent la fuite toutes deux en même temps."—
Ibid., ch. xviii.

An officer in the French service who was present in this affair gives

There is throughout, the weary routine of inde-
cisive battles during the campaigning season, and
then the retirement of both armies into "winter
quarters," to abide in impatient idleness until they are
again let loose upon each other to play on the too
equal game. Whether the casualties in the armies
were great or small, that was one ever-certain repetition, heaping an accumulation of dire misery and
calamity upon the people cursed by their presence.
It was such a process as put it in men's hearts to
pray for the apparition of some mighty captain who
could deal his enemy such a fatal blow that thereafter
one half of the world's torturers should be paralysed,
and the other half find their occupation gone.

Even for some time after Marlborough returned to
his command, the army did not aim at high achievements. Bonn was invested and taken, and next Huy,
on the Maas : this was a dependency of Liege, occupied, like the principal fortresses, by the French ; and
it had to be taken from them to clear the course of
the Maas. The town of Bonn was not heavily fortified ; but a fortress on the opposite side of the river
seems to have been troublesome, and Marlborough

an account of it in details whence one would not infer so decided a
double flight. He mentions, however, an incident causing confusion,
and likely to have caused panic. The French and Bavarian divisions
arranged that the first to sight the enemy should announce the fact by
three guns, to be acknowledged by three guns from the other division.
But D'Usson, the French general, "trompé par trois coups que les
Impériaux tirerent à son approche, et qu'il jugea être le signal que
l'Electeur lui avait marqué, passa la rivière de Hochstet, et se mit
en bataille, faisant un grand feu d'artillerie, qui ne fut point entendu
de l'armée de l'Electeur à cause du vent contraire. Ce contretemps
l'obligea à se retirer vers les lignes de Dilingen, parceque les ennemis,
qui ignoraient que l'Electeur fut si près d'eux avec tout l'armée, march-
erent à lui avec toutes leurs forces."—Mém. de Marquis Maffei, i. 174.

chafed somewhat at the delay in accomplishing a surrender. Far grander projects were arising before his eye; but there was a reason why Bonn must be taken. It contained the Court residence of the Elector of Cologne—one of those smaller German princes who had cast their lot with France. It seemed a better policy than any immediate attack on French territory, that the German adherents of France should be smitten one by one, and taught by heavy punishment that their choice had been a mistake. This secured the Germans who had joined the Empire and Britain in their allegiance, and might possibly bring back some of those others who had gone astray, to the cause of their Fatherland.[1] The siege of Huy on the Maas, following that of Bonn on the Rhine, inferred a return towards the Netherlands. There is at this point an uncertainty in Marlborough's motions, and

[1] There is a curious letter about the siege of Bonn, by Marlborough to Yres, Marquis d'Alegre, a French officer in the service of the Elector of Bavaria. Marlborough appears, in his courteous way, to make something like a threat. He says : "Je puis vous assurer, que partout où j'ai en l'honneur de commander, çà toujours été mon dessein de conserver autant qu'il m'a été possible les églises et autres édifices publics ; nous tâcherons aussi d'en user de même dans la présente occasion. Il n'y a pas besoin, monsieur, que je vous dise pourquoi nous sommes venus ici avec les troupes de la Reine ma maîtresse et de MM. les Etats, qui forment ce siège, et vous pouvez bien croire que nous tâcherons de perdre le moins de temps que nous pourrons pour venir au plus-tôt à la brèche. Je serai pourtant bien marri si en faisant notre devoir aucun des boulets ou bombes en échappe pour endommager les églises et édifices publics, n'étant nullement notre dessein, encore que nous nous croyons en droit de nous servir de toutes sortes de voies légitimes pour parvenir à notre but, sans aucun égard aux menaces que vous nous faites de la part de M. l'Electeur de Bavière, étant toujours en état de user de représailles, que nous ne manquerons pas aussi de faire avec la même sévérité dont vous parlez dans votre lettre."—Letters and Despatches, i. 91. The archæological student will recognise in the object of Marlborough's care what may claim to be the noblest specimen of Norman-Gothic in Rhenish Germany.

it becomes part of our story to notice some events in the war, not as in themselves great or glorious, but as so checking the projects of Marlborough as to require that he should change the current of the war.

Antwerp was then, as in later times, the key to the fortified towns on the Scheldt, and indeed throughout Brabant and West Flanders. It might otherwise be described as representing in enlargement the relation of its own citadel to the minor fortified works attached to its walls, since it was the centre of convergence to a group of fortified towns bound to it by an apparatus of dikes and canals. An ordinary soldier would have begun at one of the extremities and crept to the centre, but it was Marlborough's intention to strike at the heart. "I shall," he says, writing to Godolphin from Maastricht on the 19th of May, "to-morrow send an express to the Hague to see how far they have prepared *for what I call the great design;* so that we may not lose time in endeavouring to put it in execution. Before I left Bonn measures were taken for the embarking of twenty battalions of foot, if it be possible to get boats enough, and twenty-one squadrons of horse are to march the nearest way to Bergen-op-Zoom, where they are to meet the twenty battalions that go by water. These troops are to take the most advantageous post near Antwerp, after which there will be care taken to join more troops to them. If this design of Antwerp can be brought to perfection, I hope we shall make it very uneasy for them to protect Brussels and the rest of their great towns. I am speaking as if we were masters of Antwerp, but as yet the two marshals threaten." [1]

The hint about the " two marshals" reveals a presentiment too amply realised. Boufflers entered Antwerp with an overwhelming force, and passed through to the suburb of Eckern towards the north. Here was a Dutch force under Opdam, a veteran Dutch officer of good repute, though his career had not been adorned by triumphs. His immediate object, when he found himself in the presence of Boufflers's force, seems to have been to get a strong position among the many dikes scattered through the flat plain, either as embankments to canals or as fortified ramparts. Evil rumours about his fate reached England—one the matter of so much moment that Nottingham desired full information. An emissary gave him first the brief announcement: "Opdam is very much censured as having coolly run away, which left his party to the discretion of their enemies, being without a commander to direct them." [2] A Dutch officer, General Hop, reported the affair to the States-General: "It is impossible for me to mention as yet how many of our side are either dead or wounded in this long and sharp fight. Monsieur Opdam, who went up and down everywhere for a good while, is since amissing, and one of the prisoners, who is a lieutenant, affirms that he was sent prisoner to Antwerp." [3]

As it was known that Opdam had rendered to the States a report of his own conduct and adventures,

[1] Coxe, i. 245.
[2] Mus. Brit. Addl. MSS., 29589, f. 4.   [3] Ibid., f. 1.

that document was sent to the English Government. It exists in the form of a translation into English; and from this being thought necessary for rendering it available, we may be sure that the original was not in French but in Dutch.

This unhappy man's own account of the affair is valuable, as an instance of the utter dependence of an army for safety on the exactness of its commander, and the calamities that may follow any small omission or neglect. We have a minute account of a struggle for the dike as a strong position if it could be gained; but without plans or models it gives a confused succession of waverings and casual successes and disasters, till we come to the point where he tells how "one of the under officers came and told me that our men had no more powder or shot, upon which I desired Colonel Verschuner to send some immediately to them. But he told me it was impossible to come by his ammunition-waggons though they stood hard by, because the dike on the right hand near Wilmerdonck, and the ways that run there alongst, were so stopped up, not only with the artillery and ammunition-waggons, but also with the baggage-waggons and carts of the artillery and led-horses of the whole army, so that there was no getting at them. As soon as I had sent the two battalions to Orderen, as has been said, I presently sent some of my adjutants and other officers back towards the right hand to see if any assistance could be had to maintain the post at Orderen, being the only retreat left us; but there was none to be had, for the rest of our infantry were so hotly engaged, and so vigorously attacked on all sides—the enemy being three to one and having surrounded us—that it was impossible to send any to my assistance; so that I stood on the corner of the dike by Wilmerdonck alone with Treasurer-General Hop, Colonel Verschuner—who was by his cannons—and some servants and led-horses, having not so much as one battalion or squadron by me; nor could I possibly get any, for the enemy, having attacked our men in Orderen anew with cannon and great numbers on all sides, obliged them to retire, some into the enclosure and others on the skirts without the dike, not being able to stay upon the dike nor the ways that run along it, because they were closely pursued by great troops of horse and dragoons, who came presently riding along the dike of Orderen just under our cannon, when I, having none by me that I could oppose to them, in a great crowd of all sorts of people—servants and horses—was forced behind the dike. I rid a little way upon the great road which seemed to lead to Antwerp, until behind Wilmedook I found a little path, which I turned down, being followed by 25 or 30 men and horse of all sorts, hoping by that to get to our troops one way or other; but I was no sooner past Wilmerdonck than I found we were surrounded by the enemy's soldiers, who were scattered on both sides the way," and so deeper and deeper into the hostile force, until the strangeness of their isolation seems to have been in some measure a protection to them. They entered a village "full of French both foot and horse, the most of them dismounted. They presently mounted again, being surprised to see us come in there, and not knowing if we had more following us. We no less surprised to find ourselves, contrary to our expectations, so suddenly in the midst of them, began all to speak French as if we were of their army, which hindered them from firing on us, notwithstanding they observed us very narrowly, not knowing what to make of us." At length he reached Breda in safety.

The poor man concludes his story thus : " It being most sensibly afflicting to me, that after having served the State these thirty years with all faith, fulness, and fidelity, and having been in so many battles, fights, and sieges without ever being guilty of one step which deserved the least reproach or blame, that now in my own country where I have lived so long with honour and reputation, as well as in all foreign countries where I have been, must see myself so invidiously treated by so many people, without having the least knowledge or information of what passed, nor of the situation of the country where the fight happened." [1]

Here was suddenly stopped a career that seemed shaping itself in Marlborough's mind into a conquest of the Low Countries and a march into France. Before the check had occurred, we find his sagacity leading him to an expectation of it. Thus : " If M. Opdam be not upon his guard, he may be beat before we can

---

[1] A Relation of what passed at the Battle of Eckern, by Monsieur Opdam. Translation for the use of Lord Nottingham. — Hatton : Finch Papers, vol. ii., Addl. MS. B.M., 29589. In the local conditions on the side of Antwerp where this preposterous adventure occurred, it is easy to find causes of perplexity to a leader not fully acquainted with them. There are canals and detached morsels of fortification, and paved roads crossing each other. A long street, too, accompanies the road leading out of the fortifications, and old maps show it to have existed in Opdam's day. But these were all difficulties that should have been familiar to and expected by a Dutch soldier.

help him." He is sending off the closed despatch, when he opens it to say, "Since I sealed my letter, we have a report from Breda that M. Opdam is beaten. I pray God it may be not so, for he is very capable of having it happen to him."[1] This is all that, so far as any vestiges tell us, Marlborough ever said on the affair.

Waiting to be turned by events into a definite course, and seeing nothing immediately likely to effect this object, he returned to England, and mixed in home politics. It is said that at this time he had a misgiving that, with his mixed army, there would be no opportunity for the career he saw before him, had he so large a force disciplined to work in harmony under his sole command. It may perhaps have been, too, that his domestic bereavement assisted the depression of a forced inaction and a fettered will.

Marlborough, when he returned to his army, found himself in the midst of a general feeling of depression. It was felt in London while he was there, and he went to find it more deeply seated in the hearts of his allies and subordinates. The risings in Hungary had grown in strength, from two causes—the inability of the imperial forces to suppress them while engaged for the safety of the empire elsewhere, and the inducements naturally offered to them by France and Bavaria to hold out. Along with this it was rumoured, and by degrees became certain, that France and Bavaria would seize the opportunity for marching a large army down the Danube and striking a great blow at the empire in its hour of weakness. So vividly had

[1] Coxe, i. 255.

alarm penetrated into the heart of Austria, that there was hasty preparation in Vienna to stand a siege. Such was the situation when Marlborough landed at Rotterdam on the 18th of January 1704.

King Louis was now prepared to give effect to his determination to carry the war into Germany — a determination that brought him to the great disaster of his reign, the one that, though the first of many disasters, is still the most signal of all. But he would show that he was marching on to the empire of the world by hand to hand conflict with the sovereign who professed to wield that empire—at least in diplomatic courtesy. It was to this end that Monsieur de Bavière would be useful—his dominions adjoined and penetrated those of the house of Hapsburg, while the king was clear for a junction and the crossing of the Rhine. But the marshals had their doubts about the devotion to the cause of France of the Elector of Bavaria. If the joint armies were unsuccessful, the Elector might be in some measure liable to be treated, not as a fair enemy in the field, but a liegeman of the Empire in revolt. He seemed loath to quit his own territory, giving for excuse the danger of attack from the Elector of Baden. He proposed a junction by paths of such direction and difficult character that Villars warned him that they would fail in bringing him to the junction. He had let slip good opportunities for effecting this junction. Villars believed he had no more than ten thousand men in the field, while the obligation for which he drew subsidies was to maintain at least twenty-four thousand at the service of King Louis.[1]

[1] Mém. Militaires, ii. 421 et seq.

There was a suspicious levity in his dealing with
Austrian troops on occasions when he could have
struck a heavy blow.   Among speculations about the
possibilities of his conduct, one was a suspicion, not
unfounded, that, if not in absolute treaty with the
enemy, he laid himself out towards them as one who
was open to a desirable offer.   But he appears not to
have been deemed worthy of the expected price.   We
find Godolphin writing to Nottingham on the 30th
of August 1702, that except it were merely " to
strengthen Prince Eugene with reinforcements," the
cause "may pay too dear for his friendship;" and
further, " If the Elector of Bavaria would offer to
carry two thousand men into Italy for the emperor's
service, the consequence would be that he must have
the chief command there.   I don't think England
would contribute one farthing to such a treaty.   But
if he will be content to send any part of his troops to
strengthen the emperor's army under Prince Eugene,
that article would, I believe, be very agreeable to the
Parliament of England." [1]

But the Elector a few days afterwards settled the
question in a manner to remind the world of his
dexterity in substituting French for Dutch garrisons
in the barrier towns.

" *22d Sept.* 1702.—I have taken pen in hand to
acquaint you of a strange overture from the Duke of
Bavaria, who having long in several treaties given
hopes to his imperial majesty of affording him assistance with his troops—not directly against the two
kings, but in Hungary—hath now at last surprised
Ulm, the chief city in the circle of Swabia—upon

[1] Mus. Brit. Addl. MSS.. 29588. f. 157.

pretence that this circle and that of Franconia have not kept the treaty of association concluded at Ryswick. The manner thus. About forty soldiers in boer's habits, attended the opening of the gates, upon which they rushed in, slew the watch, and let in a body of dragoons which lay near in ambush, and having the advantage of a misty morning, got into the city and secured it till more forces that followed entered and possessed themselves thereof." [1]

The Elector had thus done services to the cause of France, creating probabilities in favour of his fidelity. Foremost for consideration among these, of course, was his brilliant achievement in the sudden seizure of the towns. He had reaped the gratitude of King Louis by this performance, and till there should be special reason for it, there was no occasion to mix with that gratitude suspicion that the person who had so expertly performed one feat of treachery with these strongholds, might perhaps perform another. Then he was beset by a moral infirmity that afforded a separate and peculiar hold, though it did not enhance the value of what was held. He was an inveterate and profuse gambler; and Boufflers, in a report to his own master explained that at one time the moneys he had raised to feed this appetite would detain him in the Netherlands; the wealthy and powerful burgesses who had accommodated him had power to control his motions. [2] But now, on the other side, there had

---

[1] Richard Hill to Godolphin, ibid., f. 261.

[2] "Le dit Sieur de Chassonville dit encore qu'il croit que M. de Bavière aurait peine à quitter les Pays-Bas quand il le voudrait à cause des sommes considérables qu'il y doit, particulièrement à Bruxelles; et il est persuadé que les bourgeois se mettraient en devoir de l'arrêter, s'il partait sans les avoir payés."—Mém. Militaires, i. 13. The docu-

arisen a pecuniary consideration of greater weight. The King of Spain owed money to the Elector. It does not appear whether the debt was national or personal, but the Elector felt that his best hopes of recovering his own was by commending himself to King Philip, and so he might be expected to remain true in that cause.[1] And if he were so, King Louis not only had a friend whose states were the highway to the country of his enemy the emperor, but he secured the alliance of Monsieur de Bavière's brother, the Elector of Cologne.

M. de Bavière was one of those facile and restless beings, who when they are driven to a point and fairly committed, compensate by impetuous manifestations of attachment for the hesitations and fluctuations of the past. Villars, writing from the camp at Möhringen, describes their meeting in such fashion as to give the impression that it was signally stripped of the decorum to be expected in an official and political interview between a prince of the Empire and a marshal of France. The Elector had in the meantime expressed a burning impatience to find how he could reach Villars. He sent courier after courier. At last he was seen dashing forward on horseback. Villars

ment whence this is extracted is a letter from Boufflers to King Louis, pp. 12-14. It is almost entirely occupied with speculations on the probabilities of the Elector being worthy of trust. On the general appearance of the case in the eyes of the writer's informant, Chassonville, "Il m'a dit qu'il a trouvé M. l'Electeur d'un air fort libre et point du tout embarrassé comme le serait un homme qui jouerait les deux."—13.

[1] "Le Sieur de Chassonville m'a encore dit qu'une des raisons qui engageront M. l'Electeur de Bavière à demeurer dans les intérêts du Roy d'Espagne, est le crainte de perdre les sommes considérables qui lui sont dués par L'Espagne, au cas qu'il entrât dans un parti contraire, et qu'ainsi il est persuadé qu'il donnera tout sujet d'être satisfait de sa conduite."—Mém. Militaires, i. 14.

prepared to dismount, but the Elector rushed on him
and fastened him in an embrace that drew from the
other the complaint that he narrowly escaped being
pitched from the saddle.   When the Elector's excitement permitted him to speak, he was eloquent in
gratitude to King Louis and the great French army
that had rescued him from danger, despondency, and
gloom, saving his life, his honour, and his family,
and raising him to the pitch of glory as a partaker in
the success of a triumphant army.[1]

The companions thus fantastically associated set
off together on the journey that was to be fatal to the
cause of both.   King Louis was not only determined
to push the war in Germany, but he would take it to
the south bank of the Rhine, and would thence carry
it to the Danube.   It was there that the Elector of
Bavaria could serve him by a material enhancement
of his power to threaten at once Austria, Bohemia,
Tyrol, and the German remnant of the Palatinate,
and strike wherever there was temptation and opportunity.   Catinat, the best of the French marshals,
estimated by the combination of military science and
bravery with sagacity in applying these qualities,
doubted the fitness of the forces at his disposal for
this mighty enterprise, and it fell to Villars.   His command began with a flush of success.   Among other
exploits, Kehl, on the German side of the Rhine, was
seized.   This was a casualty that would have been
signally mortifying had there been a lively feeling of
German nationality.   Kehl was a small place, strongly
fortified, to protect the German side from the dangers
inevitable in the French possession of Strasburg.

[1] Mém. Militaires. iii. 583. 584.

The tourist on the Rhine will remember Kehl, when in time of tranquillity it did part as a suburb of Strasburg, and the passport could be left in Kehl during the stroll through the capital of Alsace, lost to Germany. The loss must have been embittered when Kehl also fell into the hands of all-conquering France; but now both Strasburg and Kehl are again German, after a time when the city and the district round it had become so assimilated to French rule that the transference was a painful revolution even to persons of Teutonic name and origin.

The passage of the Rhine became now a serious question for Villars to solve. He thought at first that this could not be done nearer than Switzerland, As an operation of their force, the passage would be an easy affair; but the Swiss confederacy was a darling creation of the law of nations, and any violence on the neutrality of the defenceless cantons would, as Villars and his master knew well, be more fiercely resented than the subjugation of any of the great warlike states. It was considered at the time one of the happiest incidents in the conquering career of France, that the passage was found practicable by seizing and fortifying the small town of Neuburg, some five leagues below Basle, and building a bridge across the river. This was not accomplished without bloodshed. A smart attack was made on Villars by the Prince of Baden, who was driven back with serious casualties.

The French commander, after the passage had been accomplished, had the satisfaction to find a prevalent impression that his object was to besiege Freiburg, a strength in the territories of the Duke of Wurtemberg. Though a consciousness of bold adventure and of possible risk give a tone to the despatches of the French commander, the only immediate prospect of an enemy starting up in his path is from the two small territories adhering to the cause of the Empire—Wurtemberg and Baden. Danger from the rapid movements of Prince Eugene may come afterwards, but he is still far off. Of the possibility of an encounter with British troops there is as yet no hint.

In autumn there had dawned on King Louis and his advisers the mighty project of marching to Vienna with an irresistible force and striking a blow at the heart of the Empire. The wisest adepts in military affairs were set to work during the winter to exhaust all the difficulties likely to test such a project, and to devise methods for conquering them. They especially applied themselves to the first and the greatest difficulty—that of conveying a large army, well equipped and provisioned, into the valley of the Danube, to meet the force under the Elector of Bavaria. That once accomplished, all the rest seemed clear.[1]

It is to this first step, not the ultimate conclusion,

---

[1] Marshal Catinat was one of those whose counsel was taken. We shall hear more of him presently. In the meantime we find him precisely defining the great problem to be solved thus : " Quelles sont les mesures nécessaires pour que cette corps et les recrues destinées pour la Bavière puissent passer avec sûreté les montagnes qui séparent la vallée du Rhin d'avec la Souabe ; quel est le temps le plus propre pour cela ; quels sont les preparatifs qu'il faut faire pour y réussir ; quels sont les projets les plus utiles à suivre quand on aura passé ; et enfin, quels sont les moyens de se précautionner, contre ce que les ennemis pourvaient enterprendre, s'ils ne portaient pas toutes les forces dont ils ont à disposer, en Souabe et en Franconie, et qu'ils restassent supérieurs à nous sur les frontières du royaume."—Mém. Militaires, iv. 374.

that the still extant military correspondence of the day—fortunately abundant—refers. Throughout the winter the arrangements were made with secrecy and much industry. The projected designs of France, even to the extent of effecting a junction with the Bavarian force, must be kept a dead secret, while the visible exertions are limited to the marching of troops to increase the force on the Rhenish frontier of France. As that frontier extended from the Duke of Baden's territories, where it approached the town now known as Karlsruhe, and stretched upwards as far as Basle, it is apt to create surprise that carrying an army across the Rhine and over the intervening heights into the friendly territories of the Elector of Bavaria should have been deemed an enterprise so formidable and critical as the French correspondence reveals it to have been. But every precaution that skill, labour, and ample resources could supply was to be adopted, and nothing left to chance or mere good fortune.[1] The stake was enormous : if the enterprise were successful to its utmost idea—if Vienna were besieged and taken—the house of Bourbon would be supreme over the continent of Europe. But in the meantime, and until there was a large fresh force conveyed to the Rhine, the critical part of the project was not begun, and might be at any time abandoned without leaving on French history the stain of a failure. Accurate information was carefully gathered in early spring as to the existence and conditions of roads, and the boats that might be available in supplement to the

[1] " L'intention de sa Majesté n'est pas de rien donner au hasard."— Instructions to Tallard, Versailles, 16th April 1704 ; Mém. Militaires, iv. 425.

three bridges for the passage of the Rhine.   The possible supplies of forage and farm-produce are to be ascertained, keeping in view that the spring growth is later in Germany than in France.   Suitable places for the baking of bread and biscuit are to be noted.

The French, marching still upwards, met the Bavarians near the Lake of Constance, and then the great junction was completed.   This was not merely held as a fortunate incident preparatory to future operations with possible successes and reverses—it was a completed triumph over obstacles deemed by the enemy and the world at large to be insuperable.[1]

The whole French force told off for this expedition appears to have been—12,000 infantry and 2400 cavalry, under 900 officers.   Communication with the French territories on the Rhine was preserved ; and this, while it required that a portion of the advancing force should be dropped from time to time on the march, left the passage open for reinforcements.   Between forty and fifty thousand men had in all been assigned as the completed army of the Upper Rhine.   The general centre or gathering-ground of the two armies now in the valley of the Danube was Ulm, celebrated in more than one great war.   It was not only strong and capable of being further strengthened, but from the surrounding heights and the tower of the cathedral there was a far-reaching view of the great plain of the Danube up and down,

---

[1] " Ce fut ainsi que se termina, à la grand satisfaction de l'Electeur et des généraux, une enterprise de laquelle le sort de la Bavière, et dont l'execution avait dû recontrer des difficultés et des obstacles pour ainsi dire insurmountables.   Les ennemis en avaient connu toute l'importance ; ils avaient eux-mêmes publié quelle était impracticable."—Mém. Militaires. iv. 445.

and of the slopes of the bordering hills. Whenever a sufficient force was assembled for the accomplishment of the great purpose, it had the finest marching-ground in Europe before it—a continued plain with but trifling interruptions all the way to Vienna.

Towards the end of May perplexing news reached Tallard. Marlborough was marching up the Rhine, and had reached Coblentz. At this juncture in the war the French were ever nervous about the possession of Landau. This fortress stands on the Legh, an affluent of the Rhine, a few miles from its junction, and also a few miles on the German side of the frontier of French Alsace. It had been strongly fortified as an advanced post. It had been taken from Bavaria, now the ally of France. But however it might be disposed of between the two allied Powers, it was not to be left a prey to the enemy. Never in high esteem with the French, it was naturally believed to be an object of great attraction to the enemy, and must be saved if possible. It was a hard alternative to Tallard whether he should retrace his march so far as to save Ulm. He sent orders that the garrison of Landau should be strengthened by a thousand men from the available French forces left behind. Then came the rumour that Marlborough possibly had greater views. He might be audacious enough to attack French territory by ascending the Moselle or the Saar.

Tallard marched back towards the Rhine with a large portion of his force. This left his ally, the Elector, in great peril, for the Prince of Baden was so close upon his track that outposts made narrow escapes; and he learned that Prince Eugene, knowing

him to be but scantily aided from France, was marching upon him.[1]　At length came more specific news
about Marlborough's designs.　He was to ascend the
Moselle and besiege Trierbach and Treves.　Marshal
Boufflers had been ordered to meet and fight him on
the way, and just a sufficient force had been left in
the Netherlands to protect the French and Spanish
possessions there.[2]　On this trod the news that Marlborough had passed the Moselle and crossed the
Rhine, so that he must have determined to carry the
war into Austria and Bavaria.[3]

Some months before these flutterings in the French
and Bavarian army, it had gradually formed itself
as a fixed idea in Marlborough's mind that the true
way to strike a conclusive blow was to change his
seat of war by secretly crossing the watershed of
Europe, and unexpected by the joint armies on
the Danube, drop on them like a bird of prey.　He
might thus accomplish two objects,—save the Empire by protecting Vienna, and punish the Elector of
Bavaria for deserting the cause proper to every German Power—that of the Fatherland against France.
He had, before beginning his march, to make another
journey to England, for he had secrets to discuss
not to be safely put on paper : and to give effect to
his designs, he must draw largely on the resources of
Britain ; but he found a steady supporter in his great
kinsman.　Yet he returned to the head of his army
with a renewed sense of depression.　He chafed
against those obstinate conditions that seemed to
bind his army to peace, when his soul yearned for
war ; and in his own home, where he dearly loved

[1] Mém. Militaires, iv. 455-460.　　[2] Ibid., 460.　　[3] Ibid., 462.

peace, it had been lacking. Sarah had been overtaken by one of those furious outbursts of rage, as absolutely a necessity to her life as the occasional eruption is to the volcano. On this occasion the storm happened to alight where it was ever most effective—on the head of her gentle husband. She sent him a sweet, penitent letter to meet him on his return to the camp, and his soul was in Elysium again. Its kindness and devotion seem indeed to have overflowed, for he was put to the painful necessity of demurring when she proposed to join him in the camp.

"Your dear letter of the 15th," he says, "came to me but this minute. My Lord Treasurer's letter, in which it was enclosed by some mistake, was sent to Amsterdam. I would not for anything in my power it had been lost; for it is so very kind, that I would in return lose a thousand lives if I had them to make you happy. . . . It will be a great pleasure to me to have it in my power to read this dear letter often, and that it may be found in my strong-box when I am dead. I do this minute love you better than ever I did before; this letter of yours has made me so happy, that I do from my soul wish we could retire and not be blamed. What you purpose as to coming over I should be extremely pleased with; for your letter has so transported me, that I think you would be happier in being here than where you are—although I should not be able to see you often. But you will see by my last letter, as well as this, that what you desire is impossible; for I am going up into Germany, where it would be impossible for you to follow me: but love me as you now do, and no hurt can come to me. You have by this kindness preserved my quiet, and I believe my life; for till I had this letter I have been very indifferent as to what should become of myself."[1]

[1] Coxe. i. 323.

The States were naturally opposed to Marlborough's project. It was their instinct to demur at anything likely to weaken the protecting army so happily posted at their own gate. But Marlborough's hand was strengthened by the 10,000 additional troops, and the hope of more, as well as by the punctual payment of the subsidies, and the general disposition of Britain to make the greatest amount of contribution to the conduct of the war, while her benefits from success were prospective and doubtful. The Dutch paid portions of the subsidies, and Marlborough made account of this very adroitly by proposing that they should let him take these subsidised troops and keep their own. They were thus asked to give that of the two which they were the less anxious to retain; and the commander of the army was rid of those troublesome field deputies, who must have haunted him had he taken native Dutch soldiers.

On the 16th of May the army assembled at Bedburg, near Maastricht. Thence on the 19th began the great march. Coblentz was reached on the 25th, and Mentz on the 29th. An instructive volume might perhaps be written on the complicated mechanism—the wheels in the midst of wheels—that kept in its own distinct and separate organisation the troops of each nation, and the constituent elements of each division and subdivision, while all concentrated into a harmonious whole, moving at the direction of one man. But a few particulars, in technical phrase, culled from general orders, reports, and despatches, would make mere idle pedantry teaching nothing. It must suffice that the whole organisation was so perfect, and worked so smoothly, as to inspire throughout the motley crowd of various populations and languages an implicit reliance. And yet, what he designed to do with them was a dead secret. The most confidential of his communications were in the possession of his kinsman in the English Treasury, who so faithfully supplied him with the equipments and material supplies for the great project. But even Godolphin knew not whither the army was ultimately to march; and, indeed, Marlborough himself did not know; but it was part of the flexible power that led him always to a victory, and never to a defeat, or even a failure, that he could change his purpose at a moment's warning when he examined the surrounding conditions. He was like the engineer among a vast apparatus of powerful machinery, who, by gently turning a handle in a disc, can change the direction in which his potent enginery works, or even utterly reverse the whole process. His passing on from Coblentz to Mentz showed, that if he had at first proposed to himself an attack on French territory by ascending the Moselle, that was not now his design. He had ever, however, a hankering after this project. He afterwards, as we shall see, made serious progress in such an attempt, and suddenly abandoned it, passing to another and more propitious field of action. On the present occasion, it was said that he had made a diversion towards the Moselle; but diversions were not a favourite strategy with Marlborough. There is nothing so apt to impress people with the fact that one intends to go to a place as movements forward in an actual intention; and Marlborough seems to have reaped the benefit of this effectual method of drawing attention to the course which, in the end, he did not take.

There are now necessary revelations. The Landgrave of Hesse is directed to send to Mannheim the artillery that had been destined for the Moselle. But though there are indications that, instead of the frontiers of France, Germany and the right bank of the Rhine are to be the object, there is nothing as yet determining the crossing of the watershed into the regions of the Danube. We follow the army by the pleasant slopes of the Odenwald towards Mannheim. Hence he writes home. Sarah had been still in an affectionate humour, and he says: "I take it extremely kindly that you persist in desiring to come to me," but there are obvious difficulties in the way; and "besides, my dear soul, how could I be at any ease? for if we should not have good success, I could not put you into any place where you would be safe. I am now in a house of the Elector Palatine, that has a prospect over the finest country that is possible to be seen. I see out of my chamber-window the Rhine and the Neckar, and his two principal towns of Mannheim and Heidelberg, but would be much better pleased with the prospect of St Albans, which is not very famous for seeing far."[1] Still there was nothing to reveal a march across the watershed of Europe. The talk of the day was of the siege of Landau; and, in fact, a bridge had been laid across the Rhine, as if for service in this operation. Meanwhile, as a French force appeared to be approaching Landau to cover it from a siege, care must be taken that if they discover the path taken

[1] Coxe. i. 333.

by their nimble enemy, they are not to be permitted to cross the Rhine and follow him. "If," he says to Godolphin, "the Marshal de Villeroy can be kept on the other side of the Rhine, we must be contented to suffer him to do what he pleases there, while we are acting in Bavaria."[1]

At Hippach there was a halt of three days for the gathering up of outlying detachments. Here Marlborough met two men who were destined to be his chief co-operators — Prince Eugene of Savoy, and Louis, Margrave of Baden. It is recorded that Prince Eugene expressed his surprise at the fresh and hearty condition of the men who had sustained so long a march. But at that period the equipments and commissariat furnished by the British Government made perhaps a stronger contrast with the impoverished condition of the troops of France and Germany than they ever made before or since.

The meeting between Marlborough and Eugene was a great historical event. The two men took cordially to each other. It was a phenomenon almost unknown in warfare that two commanders who had hitherto each found himself supreme among his own people, should agree together that each should be free to devote the peculiar faculties he was endowed with to the common cause, so as to give it the strength of united action, instead of exhibiting the jealous rivalry apt to take possession of the greatest natures when their high qualities are cast into competition.

It is evident that Prince Louis of Baden was from the first a less welcome coadjutor. He asserted claims to consideration, and even supremacy, which could not

[1] Coxe, i. 336.

be easily met. He was on a small scale a sovereign prince, while Marlborough was a mere subject. But further, he had a reputation more brilliant than Marlborough had yet obtained, for it was earned by successes in actual battle; and Marlborough had not as yet fought a battle. The Prince had been trained by Montecuculi, and was master of all the rules of strategy and military etiquette in the most accomplished school that the world had yet seen. He had performed in some brilliant affairs along with John Sobieski in the defence of Vienna; and although it was difficult to estimate the effect of generalship and fighting in the mysterious rolling away of the danger, yet there was something indefinitely grand in military feats connected with the dispersal of some hundreds of thousands of the infidels who threatened the subjugation of Christendom. The sieges and battles he had taken part in formed a long list in his portion of the family-tree, and the trophies assigned to his military rank in those affairs where trophies had been captured, made a museum that was one of the wonders of the world. But in Marlborough's estimate all these glories went for little or nothing against the fatal fact that the Margrave could have prevented the junction of the French and Bavarian army, and had allowed them to join. But for all, it was necessary for the sake of the great cause to bear with the Margrave. It had been difficult to secure him for the cause; he had been bought at a high price; and at the juncture now reached, it would be a calamity if he were to take a haughty fit and break off.

An odd arrangement was at last effected—that Marlborough and he should take the command-in-

chief on alternate days. Over subordinate detachments
there was sometimes a captain of the day; but as an
arrangement for the command of a great force, it has
so dangerous a look, that only the abundant testimony
of the correspondence of the army would make it be
believed. Marlborough accepted the arrangement
with his usual imperturbable tranquillity. For all, he
would yet find his opportunity; and when he did, it
would be a strong hand that could restrain him from
seizing it. Meanwhile one of the three generals must
go westward for the protection of the Rhine on the
Low Countries. This fell to Prince Eugene, though
both he and Marlborough would fain have been
comrades.

On the 15th of June the army reached the village
of Gieslingen, on the heights bordering the Danube.
Their next march, beginning with a steep descent,
brought them to the cold table-land where the waters
on one side travel towards the German Ocean, and
those on the other towards the Black Sea. The path
before them led down to the Danube. If they had
ever been in danger, they were now safe. Had the
rocky pass been defended, to march through it would
have been as impossible as to march through a fortress.
But except to the few who were in the secret, this
great army had accomplished as complete an evasion
from the cognisance of mankind as a bird that makes
itself invisible in the sky.

The course of the Danube up and down was now
before the army. The source of all doubt and terror
had been, that the way was open for the French and
Bavarians marching on Vienna. And now, on any
such expedition, the allies could intercept them.

There was one critical point where the command of the Danube might be disputed—the old town of Donauworth, where the narrow, rapid Wörmitz pours into the Danube. This was an old imperial city. It was fortified, and very strong; but its strength depended not on the works of the engineer, but in the Danube and the Wörmitz sweeping some two-thirds round it, and the Schellenberg rising over the remainder.

Up and down, the river flows between plains of diluvium as flat as an English race-course. This plain is from four to eight miles wide, and bordered by steep hills. The Schellenberg is a branch or spur from these hills on the left side crossing the plain, and dropping abruptly to the Danube. It is one of the critical points where contests had been frequent in the old wars, and it had been fortified in different ways at different periods. On the highest level of its undulating surface there was a fort, then old, though on its site there now stands a fragment like the remnant of a small bastion. Donauworth lay in the lap of the Schellenberg. Works connected with the Schellenberg defences stretched out in the shape of a rampart and covered-way, and seemed to embrace the town, until it was handed over to the protection of the Wörmitz, and then of the Danube. With the Schellenberg in friendly hands, it might be fairly judged that no town in Europe was safer than the old imperial city of Donauworth.

If the French and Bavarian army, now again gathering round Ulm, were in occupation of the Schellenberg, and held fortified lines there, it would seem obvious that they could not be attacked with any hope of success. They might be detained there, and disabled from mischief by besieging Vienna or otherwise. But that was not a conclusion likely to satisfy the ambition of Marlborough. Naturally, he was curious to see how affairs stood on the Schellenberg. The first view disclosed that it was covered with men, who were in a state of restless activity.

Marlborough, in his ardent anxiety, approached so near that the enemy fired at his party, and balls were strewn round them. He satisfied himself that the army was not there—only a detachment: but that detachment was raising a line of field-fortresses, and if they were allowed to complete this work, the Schellenberg would be a great intrenched camp for the whole army; for the surface of the hilly ground is so extensive, that it is not easy to imagine an army so large that it would not find on the Schellenberg sufficient camping and parade ground, as well as outlets for deploying.[1]

The plan of the line of fortifications did not profess to run along the base of the hill, but to shield its upper level, seeking in its course the protection of abrupt declivities and marshy places. The line was to terminate at either end with the descent to the

---

[1] In some histories the Schellenberg is spoken of as a detached conical hill, with a flat top half a mile in diameter. Such a conception of the spot excited the puzzling question why it should be attacked. If such a place of retreat was selected for a detachment, why meddle with them? This idea of the Schellenberg might perhaps have been suggested by a book called 'The Military History of the late Prince Eugene of Savoy, and of the late John, Duke of Marlborough, including, &c., with engravings,' by Charles du Bosc. One of these professes to represent the fighting on the Schellenberg; but it is not from below, but from a point on the hill, and gives so exaggerated a rendering of the fort and its escarpment, that these might be taken for a conical hill.

Danube. It was not yet completed; but in a day, perhaps a few hours, it might be completed. Behind this rampart there were 12,000 men—some two-thirds Bavarians, the rest French—under the command of General D'Arco. The troops were fatigued with long marching; but it was Marlborough's day of command, and he determined to storm the Schellenberg. It was mercy to his own wearied troops to take the place, for every hour gave it new strength, and Marlborough learned from the motions of the men behind the works that they did not expect to be attacked on that evening.

The enemy had ninety guns and forty mortars. If Marlborough could bring men on whom he could rely to face a fire from these, the nature of the ground itself did not make much inequality between the two armies. It would have exhausted a much larger force than D'Arco had at his command to have attempted to hold the Schellenberg from its base; and once on the hill, the only absolute inequality was, that D'Arco's force was in great part protected by the field-works, and could concentrate men for the protection of the unfortified entrances.

Marlborough picked 6000 men for the first charge. His whole army was at hand, and his resources virtually inexhaustible. Before being formed, the men were directed to cut branches from the abundant neighbouring woods. These branches were to do duty as fascines in filling the ditch. The charge was made partly in the undefended spaces, and partly by running along the ditch and finding spots where the embankment might be mounted. It was sheer hand-to-hand fighting. Three times the assailants were driven back and pursued down the hill, but each time flanking attacks on the pursuers drove them back in confusion within their lines. More men had to be drawn from the army. It was the terrible alternative that life must be poured out that life might be saved.

Assistance came from an unexpected quarter— assistance very creditable to him who brought it. D'Arco had naturally told off a party to man the rampart and protect the covered-way stretching along the part of the town of Donauworth unprotected by nature. In the hurry and excitement caused by the unexpected charge, this duty was neglected. The Duke of Baden objected to Marlborough's enterprise as a piece of foolish rashness. To his amazement, however, he found that while his rash comrade was in the midst of a furious fight, a way was open to himself to mount the Schellenberg undisturbed. This was a feat thoroughly canonical in the community of trained commanders, of which he was a distinguished member. The appearance of the head of a new army marching up from the flank was encouraging to the attackers, and intimidating to the attacked. They wavered, and Marlborough's force getting well within the lines, charged irresistibly.

The Schellenberg was an admirable place to be defended, but a fatal place to be beaten in. The very defences took every resource from the defeated. A surrender would have been their policy, but there does not appear to have been collected thought among the leaders sufficient to devise such an act. Not only was an orderly retreat impossible, but there was no opening even for flight. If the fugitives were received within the walls of Donauworth, Donauworth was in the absolute possession of whoever had command of the Schellenberg. Supposing that while there was yet time the fugitives could run through the town to get at the open country, the end of the long street opened on the suburb of Berg, scattered over high ground, where a great portion of the allied army were posted. There was a bridge over the Danube, but it broke under the weight of the fugitives rushing upon it. Those only who could swim the stream had a chance of escape. The Danube makes a rapid, deep sweep round the abrupt ascent of the Schellenberg. Here a great portion of the force were tumbled down into the stream, where they sank or got across, according to the extent of their capacity in swimming.

This success was bought at a heavy cost to the small victorious army,—the killed are admitted by its own partisans to have been 1500, the wounded 4000. These numbers are enlarged by estimates on the other side, and contrasted with the small number of French and Bavarians slain and wounded : but their chief losses were not in the field, but in the flight, and especially in the despairing efforts to swim the Danube; and it is easy to believe it true that only 3000 of them returned to the banner of the Elector.[1]

It was inevitable that the fortified town of Donauworth should fall to the captor of the Schellenberg. The difficulties of the Wörmitz river and the fortifications could only give the garrison a short reprieve, and they occupied the time in an attempt to destroy their magazines and burn the town. In this they had partial and small success, and they had to leave to

[1] Coxe. i. 358.

their successors abundant provender and camp equipage. Marlborough was now master of the main passages of the Danube, in a strong place, well provided with quarters for his troops.

This was the first occasion since the old invasions by the Plantagenets, or, at least, since the battle of Pavia, where French soldiers had ignominiously fled before an enemy. A success that, though small, was so complete, augured well for the coming winter, and cheered the hearts of all communities fearing and disliking France. But exultation was dashed with pity for the poor Bavarians. It was felt that they might have fought better had some good cause stirred their blood—the cause of freedom and Fatherland. But they were fighting for the great tyrant of Europe and the enemy of their race, and those who smote them so heavily for doing so were men of the same Teutonic stock, with languages kindred to their own —English, Dutch, Danes, Swedes, and brother Germans. They were not marshalled under the banners of a paternal prince in the cause of his own people or in the interests of the great combination of German States. His ambition was both selfish and tawdry, for it gained him nothing but the grace of the insolent, aggrandising potentate, whose acquisitions by power and policy were eating into the heart of Germany.

There was no pity for the Elector. On the contrary, the ruin he had brought on his poor subjects intensified the tendency to count him a traitor to his German allegiance, rather than an independent prince making his own alliances.

The Dutch—or, let us hope, only a faction among

them—took occasion to punish Marlborough for deserting the defence of the States and fighting elsewhere. They struck a commemorative medal as appropriate to the victory, remarkable only by Marlborough being neither named nor alluded to. The legend proclaims the enemy all either slain or routed ; and that the hero of the achievement may be recognised, the medal is charged with a portrait of the Margrave of Baden.[1]

[1] The legend was HOSTE CÆSO, FVGATO, CASTRIS DIREPTIS AD SCHELLENBERGAM DONAWERDAM, 1704.—Histoire de Jean Churchill, Duc de Marlborough, 1808, iii. 556. It is to this book, written and printed under the direction of the great Napoleon, that we owe the resuscitation of the little affair of the Dutch medal. It is announced with the emphatic comment, " Les Hollandois firent frapper une médaille à cette occasion ; ce qu'il y a de bien étrange c'est que sur la face on voyoit le buste du Prince de Bade à la place de celui de Marlborough, qui avoit exécuté l'enterprise, et qui avoit joné le principal rôle dans cette scène également heureuse et sanglante."—Ibid., i. 328.

The Margrave had the fortune to find and the merit to seize an unexpected opportunity for completing the work ; but there is preponderating testimony to the fact that he thought it a rash project after the day's march, and that Marlborough took advantage of his day of command to effect it. A recent German historian of the war, the careful Carl Von Noorden, says : " Zur Verschiebung des Angriffes mahnte in den Erwagungen des Englisch - kaiserlichen Kriegsrathes nicht nur die vorgeruckte Tagesstunde, sondern auch die sichtliche Ermudung der Truppen: in diesem Sinne legte der Markgraf seine Meinunung ein. Aber am 2d Juli fuhrte der Herzog von Marlborough in namen seiner Königin der oberbefehl. . . . Schon waren weitere Verstarkungen des Schellenberges im Anmarsche. Im Saufe der Nacht könnte Graf d'Arco die Schanzwerhe Villig in Stand setzen. Marlborough ergriff den nachsten Moment ; die noch ubringen Stunden des Tages sollten uber den Eintritt ins Kurfurstenthum Baiern entscheiden."—Europäische Geschichte im achtzehnten Jahrhundert der Spanische Erbfolgekrieg, i. 542, 543.

The momentous influence of the storming of the Schellenberg was not felt until it was seen to open the path to greater events. France was not yet accustomed to realise disasters, and the following announcement in the ' Paris Gazette ' of 26th June, sounds like an account of some trifle of a different character : " Toute fois le comte d'Arco voyant ses troupes fatiguées d'un combat de près de trois heures, et

In the view that the Elector was a deserter and a traitor, the storming of the Schellenberg was set down as the first instalment of his castigation; and if he persisted in his course he must expect more castigation still, and with good reason, since Marlborough was the avenging Nemesis who was henceforth to pursue him, and bring him to reason or to ruin. A slight flush of vindictive wrath seems at this juncture to cross the calm surface of Marlborough's official correspondence, and his wrath is held in surly and distrustful suspense, while his course of action is not stopped, on understanding that the Elector is in treaty to return to his duty for a sufficient price. It is clear that the Elector hesitated and treated; but little more is known of the negotiations, except that he found himself bound to France by ties not to be broken.[1]

qu'elles pourvoient estre envelopées, jugea à propos de se retirer à Donawert, ce qu'il fit en très bon ordre, sans perdre ni drapeaux, ni étandarts, ayant seulement laissé huit pièces de canon qu'il fit enclouer, ne pouvant les emmener."—P. 357.

[1] Marlborough does not appear to have had any personal negotiation with the Elector. A deciphered cipher says: "The Elector of Bavaria hath desired to see Count Wratislau, and this evening he is to name the place where they may meet, so that by my next you may expect to know the result of their conference. In the meantime you may be assured we shall not delay our operations one moment on this account." —Despatches, i. 348. The "operations" are occasionally alluded to thus: "De presser M. l'Electeur, le plus qu'il sera possible, encore qu'il ait le Lech devant lui, afin de ne perdre aucun temps à le reduire à la raison." —Ibid., p. 343. "We are making the necessary preparations for forcing our passage over the Lech. We shall then be in the heart of the enemy's country, and shall continue to press them without giving them the least time to recover" (ibid., p. 344): and three days later,—"We have now got into Bavaria, over two great rivers, without any opposition, so that the Elector must soon come to terms, or run the risk of having his whole country ruined; for since our victory on the Schellenberg they have not made any head against us" (ibid., p. 348). "We shall to-morrow have all the army in the Elector's country, so that if he will ever think of terms it must be now; for we shall do our utmost to ruin his country."—Coxe, i. 369.

In fact, while yet wavering, he was secretly informed of the great force that his master, King Louis, had determined to send for his assistance and support, and he knew that what was destined for his support if he remained true would avail for his punishment if he proved false.   His was one of those light, helpless natures that shrink from an estimate of existing operative forces, and attach themselves to the cause favoured by fortune—and France ever had been the favourite of fortune.   A sad check reminded him that fortune was fickle ; but with fuller assistance from powerful and fortunate France, it might have been otherwise,—and now France was to throw her vast resources into his cause.   For the security of himself and the remnant of his army, he left the Danube and ascended the Lech, where he encamped round the strong fortifications of Augsburg.   Marlborough examined his position with greedy eyes, but it was not to be attacked unless he could obtain a sufficiency of battering-guns.   For these he had depended on the resources of the Margrave of Baden, who failed to furnish them.   This want crippled him severely, and we find him writing on the 31st of July to Godolphin : " For want of cannon, and the King of France doing all he can to succour the Elector, we shall be obliged to take such measures as our wants will permit us ; but you may be assured, if they give us opportunity, we shall be glad to come to a battle, for that would decide the whole, because our troops are very good.   But our misfortune is, that we want everything for attacking towns, otherwise this would have been dated from Munich." [1]

[1] Coxe. i. 373.

Master of the capital and of the strong places, Marlborough could have put in execution the ban of the Empire, deposing the Elector, and placing the government of the country and the command of the troops at the disposal of the Diet. The mode of punishment left to him was to Marlborough a sorry alternative to the glorious task of seizing the capital and dragging the Elector out of his stronghold. He announces the final resolution of the Elector to cast his lot with France, and then—" However, we are in his country, and he will find it difficult to persuade us to quit it. We sent this morning 3000 horse to his chief city of Munich, with orders to burn and destroy all the country about it. This is so contrary to my nature, that nothing but absolute necessity could have obliged me to consent to it, for these poor people suffer for their master's ambition. There having been no war in this country for above sixty years, these towns and villages are so clean that you would be pleased with them." And again : " You will, I hope, believe me that my nature suffers when I see so many fine places burnt, and that must be burnt, if the Elector will not hinder it."[1]

He occupied his force meanwhile in taking the secondary fortifications scattered around his post at Neuburg, Rain, Aich, and Friedelberg. He was thus gradually acquiring such a miscellaneous collection of cannon as might in the end serve him in crushing the Elector by the capture of Augsburg ; but it was in the decrees of fate that this end was to be reached by another method.

The position occupied by each of the two main

<hr>

[1] Coxe, i. 376. 377.

bodies of the army of the allies becomes now of vital importance. Marlborough was, as we have seen, wandering over Bavaria, punishing the country for the sins of its rulers, and at the same time foraging for his army. He was unable to take the strong places ; but he was himself too strong to be attacked by the residue of the enemy's army left in Bavaria : he had marched in detachments as far up the Danube as Neuburg and Ingolstadt. Prince Eugene found that Donauworth and the Schellenberg formed a strong post for his camp, and to that point he gathered all his force. Marlborough and he were thus some forty miles distant from each other when both received the astounding intimation that a new French army of 35,000 men was on the march to join the Elector of Bavaria, and that on the 6th of August this force had reached the valley of the Danube, and formed a line of communication with the main body of the Elector's army in Augsburg. King Louis, on hearing of the affair of the Schellenberg, had shown his old prompt decision. Such a disgrace, though small, must not be permitted to remain as a precedent. It must be overwhelmed in achievements that would hide it out of sight. Hence a force not to be resisted —a force such as France alone could raise and send to distant regions as rapidly as the unencumbered traveller could pass from place to place—was sent to end the controversy. It was led by two Marshals of France, illustrious as conquering commanders—Tallard, who was first, and Marsin, who was second in command.

When this was known Prince Eugene rushed hastily to Marlborough's camp, and the two had an anxious discussion on their common peril. It was the nearest thing that ever befell Marlborough to those overwhelming surprises that were his own favourite kind of exploit. It was clear to both these keen-sighted commanders what the large army between them would do. It would first fall on Eugene's separate force, and when that was destroyed, march upon Marlborough's.

The immediate impulse of Marlborough was to carry his army across the Danube and join Prince Eugene by a rapid march; and, as usual, the immediate impulse speedily settled into a resolute purpose. Everything depended on rapidity of movement; but in the interval, ere the march could begin, he had an opportunity for completing a separate arrangement of importance. He felt the want of a base of operations—of strong places, where he might find rest and support in a possible hour of need. Donauworth and the Schellenberg were valuable for this end; but it was desirable to have at least one more stronghold, and he arranged that the Margrave of Baden with his own force should remain behind and besiege Ingolstadt. This was in several respects a satisfactory adjustment. It rid the two great commanders of one whose pertinacious assertion of superiority of command through precedence in rank had been troublesome and even dangerous, while the Margrave himself had the satisfaction to rule over a camp which, if small, was yet entirely his own.

At four o'clock in the afternoon of August the 11th the advanced columns of the army reached Donauworth, and the junction was so far completed as much to reduce the danger of Eugene's force being destroyed. It is told, as a testimony to the rapidity of the whole operation, that on the dawn of the 12th the baggage and artillery arrived after they had on the previous day been carried twenty-four miles. We have seen that the Schellenberg is a hill running as a sort of spur from the mountain-range bordering the plain of the Danube, across that plain, and dropping abruptly into the river. Descending the river, after crossing the Schellenberg, the flat plain recommences, and may be trodden for several miles. It then breaks up into slightly broken ground, such as naturally adapts itself for war. No army remains on a perfectly flat plain to risk a battle if it can find ground where there is shelter and impediments to an enemy. On the other hand, if an army encamps on high ground, and makes lines, it is not likely to be attacked by an enemy of anything approaching to an equality in strength. Hence we find that great battles are generally fought on ground where there is no decided and palpable inequality, and where the superiority of ground goes no further for either army than the opportunity of dexterously seizing casual advantages ; and into such ground the great plain on the right bank of the Danube breaks itself up, about twelve miles below Donauworth and the Schellenberg.

Hochstadt was then, and still is, a considerable town. It has a *Schloss*, or castle ; and though we hear of the capture of the castle by the French, with so many men taken prisoners in it, yet it was no fortress, but merely a large house, incapable of separate defence, but useful to troops occupying the district. The great highroad of the Danube runs through the town ; and that the present highroad is identical with, or but slightly varies from the old, may be inferred from the enclosures on either side, and the old houses with windows protected by heavy iron bars. Blenheim, about four miles up the river, where it makes a curve, is on by-ways off the great road. By comparing old representations with its present condition, it may be seen that, like many of the agricultural villages in that part of Bavaria, it was not a town in anything but the number of its dwellings and inhabitants. The houses were stuck one against the other, as personal convenience or chance dictated—the whole lying like so many stones casually dropped beside each other on a road. It will be seen that this peculiarity had a signal influence on coming events.

It would appear that Marlborough expected to occupy Blenheim, his adversary being posted at Hochstadt. When he saw that adversary posted in Blenheim also, we may believe that the sight did not appal or disappoint him. It was one of those instances where his fertile genius drew fresh resources out of the thwarting of his original idea of the course before him. He saw at once that the enemy had grasped more than that enemy could hold.

On the evening of the 12th all was on the selected ground—men, horses, equipments, provisions, and artillery. The terrible anxiety and the desperate effort to remove its cause were over, and there was peace, order, and repose in the tired hosts. Marlborough's was ever an orderly and decorous camp. He had no doubt many social waifs in his ranks, but the bulk of them seem to have come from the class who either were conformists with the unexacting conditions of the Church of England, or were fired by the zeal of dissent from it, or conformed with the more exacting Church of Scotland. Their great general encouraged religious observances. There had been a solemn thanksgiving for the victory of the Schellenberg. When the tired troops had gone to rest, Marlborough had the Sacrament administered to him. Next day, in the anxious interval, Marlborough, having ranged his own force, waited for the intimation that at the head of every regiment the service of the Church of England, or of that communion to which the chaplain belonged, was celebrated. Thus the army became for the time a vast congregation devoting itself to Christian worship. The numbers marshalled on both sides have of course been matter of doubt and dispute. It is generally admitted that the French exceeded the allied force by at least ten per cent. It is certain that the French had by far the larger park of field-guns.[1]

Marlborough and Eugene took each the separate command of his own army—Marlborough's being a mixed force of English and allies subsidised or self-supporting, while Eugene's was the army of the Empire. As Marlborough had by far the larger force, it was determined that he should take the front and

---

[1] It is satisfactory to be able on this point to refer to the following analysis of the two forces, made by one whose ambition it was to achieve a special skill in estimating the numbers engaged in the chief historical battles of the world, and who perhaps may be counted the highest authority on all such questions :—

GERMANS UNDER PRINCE EUGENE.

92 squadrons .	.	.	.	.	⎱
11 battalions (Prussian) .		.	.	⎰ 20,000 men.
7 „ (Danish) .		.	.	.	

open the battle ; and in this arrangement he felt the
assurance that whatever befell, his illustrious companion in arms would do precisely what ought to be
done.   Marlborough's system of warfare was ever the
aggressive ; and when the ranks were completed, he
ordered an instant march on the ground occupied by

UNDER MARLBOROUGH.

14 squadrons } English.
14 battalions }

72 squadrons { Dutch, Danes, Lineburg Fran- conians, Wur- temburgers. } Called sold to Uppen, or Mercenaries. } 36,000 men.

66 battalions, 178 squadrons = 56,000 men.
52 cannons.

FRENCH.

84 battalions .   .   .   .   . } 60,000 men
147 squadrons .   .   .   .   . } (of whom 12,000 Bavarians).

90 cannons.

—Kausler : Atlas der merkwurdigsten Schlachten, p. 108.

The estimate by an officer in high command on the French side who
was in the battle was—

THE ENEMY (*i. e.*, MARLBOROUGH AND EUGENE).

182 squadrons.
63 battalions.
60 cannon.

ON THE FRENCH SIDE.
140 squadrons.
84 battalions.
94 cannon.

As appropriate to this estimate, we are told : "Leurs bataillons
étoient d'un tiers plus forts que les nôtres, et, pour nos escadrons, il
n'y en avoit pas un de cent maîtres combattants, mais beaucoup de
soixante-dix et de quatre-vingts. Les troupes Bavaroises et les miennes
étoient les plus complètes, car un bataillon françois parmi l'autre ne
pouvoit être compté qu'à trois cent cinquante."—Mémoires de Feld-
Maréchal Comte de Mérode Westerloo, i. 297.

the enemy. To reach this it was necessary to cross the small river Nebel and its marshy banks. Among the many errors attributed to Tallard is the negligence, almost inconceivable, of believing without examination that the marsh was as impassable as those who had been in the small affair on the same ground between Villars and the Imperialists, remembered it to have been some months earlier.[1] There are few parts of the surface of the earth where the conditions of to-day are so uncertain to-morrow, as the great diluvial plain of the Danube. It is troubled by distant unknown powers. The melting of the snow on the Tyrolese mountains, and the swelling or subsiding of the Salz, the Iser, the Inn, and other affluents; and the pilgrim seeking his favourite walk by the side of the grand river, may find that a few minutes have sufficed to divide it from him by a roaring torrent. It was at the same time a consequence of far too great dependence on the concentration of his troops in the villages that Tallard did not carry his front line down to the border of the Nebel and its marsh, but left room on his own side for Marlborough's army to form on good firm ground.[2] Westerloo

---

[1] "On compta trop sur un marais qui couvroit le front, et que l'on avoit trouvé impracticable au mois d'octobre de l'année précedente : il auroit fallu l'examiner de nouveau, et l'on auroit vu qu'il n'en étoit pas de même au mois d'août et qu'il étoit presque entièrement desséché.— Mém. du Marquis Maffei, ii. 41.

[2] Mérode Westerloo, with the hesitating criticism natural to one who feels that it has been his misfortune to serve under an incompetent commander, shows how ground could have been taken where the hostile force could have found no room : " Nos gardes du camp de la droite furent postées au delà du village de Bleinheim, notre gauche s'étendit trop loin, à mon avis, mais c'étoit à la françoise, pour imposer; car l'Électeur, avec ses troupes, alla jusqu'au village de Lutzingen, où il prit son quartier, et avoit devant lui les bois qui s'élargissoient

tells us how he was wakened by his valet with the information that the enemy was at hand; and rubbing his eyes, as one questioning if he sees aright, he satisfied himself that there they were arranged in perfect order on his own side of the morass. The sun shone bright on both armies, and, in the true spirit of the soldier, the general describes in a few glowing words the beauty and splendour of the scene wherever the sunshine fell.[1] The morning was slightly hazy. The enemy were not prepared for the suddenness of the attack, and they were not conscious that they must fight, until they saw the heads of the columns on the ascent from their own side of the river. Hence the French troops were disposed of to some extent under the influence of a surprise; and to this is attributed a tendency to seek immediate security by finding cover or getting behind impediments, instead of studying the motions of those

vers Nordlingen. Dans cet endroit-là, nous avions devant nous, au centre, ce terrain marécageux, un ou deux hameaux, et des moulins sur ce petit ruisseau. Le village de Bleinheim étoit environné de haies et d'enclos de jardins et prairies, avec des planches ou palissades. Ce camp n'étoit pas mauvais, mais, si nous nous fussions avancés de huit cents ou mille pas de plus, nous aurions fait un front moins étendu, en appuyant toujours notre droite au Danube et notre gauche au bois, en occupant la plaine qui étoit plus étroite dans cet endroit."—I. 295.

[1] "On ne sauroit imaginer un plus beau spectacle. . . . Le plus beau soleil du monde faisoit briller les armes de ces deux armées rangées dans une plaine; de l'une à l'autre, on distinguoit la couleur des regiments; une quantité d'officiers généraux et d'aides de camp couroient et alloient çà et là; c'étoit un coup d'œil magnifique et impossible à décrire. Mais ce fut bien autre chose un moment apres." As in the shape following: "Pendant que tout cela se passoit de mon côté, les ennemis, qui avoient traversé le marais si facilement, avoient taillé en pièces sept bataillons françois, tout nouvellement levés, qu'ils avoient trouvés tout seuls dans le centre, sans qu'il en soit échappé un seul homme. Ils étoient dans la plaine, et n'étoient soutenus par personne."
—P. 301 et seq.

who were to attack, and forming themselves so as most effectively to meet the attack. The village of Blenheim was strongly ditched and palisaded, and there a large portion of the French army was suddenly posted.

The autobiographer already cited—somewhat neutral in his sympathies, though he belonged to the defeated army—describes the occupation of Blenheim by so large a portion of the army as an act not done under specific command, and hints that it was the resource of troops heartless and timid seeking a refuge. He shows also that much of the peril and death in the great tragedy was caused by what he sarcastically calls the laudable custom of the French in setting on fire whatever they found to be combustible.

The character of Blenheim, as of the other towns and villages in the great plain, may account for the peculiarity that the troops found their way within its shelter not by distinct military organisation but in a mob. These collections of houses, rather than towns, are evidently at present such as they were then, though the historical causes of their peculiarities have long passed away. They were the resource of a people rich in agricultural produce, but so cursed by war that they dared not keep their wealth in rural homesteads. Hence the farmers of a district and their workers agglomerated themselves into groups of barns and houses. At dawn the workmen may still be seen radiating out from their abodes, all round the unarranged and streetless groups of houses; and in the evening, in the hay harvest, there are to be seen along the paved roads long processions of large waggons bringing home the produce.

Several hours passed ere the passage of the army over the Nebel was completed. The enemy's army filled a long line, inviting attack at various points; but the fighting was concentrated against the fortified village of Blenheim, with its crowd of inmates. It was repeatedly assailed in vain at the cost of many lives; and it was said that the impetuous Lord Cutts, who led the assailants, furiously attempted to tear down the palisades, as an example and encouragement to his followers to force their way through the defences. It appeared, however, that the distribution of forces whence the village had acquired its strength, was a cause of fatal weakness elsewhere. The whole line, from Hochstadt to Blenheim, was weak, and at some places destitute of defence by infantry. Marlborough directed a charge in great force upon the line, and broke it. A strong transverse force thus separated the right of the French army from the centre and the left. The condition of inequality in numbers was thus inverted; and in the inversion there was an exaggeration of the proportions, for the allies fought with an army not much above half their own in number. When the inferior force had been sufficiently weakened, Marlborough directed a general charge of cavalry, which scattered them to the right and the left, those on one side seeking safety in Hochstadt, and on the other finding no refuge save by swimming the Danube, where multitudes were drowned. The commander, Tallard, had to surrender himself to the Prince of Hesse; and it is said that, being near-sighted, he mistook the force under the Prince's command for part of his own army.

The battle was now gained, but there remained an affair of solemn import to both sides. Twelve thousand men were shut up in the village of Blenheim. All efforts by their commander, the Marquis of Clairanbault, to obtain instructions from his superiors, had failed. Perhaps he did not know the fate of the day. However this may have been, he mysteriously disappeared. It was supposed that he had crept out of the village to seek instructions at his headquarters, and that, getting entangled in the rush of fugitives from the main army, they swept him into the Danube, where he was drowned. What made the strong defence of the position against the early attacks, now only kept its holders in a trap, where they were surrounded by the whole victorious army of the allies. They showed vigour and courage, but to no possible end. They attempted to make sorties, after the manner of invested garrisons; but there were essential differences that baffled such attempts at the outset. The fortress has outworks, within the protection of which sallying-parties can form so as to fall on the besiegers in battle array; and when it is necessary, they can again come within the shelter of the outworks. But the unfortunates in Blenheim could only run out in the vain hope of forming themselves in rank outside, and with the certainty of being immediately slain. It was a period of awful suspense to the assailants as well as the assailed, for the solemn question arose, Was the victor, according to the hard law of a soldier's duty, to do the worst he could against the enemy if that enemy continued obstinate? The whole of Marlborough's army surrounded the village, with not only the cannon orig-

inally in its possession, but those taken from the
enemy. The troops in the village were so closely
packed, that we hear of the small area of the churchyard affording relief to the pressure. Must the victor
then pound the village in a cannonade, and crush
the twelve thousand under its shattered houses ? [1]

This gloomy juncture is enlivened by an incident
exemplifying the indomitable elasticity of the spirit
of the Frenchman, and his instinct for the enjoyment
of the mocking spirit of his intellect under the most
tragic conditions. Two figures were seen to approach
the doomed crowd. One was a French officer, the

---

[1] By high modern professional authority, it is held that 4000 is the
utmost number of troops that could with safety and advantage have
been posted in such a place as the village of Blenheim (Kausler, Atlas
der merkwurdigsten Schlachten, p. 112). A contemporary military
critic, however, who was in the service of the Elector, and must have
known everything that could be known of the affair, says : " C'est une
chose inouïe qu'un corps de 26 bataillons et de 12 escadrons, qui étoit
dans un village, se soit rendu prisonniers de guerre."—Mém. du Marquis Maffei, ii 41. We have this from Westerloo : " Le premier feu de
l'attaque de ce village ne fut pas plutôt commencé, que les deux lignes
d'infanterie, qui faisoient vingt-sept bataillons, et qui avoient ordre de
soutenir le village, à ce que je dois croire, y entrèrent fort prématurément
et mal à propos. On y fit encore entrer douze régiments de dragons, pied
à terre, quand dix bataillons non-seulement l'auroient pu défendre, mais
l'auroient mieux défendu que toute cette armée qui auroit été de bien
meilleur usage ailleurs. Elle fut là pour se perdre et perdre le tout ;
elle s'embarrassoit tellement, que les hommes, étant entassés les uns sur
les autres, ne pouvoient se remuer et ne pouvoient recevoir ni ordre ni
commandement. Après cela pas un seul coup des ennemis n'étoit perdu,
tandis qu'ils ne pouvoient atteindre l'ennemi que par le feu de ceux qui
se trouvoient en avant, et ne pouvoient pas toujours tirer, tant par las-
situde que parce que leurs armes crevoient. Ceux de derrière étoient
tués sans pouvoir atteindre l'ennemi, et, s'ils vouloient tirer, ce ne
pouvoit être que sur nos propres gens et sans voir où. Outre cela,
comme nos troupes elles-mêmes mirent le feu au village, ces pauvres
gens se grilloient parmi les toits et les poutres des maisons qui tom-
boient de toutes parts, et se brûloient au milieu de cette petite Troie
qu'ils s'étoient allumée eux-mêmes."—I. 303, 304.

other in his uniform proclaimed himself an officer of
rank in the British army.   Was this latter a prisoner
brought to them by one of themselves?   Were they
then able, at the conclusion of that disastrous day, to
say they had made prisoner a British officer?   Such
was the tenor of the grim merriment in which the two
were received.   The British officer was Lord Orkney,
accompanied by one of the French prisoners, to represent to his fellow-soldiers the hopelessness of their
position, and to beseech them to surrender.[1]   It was
a bitter alternative.   The true soldier, in the choice
of his profession, has thrown his life as a stake that
may be taken up at any time.   He cannot accept the
alternative of saving it by anything that has the
faintest tinge of grudging it.   Yet there may be
occasions where one who has responsibility for many
other lives as well as his own, may seek and find
the more honourable alternative in the act that must
preserve all; and such surely was the condition of
those who consented to the surrender of the village
of Blenheim.   There is little doubt that the surrender
was a mighty relief to Marlborough, looking to the
horrible work that had to be done if the imprisoned
mob continued defiant.

The dealing against the common enemy of a blow
such as this, when its weight was weighed against
that of the dubious, hesitating achievements of the

[1] Voltaire, who enjoyed this characteristic incident, had it from Lord
Orkney : "Un de ces officiers nomme Des Nouvilles, revint a cheval
un moment après dans le village avec Milord Orkney du nom D'Hamilton. ' Est-ce un Anglais prisonnier que vous nous amenez ?' lui dirent
les officiers en l'entrant. ' Non, messieurs, je suis prisonnier moi-même,
et je viens vous dire, qu'il n'y a d'autre parte pour vous que de vous
rendre prisonniers de guerre.' "—Siècle, ch. ix.

expertest generals of the age, is expressed emphatically but unconsciously by Marlborough himself when he writes to his Sarah,—" My dearest life, if we could have another such day as Wednesday last, I should then hope we might have such a peace as that I might enjoy the remaining part of my life with you." [1]

No doubt the victory was heavily paid for in the vital expenditure that all victories demand. The loss on the side of the victors was estimated at 4500 killed and 7500 wounded.[2] The dead on the other side were not to be counted—no one could tell how many had been swept away by the Danube. In intercepted correspondence, alarmists on the enemy's side were found estimating the missing at 40,000. But there were several causes besides death or wounds tending to thin the enemy's camp. The prisoners amounted to between thirteen and fourteen thousand. Of these, above a fifth, being Bavarian Germans, joined the Imperial army. Uncontrolled by the presence of a French force and the organisation of a Bavarian army in alliance with France, the Elector's scattered troops found their way in groups to the camp that represented, or went nearest in that day to representing, their Fatherland. The garrison of Ulm capitulated and surrendered on terms. They were both French and Bavarians, to be escorted to Strasburg; but the bulk of the Bavarians refused to be taken into French territory—or, as an Italian officer in the Bavarian service puts it, they deserted.[3]

[1] Coxe, i. 9.   [2] Ibid., p. 4.
[3] " Mais la plupart des Bavarois deserterent en chemin pour returner au Bavière, comme avoient fait paraillement ceux qui étoient avec l'Electeur."—Mém. du Marquis Maffei, ii. 56.

The Elector had now been taught that in preferring the service of all-conquering France to the defence of Germany in her hour of peril, he had made a mistake. He sought safety in French territory, and reached Strasburg with a rapidity that savoured of flight. The Electress fled from Munich; but she found herself among more dangerous neighbours when she was hurried on by torrents of fugitives pursued by enemies whose blood was heated by victory and the fierce excitement of the chase, and returned to her home. It is not to be supposed that, in this foolish flight, she expressed an apprehension that the British and German troops under Marlborough's command were a restoration of the hordes of Attila; but her conduct was an example of the panic-fright that shot through all the territory immediately influenced by the result of the battle.[1]

[1] On the 21st Marlborough writes to his wife, " The poor Electress has taken five of her children with her, and is following her husband." And again, on the 25th : " The Elector of Bavaria has sent his wife and children back to Munich, and this morning, by a trumpet, has writ to me, and in it a letter to the Electress, open. It has made my heart ache, being very sensible how cruel it is to be separated from what one loves. I have sent it to her by a trumpet of my own, with assurances that her answer shall be carefully delivered to the Elector ; for I take pleasure in being easy when the service does not suffer by it."—Coxe, i. 13.

Critical readers of history are well acquainted with a method by which those who have to tell an unwelcome story mask the misfortunes under successful details. There has been a gallant and effective charge —an assault has been successfully resisted — more or less, here and there, corps and divisions have covered themselves with glory, &c., until the total sum of the conclusion is covered over, and bungles pass unnoticed. The first announcement of the battle of Blenheim, in the ' Gazette of Paris,' is a fair specimen of this method :—

" Les Anglais chargerent de nouveau la Gendarmerie qu'ils rompirent : son Altesse Electorale la rallia, et avant esté sourenùe par la cavalerie, les ennemis furent encore repoussez. Cependant, l'aile gauche

Thus the two illustrious leaders who expected to be successively and separately attacked by a superior force, found by a signal fatality that their enemy, by his blunders, conferred on them the opportunity for

et l'infanterie commandée par le Marquis de Blainville, avoient en cinq differentes charges, toujours enfoncé, et rompu la droite des ennemis avec un grand carnage, gagné l'artillerie et pris beaucoup d'étandarts et de drapeaux : de manière que l'Electeur crut la victorie certain. Mais il apprit en ce temps là, que la cavalerie de l'aile droite ayant esté attaquée par les ennemis avec de nouvelles forces, ils l'avoient entièrement defaite, et qu'ayant passé la ruisseau ils au avoient rempli de leurs troupes le terrain qu'elle occupoit. Alors son Altesse Electorale voyant le nuit approcher, et craignant d'estre envelopée, jugea qu'il estoit temps de faire retraite. Il envoya avertir l'infanterie, qui estoit encore auprès du village, au nombre de vingt-sept bataillons, avec quatre régimens de dragons, et qui avoit toûjours battu les ennemis, de se retirer, ce qu'elle pouvoit faire aisement. Neanmoins ceux qui la commandoient s'opiniâtrerent à garder leur poste, ce qui causa la perte de la bataille ; les ennemis ayant jusques là, perdu beaucoup plus de gens que l'Electeur de Bavière, mais ils en furent dédommagez avec avantage par la prise de ses bataillons, et des quatre régimens de dragons, qui furent ensuite obligez de se rendre. Le reste de l'armée par les soins du Maréchal de Marcin, se retira en très bon ordre, sans qu'aucun bataillon ni escadron se rompit, faisant de temps en temps volte-face et des furieuses décharges sur les ennemis qui ne les suivrent pas long-temps, on arriva de cette manière à Lauingen, où une partie de la cavalerie de la droite s'estoit ralliée avec quelque infanterie. Les bagages n'ont pas esté perdus ainsi que les ennemis l'ont publié, et ils n'ont pris que vingt-cinq à trente pièces de canon."—Gazette, 6th September, pp. 418, 419.

Voltaire will not readily be understood as abridging the same story when he says : " Environ douze mille morts, quatorze mille prisonniers, tout le canon, un nombre prodigieux d'étandards et de drapeaux, les tentes, les équipages, le général de l'armée et douze cents officiers de marque au pouvoir du vainqueur, signalerent cette journée. Les fuyards se disperserent ; près de cent lieues de pais furent perdues en moins d'un mois."

" L'étonnement et la consternation saisirent la cour de Versailles, accoutumée à la prospérité. La nouvelle de la défaite vint au milieu des réjouissances pour la naissance d'un arrière-petit-fils de Louis XIV. Personne n'osait apprendre au roi une vérité si cruelle. Il fallut que Madame de Maintenon se chargeât de lui dire qu'il n'était plus invincible."—Voltaire : Siècle de Louis XIV.. ch. 19.

executing that powerful tactic upon himself.[1]   That
two separate battles were fought on that memorable
day is typified in the custom of one half the world
speaking of the battle of Hochstadt, and the other
of the battle of Blenheim.

The deficiencies and blunders of the French commander have been amply exposed by his countrymen.[2]
But the one fundamental error—the error that, in
itself irretrievable and the source of all the others—
was, when a general of Catinat's capacity, with such
troops as he commanded, permitted himself to be
within fighting reach of Marlborough, with an army
such, in discipline and physical condition, as Marlborough commanded.   There were many reasons on
the French side why a battle should be delayed.   It
was believed that Villeroi would soon bring up a
reinforcement, and that such a line of communication
would be laid between the Rhine and the Danube as
should enable King Louis, drawing on his inexhaustible resources, to surround Marlborough's force, and

[1] The effectiveness of the policy of striking an enemy in detail became popularly known from its high favour with the great Napoleon,
and especially from his reliance on it for success in the Waterloo
campaign.

[2] The author of the 'Life of Marlborough,' printed for the great
Napoleon, " Point d'éclaireurs, point de gardes avancées, point de pré-
cautions pour disputer avec succès le passage du ruisseau; et plus que
tout cela, un mauvais ordre de campement et de bataille, qui faisoit
des armées combinées, des armées separées,"—so completely separated
that " on eût crue qu'elles ne combattoient pour la même cause," so
was " toute disposé pour être battue " (i. 348, 349).   The author, however,
discredits, and with reason, a story told by Voltaire, how Tallard, on
the evening before the battle, wrote to Villars an account of the position
of both armies, with his proposed plan for fighting; that Villars sent
the document to his brother-in-law De Maisons, with the comment that
if Tallard carried out his intentions, he would be certainly defeated;
and that the whole was shown to King Louis and made public (i. 361).

cut off his retreat. The allies would in the meantime
be starved, for they already felt a pressure on the
resources of the accessible parts of the country. All
these considerations should have suggested to Tallard
the prudence of getting out of reach by establishing
a fortified camp, or going behind strong lines; but
the same considerations constrained Marlborough to
the alternative of immediate battle.

The letters written from the field by British officers
—those of their great leader especially—have a tone
rather of weighty responsibility and solemn thankfulness than of exultation. There is more of the duty
of using rightly the great success achieved than of
the vaunting glory of victory. The defeat of the
enemy is treated as the destiny in the hands of a
higher Power, in whose dispensations the army and
its commanders are the humble instruments; even in
the acknowledgment of a higher Power there is but
that giving of the glory which seems to express a reflection of its lustre still brightening the human instrument. So Marlborough, whose announcements of
success had chiefly to be written in the French language, of " la grande victoire, que le bon Dieu a
donnée aux hauts allies," leaves no trace that a thirst
for further glorious victories is created. All the fond-
est hopes founded on the greatness of the success—on
the terrible destruction that has overtaken the enemy
—rest on the prospect of a speedy end to the war.
But all possible resources must with all possible
promptitude be made available to the completion of
the work by driving all the French forces out of
Germany. It is no longer worth while to waste time
and force on so petty an affair as the siege of Ingol-

stadt. The fortresses will drop in when the power that holds them is paralysed, and all further blows must be aimed at the heart. It seems to have been at this point that the idea dawned on Marlborough of marching to Paris. Meanwhile even the greatness of the success carried with it its burdens of anxiety, chiefly in the possession of some 17,000 prisoners, many of them Bavarians, whose countrymen surrounded the invading army.

The news of the great victory swept through the British islands a pulsation of exulting joy that presented a rare phenomenon among a people usually exempt from flushes of excitement. But it had been a mighty relief. Depressing news had gone about, telling that the overweening commander had taken his fine army across the backbone of Europe into distant regions inhabited by enemies, and the mystery of what had become of all was solved by news that gladdened the country from the palace downwards. In Windsor Castle the window of the library is shown where the queen sat in pensive reverie when it was announced to her.

The occasion may be said to have instituted a feature peculiar to this reign, in the repeated solemn thanksgivings within the Cathedral of St Paul's for victories in the great wars. There were in all eight of these, and the queen was present at all save the last, when her infirmities would have rendered the toil oppressive. There was a happy coincidence in victory following victory just when the noble dome had been completed for rendering the national thanksgivings, with accessories unmatched throughout the world in the full conjunction of simplicity

and decorum with splendour. It has been noticed that
the place of the queen in these ceremonials had something in it that hinted at a more vitally ecclesiastical claim of supremacy than that of the Crown's
authority over benefices and dignities. Within the
house of God she took precedence of His servant the
bishop. "The council declared that the cathedral
for that day, being the queen's chapel royal, the seats
were to be disposed of and all the arrangements
made by the Lord Chamberlain. The queen's throne
was exactly as in the House of Lords, about three
feet higher than the floor of the choir, covered with
a Persian carpet, and a canopy upheld by iron rods
fastened to the organ-loft, about fifteen feet high,
with an armed chair on the throne, with a footstool
before it, and a desk for the queen's book, covered
with crimson velvet richly embroidered and fringed
with gold, and with a cushion thereon of the same."
The Lords and Commons, the great officers of State,
the ornamental part of the great corporation of
London,—all graced the ceremony, and rendered it
almost a duplicate of the coronation.[1]

[1] Milman, 'Annals of St Paul's,' p. 429, and Proclamation there
cited. The recollection of these august and memorable ceremonials
might possibly enhance the amazement that overtakes every stranger
in London when he beholds the statue of Queen Anne perched
on its hideously broken pedestal, surrounded by its shattered group
of symbolical figures before the noble tympanum of the cathedral. It is like a portion of the devastation that used to cause a
shudder in passing Leicester Square, but it might have been the
apology there that the district was in a manner consecrated to moral
filth, occasionally lifting itself to the dignity of crime. It may be
pleaded that by law and constitution there is no one responsible for
the preservation of the Queen Anne statuary group in front of St
Paul's; but is it creditable to the ecclesiastical hierarchy and to the
city of London that this defect in our institutions should be in a
loathsome shape flared in the eyes of the world? It might be expected

Among the other symptoms of joyous excitement, the poetic muse naturally had a revival, with vitality enough to send forth at least one effort destined to live, "The Campaign," by Addison. It has many happy images, but aptest of all was a description of heroic calmness and self-possession in the storm of battle adorned with imagery from a recent scene of storm and terror at home.

> "So when an angel by divine command
> With rising tempests shakes a guilty land,
> Such as of late o'er pale Britannia past,
> Calm and serene he drives the furious blast ;
> And, pleased the Almighty's orders to perform,
> Rides on the whirlwind and directs the storm."

Though on the great occasion the muse soared to this height, yet it also crawled in abundant doggerel. It might not be counted an irreverence either to the hero or the bard to cite some specimens of the humble tributes offered from the literature of the illiterate, yet such an anthology scarcely seems congenial with the occasion. But a comprehensive author of the day, who measured swords with Pope as poet and Burnet as historian, seems to demand that his ambitious claim should be tested. The 'History of England,' in three folio volumes, written by John Oldmixon, places its author as the historical champion of the Revolution policy against Brady

that of the warm and worthy citizens who pass this object in the way to their devotions, some one might at his own personal cost abate the nuisance. It is not recommended by a traditional effort of the Cockney muse to find inspiration in the queen's posture, thus :—

> "Poor Queen Anne, she is left in the lurch,—
> Her face to the gin-shop—her back to the church."

and other vindicators of what is called the Tory policy of the later years of Queen Anne's reign, though what was written in this cause would have conveniently fitted itself to the occasion had the Stewart line been restored. With this explanation, a passage from a very ambitious song of triumph is dropped into a note.[1]

[1] " A pastoral Poem on the Victories of Schellenburgh and Blein- heim, obtained by the Arms of the Confederates under the command of his Grace the Duke of Marlborough over the French and Bavarians. With a large preface, showing the antiquity and dignity of Pastoral Poetry. By Mr Oldmixon. London, 1704."

The pastorality consists in Menelaus,

> "The father of the field, whose artful strains
> Sweeten our sorrows and relieve our pains,"

assenting to the request of Thyrsis to

> "Come to this shade, and by Sabrina's stream
> Of wonders sing, and Churchill be thy theme."

Perhaps the most ambitious, if not the best part of his song :—

> "Just to himself and his intrepid troops,
> In heaven and them he centres all his hopes.
> With safe and speedy pace he moves to scour
> The Swabian woods, and curb tyrannic power :
> The Gallic wolf and the Bavarian boar
> Wide waste commit along the Danube's shore,
> But tremble as the British lions roar.
> Till then the rebel and his false ally
> Assembled Europe's distant power defy ;
> Pale terror seizes 'em at CHURCHILL'S name,
> Conscious of present guilt and future shame :
> In vain to cities or to bogs they fly,
> And with their rising ramparts reach the sky.
> No works for Britons are too strong, no walls too high.
>
> . . . . . .
>
> The thunders and the sulph'rous blaze of war
> But warm the Britons whom 'twas meant to scare ;
> Dauntless they rush amid the flames and smoke,
> And death's dread fury by their rage provoke."

The Roman eagle has " fallen so low that he despairs to rise " :—

> "But see—at CHURCHILL'S awful name he springs
> Aloft, and spreading his imperial wings,
> With steady eye to prove his rightful sway,
> Awhile he gazes on the burning day,
> Then towers above his foe, his right maintains,
> And drives the rout obscene from the ethereal plains."

The first material effect of the battle was to neutralise Bavaria. The Elector was in Flanders; and the Electress, as regent, had no alternative but compliance with the demand to disband the Electoral army and conclude a peace. The French army wandered rather than retreated through the Black Forest to the Rhine. Ulm surrendered, but Landau was still an obstacle, and Prince Eugene remained before it with a besieging force. In an estimate of the military and the geographical conditions, it was decided that the valley of the Moselle was the best road to the heart of France; and the first stage in that direction was the taking and occupation of the ancient Roman city of Treves, with its fortifications and its serviceable old stone bridge over the Moselle. Meanwhile, Marlborough visited Berlin and Hanover; and in his polished diplomacy, following on so decided an acquisition of practical strength, he succeeded in obtaining from Prussia a contingent of 8000 men, to be employed in the meantime in assisting the Duke of Savoy. Quickly followed the honours appropriate to so great an achievement. At home a gift was made to Marlborough of the Honour and Manor of Woodstock, where now stands the palace of Blenheim. He obtained from the Emperor the signal distinction of being inaugurated a Prince of the Holy Roman Empire, as ruler and possessor of the principality of Mindelheim, on the tract of plains and low hills that may be seen from the steeple of the cathedral of Ulm.

CHAPTER VII.

𝕿𝖍𝖊 𝖀𝖓𝖎𝖔𝖓.

WHEN we left the question of an incorporating union
between England and Scotland, the completion of the
project appeared to stand farther off than ever, since
discussion seemed only to afford an opportunity for
discovering obstacles insuperable. Among the points
at issue both in the Scots Estates and at the meetings
of the Commissioners, Scotland's great adventure in the
Indian and African trade naturally came up along with
the question how far England would accept it as balancing in favour of Scotland the privileged companies
of England. The dealing with the matter, though

slight and casual, was significant enough to be ominous of mischief. In the course of the conference, the Scots Commissioners, on the 27th of January, offered to the English a condition that the privileges of "the Company of Scotland trading to Africa and the Indies do continue and stand in full force and vigour in favour of the proprietors of the said Company, after the union of the two kingdoms." To this there came from the English side the chilling answer: "Their lordships say, it has been found by experience that two companies existing together in the same kingdom, and carrying on the same traffic, are destructive of trade; and are therefore of opinion that to agree to this proposition will be inconsistent with the interests of Great Britain." The Scots reiterated their claim, suggesting the alternative of purchasing the pecuniary interests invested in the Company, when further discussion was closed by the queen's letter of adjournment.[1]

Through a succession of incidents unparalleled in history, it befell that this part of the national quarrel was to be fought out by the rival companies.

A vessel belonging to the Scots Company, named the Annandale, put into the Thames, either to be repaired or to raise the full complement of her crew. The vessel was to go on a trading voyage to the East Indies. Those who had control over the vessel did not commit the folly of beginning the voyage in England; that would have been, whether she was manned by Englishmen or Scotsmen, an invasion of a monopoly which no one questioned, so far as trading from England was concerned. The vessel was

[1] Bruce. ccclxi. 3.

to return to Scotland, and then it would be as independent of English law or monopoly as if it had been owned in Amsterdam or Hamburg, and had returned to its own port, after having,been for a time in English waters. The East India Company, under their prerogative powers, seized the vessel. There was evidence sufficient to prove that it was to be employed in the trade sacred to the East India Company, and it was within the jurisdiction of the English courts of law. At the conclusion of a litigation, where we are told that parties were amply heard, the Annandale was forfeited. This was not only deemed to be a notable national insult, but was a serious addition to the calamities that had befallen the Scots Company. Of course the mischief that must follow such an act was strongly urged by the Scots ministers on the English Government ; but it was one of the many occasions when the law had to take its course, be the political results what they might. In England, and scarcely anywhere else at that period, the subject's legal rights were absolute, as against prerogative and diplomacy. It was a homage to personal liberty and rights for which the nation had sometimes to pay heavily, as on the occasion of the arresting of the ambassador of the Czar for debts to London tradesmen.

Just as the Scots were roused to fury, the astounding news swept over the country that a vessel belonging to that India Company which had flung injury and insult on Scotland had been driven into the Firth of Forth by foul weather, and was seeking shelter under the coast of Fife. This vessel was named the Worcester. The Scots Government were relieved of unpleasant difficulties and responsibilities by the enterprising gallantry of the gentleman who held the office of secretary to the Scottish Company "trading to Africa and the Indies." Without any farther authority than this his official position, he determined to try to seize the Worcester. Accordingly, one sunny afternoon in August, he found a body of friends, nineteen in all, in whom he could place absolute reliance, and the matter was to be attempted after the manner of a frolic of a dangerous and possibly tragic character. There seems to have been much curiosity among the citizens of Edinburgh to see the vessel that had done business in the mighty deep at distant India; and the crew were accustomed to exchange hospitalities with visitors. The secretary with eleven of his followers sought admission as visitors, and they were the more welcome that they brought with them great store of spirits, wine, and fruit. Other two boats, arriving separately, brought the rest of his followers; and it was the policy of the three detachments to appear to have arrived fortuitously, and to know nothing of each other. It was inferred from the respect paid by his followers to the secretary, that he was some great man, and the officers of the Worcester were ambitious of making his acquaintance. This suited his project, and he had them all in the cabin joining his followers in a thoroughly jovial revel,—it was the secretary's design to seize them there, and, as he said, "render the common sailors headless." The secretary was bidding good-bye, his galley was waiting for him, when suddenly, his party being outside the door, closed it on the officers of the Worcester, and fairly entrapped them. The assailants were thoroughly armed with hidden weapons, and they found no difficulty in seizing the ordinary crew in detachments. The secretary states that the crew were double the number of his own party—they must have thus numbered thirty-eight—a crew in its size inferring business beyond the mere handling of a trading vessel in that day.

So was accomplished a feat that, if we look on it in its abstract nature, without estimating precedents and consequents, was as absolute an act of treachery as the massacre of Glencoe, and, indeed, closely resembled the strategy of that tragedy. As it befell, no one was even wounded, but there might have been bloodshed to any amount; fortunately the affair was free of any such tragic embarrassment. The name of the hero in this brilliant affair was Roderick Mackenzie. Whatever may have been his capacity as a secretary, he proved himself to be a skilful and intrepid military commander, yet his name is unknown to fame, and is only to be found after diligent search.

The hatches, gunroom, and other "keepings" being closed, and sealed with the seal of the great Scots Company, a force under the order of the Company was drafted on board, so that it might be unnecessary to hold the crew of the Worcester, against whom no man then felt enmity, in bondage. It was whispered that this was not a just act of retaliation; that the Worcester, instead of belonging to the great English East India Company which had seized the Annandale, belonged to another company of recent formation, which the India Company was treating despitefully in its usual tyrannical way. But the affair was not a paltry rivalry among trading companies. The seizure of the Worcester was a blow dealt by Scotland against England. It was essentially a *casus belli*, taking that diplomatic definition in its exact sense, not as a ground for declaring war, but as an act inferring the existence of war—an act such as a nation does not commit unless it is already virtually at war, whether the war has been declared or not.

But fate had still further stimulants in store for feeding the fires of national wrath blazing throughout Scotland. News were received of the capture of one of the Scots Company's vessels, and the slaughter of all the crew, in distant Eastern waters; and that the perpetrators of the crime were Englishmen required little evidence to gain belief. By a concurrence that seemed to imply some more solemn agency than mere chance and coincidence, the crew of the Worcester in their tipsy orgies had afforded glimpses of dark secrets, hinting at deeds of violence that let them see the finger of God in their present troubles.

Daniel Defoe, with all his sound English sense, had a fervid hankering after special providences and other preternatural interventions in human affairs, especially when they pointed to tragic conclusions; and on this occasion his ears were greedily open to all rumours of incidents tending to the revelation of a special providence, the while decorating the rumours as they came with his own solemn meditations thus:—

"Some of the ship's crew, whether in their drink or otherwise, let fall some words implying that they had been pirating, and particularly some very suspicious discourses, intimating that there had been blood in the case. . . . From a little to more—from dark expressions they fell to downright quarrelling and calling one another names, which there seems to be good reason to believe might in part be true on both sides; for some of them, however innocent of this matter, had been, it seems, guilty of wickednesses of other sorts black enough. This folly of theirs came at last to such a height that it could be no longer concealed; for it became the public discourse that they had been guilty not of murder and piracy only, but of uncommon barbarities; and not that only, but that it was particularly on a Scots ship and Scotsmen —particularly Captain Drummond and his crew.

"At length it was brought to the ears of the Government, and as the public justice of all nations is obliged to take cognisance of such horrid things as were here suggested, the fellows were examined, and they frankly confessing, Green and five of his men were taken up. The positive evidence was only two negroes, but others so corroborated what they said, and circumstances concurring to make almost everybody believe the fact, at least in that hurry, they were, upon a long hearing, severally found guilty of piracy and murder.

"There are sometimes such crises, such junctures in matters, when all things shall concur to possess, not a man but even a nation, with a belief of what at another time they would not believe even upon the same evidence; and in this, man seems actuated by a sort of preternatural influence, as if invisibly directed to bring to pass some particular thing pointed out by Providence to be done for reasons of His own, and known only to His inscrutable wisdom.

"Just such a case this seems to be. The circumstances of Green and his crew were very unhappy for them ; their being put into Scotland, where they had no manner of business—no distress to force them in ; their being seized by the Company ; the men falling out among themselves, and being the only instruments of detecting what no one ever could have charged them with ; their staying there when they might have gone and had no more business there— from whence some alleged that they had no power to depart. These and more concurring circumstances, which were observed by the most curious—and some of which were noted in the trial—seemed to jump together so visibly, that all people seemed to acknowledge a wonderful and invisible hand in it, directing and pointing out the detecting some horrible crime, which vengeance suffered not to go unpunished." [1]

It would be difficult to find, in the history of the administration of justice, a trial conducted with more solemnity and deliberation, and bearing on the face of the proceedings more anxiety for fair dealing, than that of Captain Green and his crew. The first step in it was a long investigation by the Secret Council. [2] As the result of this preliminary investigation, the Council gave order that Thomas Green, the commander of the Worcester, and eighteen others from among the subordinate officers and seamen, ultimately limited to fourteen, should be brought to trial before the Justiciary Court of the Admiralty, for the crimes

[1] Hist. of the Union, 4to, 1786, pp. 78-80.
[2] See " The Trial of Captain Thomas Green and his crew at the High Court of Admiralty of Scotland, 4th Anne, A.D. 1705."—St. Tr., xiv. 1199 *et seq.*

of piracy, robbery, and murder.   The judge of the
Court of Admiralty representing to the Council the
importance of the case, desired that he might have
" assessors " or skilled advisers to assist him ; and
there were to this end named Lords Loudon and
Belhaven, Home of Blackadder, and two judges of
the Court of Session, Dundas of Arniston and Cockburn of Ormiston.   There were six counsel for the
defence.   An ordinary reader of the trial in the present
day would probably be surprised by the quantity of
inappropriate learning scattered through it in citations
from the ' Corpus Juris,' and from eminent foreign
commentators on that majestic collection,—as Math-
æus, Monocheus, Carpzovius, and Andreas Gailius.
There was something in this parade of learning beyond
either the reality or the display of signal impartiality
in the trial.   Where the law of nations was concerned,
England was driven out of the provincial strongholds
of her common law.   This process of ejectment was
at the time in rapid operation ; for the country could
not protect its advancing foreign commerce unless
it admitted the quick and simple processes of the general mercantile law of Europe, founded on the civil
law, the simplicity and flexibility of which fitted it
for immediately dealing with notes of hand, bills of
exchange, policies of insurance, and other novelties in
advancing commerce.   Especially was the practice in
questions of shipping and navigation a creature of this
law—in other words, of the imperial law which the
Romans had left for the service of all the civilised
world.   Excepting the feudal customs for the tenure
of land rights, the Scots had no other law but the
civil, and this was an occasion for displaying their

mastership of its mysteries before the world, and especially before the lawyers of England less endowed in the same accomplishments.

It had been found on an examination by experts sent to search and unload the Worcester, "that the goods aboard her were not stowed as merchant goods used to be, but were found in the hold in such confusion as if taken by piracy and no otherwise." It seemed to be put beyond doubt that the Worcester with part of her crew had fought another vessel, and though it was not proved which was the aggressor, the Worcester was victorious, and the crew of the other were killed and thrown overboard. Of what was heard during the scuffle, enough was reported to identify the victims as natives of Britain. This affair occurred on the coast of Malabar.

The scattered evidence leading to this conclusion revealed the source of all the difficulties of the case. This was the prevalence of piracy at that period, as not only the sole business of a community of avowed sea rovers and robbers, but as affording inducement to the professed trader to transact casual piracies as any dispute on the waters national or personal gave him the opportunity. Persons who have occasion for closely observing the administration of criminal justice in this day, believe the condemnation and punishment of a purely innocent person are, in this country at least, next to impossible, but that it is a thing very likely to happen that a habitual criminal is punished for some act not committed by him, and he accepts his fate with equanimity, and possibly a touch of thankfulness that the eyes of justice took the direction that they did take, instead of

tracking him more accurately in to some more
serious disaster. Many a sea commander at that
time could feel with Green, that "conscience doth
make cowards of us all."

And somehow conscience seemed to aid the conclusion that suited the feeling of Scotland. A vessel
called The Speedy Return, belonging to the great
national company, had been long absent. Those
who were most interested and anxious about her fate
heard through indefinite rumours that she had fallen
into the hands of pirates, and that her commander,
Captain Drummond, and all his crew, had been murdered. Was this, then, the feat that the Worcester
had performed? Suspicion strengthened into a
fixed certainty; and by a strange fatality the con-
vivial and penitential talk of the crew of the Worcester had appeared to accept the same conclusion.
Whether it was that they could not or that they
dared not tell who they were who had been fought
with, they said nothing to contradict the story about
Drummond, but rather gave hints to confirm it.

The preliminary adjustments for the trial began
on the 12th of February, the trial itself began on the
5th of March, and the jury rendered their verdict on
the 14th. It involved guilt against all the accused
except John Reynold, the second mate, who was
found to "have been ashore at the time of the action
libelled." Here, then, were fourteen men to be condemned to death. Perhaps the judges shrank from
the exhibition of so many human beings hanged at
once—perhaps they felt that the affair would have
less the aspect of a triumphal sacrifice to national
vengeance were the executions adjusted deliberately

and in detail. Green with four others were sentenced to suffer on the 4th of April; other four on the 11th of April; other five on the 18th. The place of execution was the open beach adjoining Leith, within high-water mark.

The tragic history was nearly closed, when a story was told to account otherwise for the disappearance of Captain Drummond. He had fallen into the hands of pirates, not on the Malabar coast where the Worcester had seized a vessel, but at the great island of Madagascar. The Scots Company's vessel was picking up negroes for the slave market, when " five several persons who afterwards appeared to be pirates, armed with pistols, swords, and other weapons, came on board the said Speedy Return, with a pretence to buy something, and taking advantage of the said Thomas Drummond, Andrew Wilkie his surgeon, and several of the said ship's company being on shore and others working in the hold, the said five persons by force of arms took possession of the said ship, and immediately made a signal, upon which about forty or fifty other pirates came on board." And so The Speedy Return was taken and burnt, her commander Captain Drummond remaining in Madagascar. Such was the purport of an affidavit made at Portsmouth on the 31st of March. More than twenty years afterwards, when the affair had been obliterated by other political influences, a book confirming the material part of this story in an account of Drummond's adventures in Madagascar, scarcely attracted attention as a historical revelation.[1]

[1] Madagascar; or, Robert Drury's Journal during Fifteen Years'

This trial is often cited as exemplifying the value of, and the danger of deserting, the great principle of the English law called the *corpus delicti*—the proving separately by full evidence that a crime, especially if the crime charged be murder, has been committed, as a separate process of evidence from that which brings it home to the guilty party. The English law in its especial fastidiousness, when the charge is for taking life, has established the preliminary process of a coroner's inquest. But it was found necessary to make the practice of piracy, or the adoption of the profession of a pirate, in itself a crime. Indefiniteness was pleaded in Green's case. The references to Drummond and The Speedy Return were collateral matters casually fitting themselves to the evidence; and against the substantive charge in the indictment it was pleaded that there was no " name, designation, or any other sign or evidence by which the ship alleged to be seized might be particularly distinguished, nor yet the persons' names alleged to be murdered, or to whom the ship and goods robbed did belong." But it was maintained for the Crown that under this plea of indefiniteness, " if in the road of Leith, before hundreds of spectators, one ship should invade another, destroy her men, seize her goods, and sink the vessel, whereby none of all these could be condescended upon, there could be no criminal libel upon it because of the defence of indefiniteness." [1]

The criminal law of Scotland had been driven to indefiniteness in dealing with the Highland and

Captivity in that Island : 1729.   See also the 'Gentleman's Magazine for 1769, p. 17.   [1] St. Tr., xiv. 1242.

Border reivers in their depredations and slaughters.
Yet even the loose lessons taught by such practice could hardly impart more indefiniteness to the
dealing with cases of piracy than a great oracle of
the English law has definitely expressed : " The
crime of piracy, or robbery and depredation upon the
high seas, is an offence against the universal law of
society,—a pirate being, according to Sir Edward
Coke, *hostis humani generis.* As, therefore, he has
renounced all the benefits of society and government,
and has reduced himself afresh to the savage state
of nature by declaring war against all mankind, all
mankind must declare war against him ; so that
every community hath a right by the rule of self-
defence to inflict that punishment upon him which
every individual would in a state of nature have
been otherwise entitled to do, for any invasion of his
person or personal property." [1]

The Worcester was so heavily armed as to supply
her captors with eight guns, afterwards mounted on
a fort for the protection of the Firth of Forth. Any
positive evidence of her use in piracy is aided by
silence where contradiction or intervention might
have been expected. Here is a vessel apparently
seized and forfeited, and no one appears to have any
claim on her but the crew. She did not belong to
the old East India Company, and that she was originally freighted by a rival company is only put hypo-
thetically. Among the protestations against the
seizure of the vessel and condemnation of the crew,
no worshipful public company or body of merchants
claiming ownership ventures to appear.

[1] Blackstone's Commentaries, iv. 21.

Two of the condemned crew confessed that they had committed piracy and murder. So far they admitted what, on the whole evidence as we now have it, was hardly to be doubted; but when they said their victims spoke as Scotsmen, and they understood them to be Captain Drummond and his crew, we know that they must have been endeavouring to propitiate their enemies. And, indeed, to this end they gave what was more than compensation for the Portsmouth affidavit. There was in the interval between condemnation and execution a rapid correspondence between Whitehall and Holyrood. Scotland was tossed with rumours and suspicions. It went abroad that the English fleet was to blockade the Forth so far as to stop communication with France as a preliminary to the coercion of Scotland. And the suspicion so far took palpable shape in Scotland, that the Council demanded the presence of the commander of an English man-of-war that he might explain his conduct in searching certain vessels in Scottish waters, with the satisfactory result that, after treating the order with something like defiance, he had to admit, apologetically, that a mistake had been made by an officer under his command. One point was yielded to the urgent pressure from England. The first execution was postponed from the 4th to the 11th of April. This became a critical day for Scotland. Farther postponement inferred farther action. Whatever action was taken must pass through the Scots office and forms — England was helpless for any civil operations in Scotland,—she could only make war, and to that all things seemed to be drifting.

Had the law not taken its course, we have in the after-history of the Porteous Mob a recital of what the history of Edinburgh on the 11th of April 1705 would have been. On both occasions there was like preparation in the flocking of multitudes of men into Edinburgh from distant parts of the country, as persons who were to take part not in a merely local, but in a national affair. But Captain Green and two victims selected from the crew were hanged on the sands of Leith amid the sanguinary rejoicings of the mob.[1]

[1] The following letter, among the recent acquisitions in the British Museum, is interesting, not so much for any new light it affords, as because, having been written by Chancellor Seafield to Godolphin, it is a testimony to the close eye kept by this great statesman on all the influences at work in Scotland :—

"EDINBURGH, *Aprile* 11*th,* 1705.

"MY LORD,—This morning the flying pacquet concerning Captain Green arrived. Her Majesty's letter was very gracious, and we being in expectation that a letter would come about that time, the night before appointed all the councillers that were in town, which were about ten or eleven in number, to be at my house at eight o'clock in the morning. They brought me accompts that the people were convening from all places, and that there was great appearances of a tumult. All we could do was to acquaint the Magistrates of Edinburgh, and generally to be careful ; and, in the meantime, we read her Majesty's letter, and a committee read those papers and affidavits that were transmitted, and reported what was contained in them to the Board. We considered that we were but few in number, and divided in opinion, and her Majesty's principal servants were all absent—nothing that I could do could persuade them to attend the two last meetings of council. However, we thought it our duty to go to the Council Chamber together, that what we did might have the greater authority. As we went along the streets the whole people and mobb were crying for justice, and desired we might grant no reprieve. After wee were some time in council we came to be convinced that there was no possibility of preserving the publik peace, without allowing some that were thought most guilty to be executed, and therefore Captain Green, Captain Madder, and Simpsone the gunner were condescended upon, and we reprieved the rest to the nineteenth instant, and appointed a full council to meet on Tuesday preceding, and I was appointed to write a letter to her Majesty, which I have done and sent herewith. As I was returning home, the people

The three victims seem to have sufficed to quench the national thirst for blood. The other eleven were one by one released, and then dropped quietly into privacy and oblivion, as is usually the way with the criminal classes when they have narrowly escaped the sword of the law.

Scotland has tacitly accepted this affair as a national crime, palliated in some measure by critical political conditions. But we may believe that had any of the Continental powers of Europe trapped Green and his crew when transacting business in the Spanish main, or any other of the favourite hunting waters of the buccaneers, there would have been the question by torture to begin with, while all who

who heard some were to be execute did give huzzas ; but at a farther distance, the mobb being informed that a reprieve was past, did first ask me what was done with these murtherers. I told them they would have satisfaction very soon; but some of them not believing, they stopt my coach, and those at a little farther distance threw stones. At last I was forced to come out and expose myself entirely to their fury ; but when they saw me they fell imediately calm, for I did not in the least seem discomposed, and they separate to each hand, and then went into a friend's house, and none of them offered to follow. The General convened some of the regiments of guards and secured the ports of the town, and then the mob went and attended the prisoners to the place of execution. Many of the city and gentry came and waited on me home to my house, and now all is quiet, and there is no disturbance. Our divisions and factions among ourselves occasion the authority of the Government to be very low, and I have but a very bad prospect of our affairs unless we come to a better understanding after my Lord Commissioner arrives. There are few of the new party have been in town since Mr Johnston was laid aside, so I cannot inform your lordship what they will do upon it. The Treasurer-depute attends very close, and I cannot deny but he gives me assistance. Both parties will be here at the time of the Commissioner coming to town, and I shall endeavour to understand their minds, and shall write fully.

"The magistrates and ministers that did attend Captain Green and the other two that are execute, do inform me that they all three dyed declaring their innocence of the crimes for which they were condemned.

"SEAFIELD."

escaped the rope would have been chained for life to the long galleys, then employed in the coasting and river navigation of the Mediterranean and the narrow seas.

Another incident of the period, effective in scattering alarming rumours over England, was known as " the Scotch Plot." The Highlanders were to be raised twenty thousand strong in the Jacobite cause. There was to be a great *tinchel* of the deer—a hunting on a national scale—bringing together all the active men of the country with arms in their hands. The project for turning the host of sportsmen so collected into an army was the idea of a great statesman—according to Celtic statecraft—Simon Fraser of Lovat, who was to call out his own clan. He was not its chief according to the administration of the law by the Scots courts, but he was accepted by the people, and all the more beloved by them that he was a fugitive for his crimes from Saxon justice. That the Highlanders, known only as mendicants and marauders, could be rapidly embodied in an effective force, was an idea much ridiculed by the sages of the period. But it was realised twelve years afterwards, precisely in the manner suggested by Lovat—a great driving of the deer. And it was so effective forty years after our present period as to bring its inventor to the block on Tower Hill.

At the crises of the "'Forty-five," indeed, the moral gulf between the Celtic Highlander and the Saxon Lowlander had become broader and deeper than it was at our present period. This came, not from any change in the Highlander, but from the progress of civilisation, law, and wealth in the Lowlands. These

elements of progress had their reaction on the necessary conduct of the Highlander, though they made no
change in his nature. He was more closely hemmed
in among his mountains. Determined not to work
for his living if he could lay hold on the fruit of other
men's industry, he found the granges and byres and
sheepfolds ever more effectively guarded, and this
made him desperate and dangerous. As agriculture
prospered, too, its fruits became more attractive. The
Highlander ate grain and vegetables only when he
could get nothing better. And now there was prey
for him in butcher-meat close at hand—the flocks
dotting the neighbouring fields, the cattle upon a
thousand hills.

Simon Fraser of Beaufort, as he called himself, was
not yet quite twenty years old. He was, however,
"young in years but in sage council old," if it be
lawful to apply Milton's noble antithetic appreciation
of his contemporary Henry Vane to one who was a
powerful combination of ferocity and dissimulation.
On his own side of the Highland line he was as
thorough a savage as any Roderick Dhu who had
never gone farther from his lair than the most available foraging ground, and he had the subtlety of
Fouché or Talleyrand. He was accomplished, too,
and could grace a Court without much exertion.[1]
He had two great objects in life : the one to succeed
to the chief peerage of the Fraser family as Lord
Lovat, the other to be chief of the clan Fraser ; and

[1] A revered friend of the author, many years ago departed, asked
Mountstuart Elphinstone if he believed there had ever been another man
endowed in such perfection with the united qualities of ferocity, cunning, and plausibility as Lovat. The Indian statesman answered "Yes ;
he knew an Affghan chief who was his absolute duplicate."

he attained both. For the peerage he trimmed his sails towards Whitehall or St Germains as the political atmosphere suggested. The other, and far more important dignity, came to him from his own people, who were not bound by the absolutely feudal rules of Lowland hereditary succession in the adjustment. Merit had its influence in the selection, and the merits of Lovat as a leader of Highlanders to their most dearly cherished objects were egregious. There was an heiress of the house of Lovat. He approached her and appealed to her with all available blandishments; but those who were responsible for her protection shifted her beyond the radius of his influence, and events showed that they acted judiciously in so doing.

On some genealogical ground, not easily traced, he thought he might do something for his claims by becoming the husband of the widow of the Lord Lovat whose death had made room for a successor, and he resolved to effect this object after his own fashion. He sent the *crossteric*—popularly called the fiery cross—through the glens; and that symbol of absolute obedience to the call of strife or danger clustered round him some three hundred ruffians. They surrounded the house of Beaufort where the widow and a body of relations, dependants, and protectors abode with her, and kidnapped the whole party. The lady he carried to his safety retreat of Eilan Agus, an isolated rock passing up through the central depth of a roaring river, whose lateral waters chafed and tossed against the precipices of a deep mountain gorge.

Simon, knowing well enough that a forced marriage

was liable to annihilation, resolved to secure himself by violating her, judging that thus she and her friends would be at least as eager for the marriage as himself. But his plans were not to be a success. There gradually arose so powerful an apparatus of hostility against him, that had all his enemies in the Highlands suddenly become his friends it must crush him. The Secret Council, the chief tribunal in Scotland—especially the tribunal that dealt with State criminals too strong for the common courts of law—was busy in preparation for war against Fraser of Beaufort and his followers. Hence he found it expedient to go abroad beyond the reach of British justice. A mystery that many of his countrymen tried to pierce, shrouded him down to the time of his return to frighten both England and Scotland with the plot. It was a strong belief among those who professed to be best acquainted with his motions, that meanwhile he had taken orders in the Church of Rome. The belief leant to his adoption rather of the regular than of the secular branch; and it was noted that one having so many crimes to set right, found it convenient to have a confessor and absolver ever at hand, and never disturbed by scruples.

When Simon Fraser next came into notice among his countrymen, it was, to the astonishment even of those who knew him best, to announce the following project for a new revolution for restoring the house of Stewart. He had solemn promises and obligations from the several Highland chiefs to raise 10,000 men among their retainers. He professed to have obtained by personal negotiation with King Louis an auxiliary force of 5000 men, who were to be landed at Dundee, the easiest access to the north Highlands; while, to perplex Government, a nominal force of 500 were to land in the wild district round Ben Nevis, whence they would find their way to the country of the Frasers. Simon Fraser made his approaches with such signal cunning that he converted himself from the position of an exiled outlaw steeped in vulgar criminality to that of a diplomatist with the policy and destinies of sovereigns in his hands. He easily reached the ear of Mary—of the gentle Mary of Este, that queen of a sorrowful lot, the widow of the exiled King James, and mother of the Pretender. She took the whole affair to King Louis personally. Sick of the world and devoted to retirement as Queen Mary was, she could command the immediate consideration and sympathy of the mighty monarch who was the terror of Europe. She could ever touch the great redeeming feature of his character—his sense of chivalry. It had been at the service of her husband, it would remain at the service of her son, and was doubly at the service of the suffering woman. There was a strong temptation in France to encourage any project that might carry Marlborough and his army home. Lovat was put in the hands of, and fully heard by, the Marquis of Torcy and other advisers of the Crown. He boasted, as we have seen, of interviews even with the great Louis; and he had effected so much that his assertions were believed. One sees through all, however, that practical French statesmen thought the 10,000 Highlanders a vain imagination; but they were safe in the conclusion that when the Highland army became visible an auxiliary force would be sent from France.[1]

Fraser did not return alone. The French statesmen hesitated to leave in the hands of one man, and he a stranger, an enterprise of so unusual an aspect. They therefore selected as his companion, and virtually as a spy upon his motions, a cadet of an old Scots family who had become naturalised in France. He is territorially identified as the brother of Murray of Abercairny, who had a commission, in the interests of France, to accompany Fraser in his visits among the chiefs. Lovat carried a colonel's commission; and the two documents were prepared with all official solemnity, being under the sign-manual "James R.," and "given at our Court of St Germains;" while, under the English constitutional usage requiring some poor officer of State to take the responsibility of all acts of regal administration, each was countersigned "Middleton." Another and more ominous shadow haunted the emissaries' steps. Sir John Maclean, an ardent Jacobite of untainted honour, hearing among the exiles something of Fraser's machinations, and

---

[1] From the French side, the mission, with its result, is pretty well told thus: "Frazer passa en France vers 1702, et se rendit a la cour de Saint-Germain, qui sous la Reine Douairière, veuve de Jacques, était comme du vivant de ce Prince un foyer d'intrigues et de bigotisme—de projets ridicules et d'espionage. Frazer commença par capter la bienveilance de la Reine en se convertissant au Catholicisme. Il déclara ensuite qu'il s'été assuré des dispositions des principaux chefs de clans Ecossais, que ces lords étaient tout disposes à s'insurger en faveur du fils du Jacques II., pourvu que le gouvernement Français leur fournit des armes, de l'argent, et un corps auxiliaire de cinq à six mille hommes. Louis XIV et ses ministres agréerent ce projet; cependant, avant de songer à l'exécution, ils voulerent verifier si les assertions de Frazer étaient exactes."—Hoefer, Nouvelle Biographie Générale, voce "Lovat."

aware of the man's nature, dreaded the commission
of some dire treachery among his unconscious Jacobite comrades, and through hardships and imminent
perils got himself landed at Folkstone, and found his
way northwards.

There were other symptoms of political restless-
ness. Between the adherents of the Revolution
Settlement on the one side, and the Jacobites at the
other, there were many important people of uncertain
tenets as to whom it was desirable to be assured.
To clear away dubieties, a proclamation, issued by
the Privy Council of Scotland, offered oblivion and
indemnity for those who should ask it, and accept
the qualifying conditions. Of course it could not be
expected that the officers of the exiled Court, and
other exiles notorious for their devotion to Jacobitism, would seek protection in this asylum; but it
was noticed that men of mark of this class were
drifting northwards, as it was said, with the object
of securing the indemnity. At the same time, there
were rumours of large sums in gold passing from
Holland to Scotland, and of busy purchasing of
horses in Ireland for the Scots market.

These threatenings in the air, however, vanished
with the failure of the main project. The Highland
chiefs would put no faith in Fraser; and his plotting
was lost. He took the opportunity, however, ere he
was stripped of all availabilities for mischief, to per-
petrate a piece of malice against his old enemy, Atholl.
He had been intrusted with a letter unaddressed, but
speaking of reliance in time of need by him for whom
it was intended. It was initialed by Mary of Este,
and the seal bore the effigy of her son. On the blank

outside Fraser wrote the address of Atholl; and then he carried the significant bit of paper to Atholl's great enemy, Queensberry, the commissioner of the Scots Parliament, who believed in the document and the meaning imparted to it. We get still further into the complicated reticulation of the plotting of the period. As a weasel watches a rat, so did a man notorious in his day by the descriptive title of "Fergusson the Plotter" keep stealthy watch on the furtive movements of Fraser, exposing them whenever he thought fit; and at last there was no resource for the ambassador of so grand a mission but to sink again into obscurity abroad.

With his departure, the romance—or the farce, if the expression is preferred—of the "Scotch Plot," otherwise called the "Queensberry Plot," vanishes, leaving a sediment of constitutional difficulties. The danger of an immediate Jacobite insurrection vanished with it; but there remained other more serious dangers of a national strife between England and Scotland. By a speech from the throne the queen drew the attention of both Houses to "unquestionable information of very ill practices and designs carried on in Scotland by emissaries from France, which might have proved extremely dangerous to the peace of these kingdoms." There was, at the same time, a royal message to the Secret Council of Scotland, requiring them to make inquiry into the affair. In England, the House of Lords began a busy investigation. It was conducted without any consideration for the fact that if offence had been committed, it had been in a separate independent State. It was enough to justify them that persons under

the sovereignty of the queen had been injuriously
entreated by persons also under that sovereignty.
Scotland was all on fire at once. It was not easy,
however, to find a constitutional battle-field where
the Scots Estates could fight the English House of
Lords. But presently the Scots saw, to their relief,
that the august House was grappled by a closer
enemy—the House of Commons. The dispute thus
opened was a supplement to the Aylesbury Election
case. It was an attack by the Commons on the
systematic policy of the Upper House to arrogate to
itself supremacy over the administration of justice.
The debates upon " the queen's speech respecting the
Scottish plot" were not nearly so significant and
fruitful in constitutional precedent and principle as
the great Aylesbury question; and the points at
issue having been examined and commented on as
appropriate to that debate, seem to require no more
attention here.[1]

Before passing on to matters of higher import,
it may be right to note two incidents where only
two persons were concerned; but the treatment
of these two was significant of what Scotland
at large might expect. Sir John Maclean was
caught in England. He pleaded that he was on his
way to Scotland to qualify for the indemnity; but
he underwent a threatening examination by a committee of the Lords, whose conduct on the occasion
left the impression that but for greater events quickly
following, harsher treatment might have been dealt.
A certain Scot named David Lindsay was apprehended and tried at the Old Bailey on a charge of

[1] See Parliamentary History, vi. 172 *et seq.*

high treason, in that, being a subject of her Majesty, he had passed into France in defiance of the proclamation denouncing that offence as high treason. He pleaded the indemnity. He was under-secretary of State to Lord Melfort, the prime minister of " King James the eighth king of Scots," but the Government in Scotland having found reason for propitiating him, had granted him a pardon for all his treasons. The Old Bailey could find nothing fit to be effectively pleaded there, either on the indemnity or the pardon, and passed sentence of death on Lindsay; but the executive was wise enough not to give effect to the sentence by hanging and embowelling. And now we pass from these small events, incident to the perilous position of the British empire, into a broader and deeper current of history.

The English statute, responding by precautions and threats to the Scots Act of Security, contained clauses for furthering an incorporating union as the only conclusive settlement of accumulating difficulties. It provided that Commissioners for England appointed by the Queen under the Great Seal shall have power "to treat and consult" with Commissioners for the same purpose, "authorised by authority of the Parliament of Scotland."[1] The statute of the Parliament of Scotland completing the adjustment, with the short title "Act for a Treaty with England," authorises such persons "as shall be nominat and appointed by her Majesty under the Great Seal of this kingdom" to treat and consult with "the Commissioners for England."[2]

The next great step was the appointment of the

<hr/>

[1] 3 & 4 Anne. c. 7.   [2] Scots Acts. 1705. ch. 4.

two Commissions, thirty-one on either side. On the English were the two archbishops ; for Scotland there was no clerical element. It was noticed that for England all the members not official were from the peerage, while in Scotland there seemed to be a desire to represent the peerage, the landed commoners, and the burgesses or city interest, in just proportions. At an early stage in the daily business, the English brought up a proposition, about the reception of which they had considerable apprehension, that there should be "the same customs, excise, and all other taxes," throughout the United Kingdom—virtually a resolution that Scotland should be taxed on the English scale. This was easily passed by means of a solvent —due, no doubt, to the financial genius of Godolphin —that, on an accounting and proof of local or personal hardships arising from the adoption of uniformity, compensation in money should be made from the English Treasury. But a more critical point was reached when, on the 24th of April, the Chancellor of Scotland brought forward, among certain preliminary articles, one "that there be free communication, and intercourse of trade and navigation, between the two kingdoms and plantations thereunto belonging, under such regulations as in the progress of this treaty shall be found most for the advantage of both kingdoms."[1] This was frankly accepted on the part of England, and faithfully adjusted in detail. It was felt to be a mighty sacrifice made to exorcise indefinite but formidable calamities in another shape.

At this point in the progress of the Union all interest resting on the excitements of political victory

[1] Proceedings of Comrs., Scots Act, xi. 165.

and defeat, or the chances of a bitter war, came to an end. There were a few small incidents in Scotland; but England was placidly indifferent. She had cheerfully paid a heavy stake as loser in the great game, and it would trouble her no more. The statesmen of the two countries knew that the Union must pass unless the Jacobites of Scotland were joined by an invading French army; and that was not a likely casualty while Marlborough was hovering on the frontiers of France. There was a touch of the native haughtiness in this placid indifference of England. No doubt it helped in clearing the way to the great conclusion; but for many years after the fusing of the two nations into one, disturbing events showed that it had been better had the English known something about the national institutions and the temper of the people who had now a right to call themselves their fellow - countrymen. It was expected that Scotland would be quietly absorbed into England —absorptions much more difficult in the first aspect were in continuous progress in Asia and America. The Englishman had great difficulty in reconciling himself to political and social conditions not his own, and his pride prompted him to demand that, if he left England, any part of the world honoured by his presence should make an England for his reception. When expecting this on the other side of the Border, he forgot that the Scot had too much of his own independence and obstinacy. True, the Scot, among the sweet uses of adversity, had imbibed more of the vagrant, and could adapt himself more easily to the usages and temper of other nations. But on the question of yielding up his own national usages and prejudices in his own country he was as obstinate as his mighty partner.

There was still a world of business to be transacted in details of the unattractive kind that belong to accountants' reports. These may be objects of vital and intense interest—as in the realising of the assets in bankruptcies, where persons immediately interested in frantic excitement hunt out the array of small figures—two, three, four, or five—that tells them whether they are safe or ruined. But the interest is not of a kind to hold its intensity through after-generations. On some items of the present accounting, however, there was, in the principle adopted, a fund of personal and political interest. The heavy debts of England had to be considered—and here, as in all pecuniary arrangements, England was free-handed. The Scots made an effort to retain their African Company ; but they fortunately offered the alternative of purchasing the stock from the holders. On the alternative of retention the English Commissioners were resolute in refusal and resistance, but they were ready to entertain the other ; and they accepted it in a liberal shape. To have bought the stock at its market value would have been a farce, after the ruin that had overcome the Company. But if it could not be even said that England had ruined the Company, the sacrifice had been made in the prevalence of English interests, and while there was yet a hold on England it should be kept. There was no difficulty in coming to a settlement satisfactory to the Scots, and willingly offered by the English. It was substantially payment of the loss on each share, as calculated from an examination of the Company's books.

The adjustment of the several pecuniary claims thus created in favour of Scotland was simply the collective summation of the losses incurred by all the stock-holders; and when the summation was completed, the total was passed into a capital sum, called the Equivalent. This sum total of the various items, with all their fractions, making up a fractional sum less than £400,000, might be otherwise described as a capital stock held by the shareholders of the old company trading to Africa and the Indies, each to the extent of his loss. Odious suspicions were, down to the present generation, propagated about an item, or group of items, in the Equivalent. A sum amounting to £20,540, 17s. 7d., had been made over by the English Treasury, to be paid to influential Scotsmen as the price of their votes or influence in favour of England. Fortunately this affair was closely investigated by the celebrated Committee of Inquiry that brought on Marlborough's dismissal and Walpole's imprisonment. It was found that the Scots Treasury had been drained; and the crisis of the Union was not a suitable time either for levying money or for leaving debts—the salaries of public offices especially —unpaid. England, therefore, lent money to clear away this difficulty. The transaction was irregular, and had not passed through the proper Treasury forms. It was ascertained, however, that the money so lent had been repaid. In discussions of the affair, before those concerned were fully cleared of the odium of bribery, taunting remarks had been made on the oddity and sordid specialties of the items of payment. Thus the allowance to the Lord Banff was, in sterling money, £11, 2s. It would have had a richer sound, and perhaps resolved itself into round numbers, in Scots money; but as it is, there is no more to be said against it than that, as a debt in some way due to the Lord Banff, the exact English book-keeper had entered it down to its fraction.[1]

There remained a few matters of adjustment of uniformities between the two countries for the advantage of both—such as a fixed standard for rating money in account. The Scots grumbled rather than complained about the English standard being always made the rule, and no reciprocity being offered. But the Scots were left considerable facilities for the use of their own customs for home purposes in pecuniary matters, and in weights and measures. If, for the

[1] Having investigated this point many years ago, I was gratified to find the following testimony to my services by one who, when he had made himself fully master of the facts, could be relied upon for absolute justice, with perhaps a tinge of generosity: " Lockhart of Carnwath, in his ' Memoirs,' made public a list of thirty-two names, with a certain sum of money assigned to each, the entire sum amounting to upwards of £20,000. This actual sum was advanced in an irregular manner, and without the customary forms, from the Treasury of England, as was proved before the Commission of Public Accounts, in 1712, of which commission Lockhart was himself a member; and he infers that the money was designed and applied for the purchase of votes. On his authority, the accusation passed current in that age with the Jacobite writers, and in later years, with those who felt more or less sympathy with them. But admitting his list to be entirely authentic, the inference which he drew from it is shown by subsequent research to be entirely erroneous." In footnote: " See especially the full details and the able arguments of Mr Burton, in his ' History of Scotland,' vol. i. pp. 484-494."—' History of England, comprising the reign of Queen Anne until the Peace of Utrecht, by Earl Stanhope,' 2d edit. p. 282. The opportunity may be here taken to note that, in the history of the period there referred to—afterwards incorporated with a History of Scotland from the Roman Invasion downwards—the author had an opportunity of dealing with the Scottish history of this period with a fulness of detail beyond what would be due to the affairs of Scotland in the present book.

general convenience of commerce and taxation, any uniformity was necessary, and the practice of the greater nation was a suitable standard for the other, it was the smaller sacrifice, and to both parties the easier arrangement, that those who were only an eighth part of the inhabitants of the island should yield to the overwhelming majority.

It was in keeping with the wisdom and tolerance prevailing throughout on the English side of the Treaty, that it should be first discussed in the Parliament of Scotland. If this was felt as a courtesy to Scotland it was an expediency for England. All opposition would be in Scotland, and it was well to know it at once, that disputes might be cleared off and a simple affirmative or negative presented to the Parliament of Scotland. The Parliament of England has ever restrained vague oratory by a rule that there must always be a question of Yes or No fitted for a division as the text of a debate. In Scotland on this occasion, as on many others, there was at first a discussion of the general question; and when this along with other sources of information had given the servants of the Crown some assurance of the fate of the measure, there was a separate debate and division on the first article, understood on all hands to be a final decision. The debate was decorated by a work of oratorical art long admired in Scotland, and indeed worthy of admiration anywhere for its brilliancy and power. It was a great philippic, taking that term in its usual acceptation, as expressing a vehement torrent of bitter epigram and denunciatory climax.

The speech of John Hamilton, Lord Belhaven, " On the subject-matter of an Union betwixt the two kingdoms of England and Scotland," was so amply dispersed in its day, that if a collector of pamphlets on the Union buys them in volumes he will generally find this speech in each volume. It is, no doubt, an effort of genius; but what will confer more interest on the following specimens selected from it is, that it was an attempt to rouse the nation to action at this perilous and momentous crisis, and succeeded only in drawing attention and admiration as a fine specimen of rhetoric art.

" I think I see the present Peers of Scotland, whose noble ancestors conquered provinces, overrun countries, reduced and subjected towns and fortified places, exacted tribute through the greater part of England, now walking in the Court of Requests like so many English attorneys, laying aside their walking swords when in company with the English peers lest their self-defence should be found murder. . . .

" I think I see the Royal State of Burrows walking their desolate streets, hanging down their heads under disappointments, wormed out of all the branches of their old trade, uncertain what hand to turn to, necessitate to become 'prentices to their unkind neighbours, and yet after all finding their trade so fortified by companies, and secured by prescriptions, that they despair of any success therein. . . . But above all, my lord, I think I see our ancient mother, Caledonia, like Cæsar sitting in the midst of our senate, ruefully looking round about her, covering herself with her royal garment, attending the fatal blow, and breathing out her last with a *et tu quoque mi fili.*"

The great remedy for all, is an end of rancorous

feuds and hatreds dividing Scotland; and this calls from him a glowing picture of the land that by union and industry has made itself too powerful to be a safe partner for humiliated Scotland.

"They are not under the afflicting hand of Providence as we are; their circumstances are great and glorious; their treaties are prudently managed both at home and abroad; their generals brave and valorous; their armies successful and victorious; their trophies and laurels memorable and surprising; their enemies subdued and routed. . . . Their royal navy is the terror of Europe; their trade and commerce extended through the universe, encircling the whole world, and rendering their own capital city the emporium for the whole inhabitants of the earth."

The speech was for the country, not for the House. The great points about trade and virtual independence had been conceded by England, and a union was looked to rather as a refuge and a gain than as oppression and plunder. It has even been said that there was some inclination to receive the speech with irony, and Defoe, who seems to have been present on the occasion, gives this account of what followed:—

"Mr Seton, who made the first speech, stood up to answer the Lord Belhaven; but as he had already spoken, the order of the House—viz., 'that the same member could not speak twice in the same cause' —was urged against his speaking, and the Earl of Marchmont standing up at the same time, the Lord Chancellor gave place to him, who indeed made a short return to so long a speech, and which answer occasioned some laughter in the House. The Earl of Marchmont's speech was to this purpose—viz., He had heard a long speech, and a very terrible one, but he was of opinion it required a short answer, which he gave in these terms: 'Behold, he dreamed, but lo! when he awoke, he found it was a dream.' This answer, some said, was as satisfactory to the members, who understood the design of that speech, as if it had been answered vision by vision." [1]

In the debates on the Union, some Scots statesmen found a tactic, infinitely valuable to them in the united Parliament, of voting in a group. They were called the "New Party," and nicknamed the "*Squadrone volante.*" In the correspondence already referred to, it was good news at St Stephen's when it was announced that the New Party had adopted the Union.

---

[1] Hist. of the Union. Defoe like other jesters—notably Swift—when chained down to serious history or narrative, seemed to drop his magic wand, as only of use for raillery or sarcasm, and to become verbose and stupid. He lightened up, however, on the occasion in his 'Review.' A ballad, the first stanza of which, if I remember right was,—

> " Come hither you dreamer of dreams,
>   You soothsayers, wizards, and witches,
> Who puzzle the world with hard names,
>   And without any meaning make speeches.
>   Here's a lord in the North,
>   Near Edinbro's Forth,
> Tho' little's been heard of his name or his worth,
> Has seen such a vision, there's no mortal can reach it,
> We may challenge the clan of Egyptians to match it."
>
> —Defoe, Review, iv. 69.

A Catechism from an old MS. :—

" There was a man and he made a speech, and it was a man that used to make a speech ; and the man that made the speech was a lord, and this lord made a long speech, and at the end of this lord's long speech, behold another lord stood up and made a speech, and this was a very short speech. But the lord that made the short speech was supposed fully to have answered the lord that made the long speech, for he said unto him that he *dreamed*, and it seemed unto him as if it were, but when he awoke, behold it was a dream."—Review, iv. 509.

On the critical division the numbers stood—118 for the article and 83 against it. The remainder of the clauses passed without division, a ready acceptance being given to amendments that were virtually improvements in giving effect to the spirit of details in the Treaty, as where it was adjusted that for trading purposes, vessels bought abroad for trade from the Scots harbours should be counted equivalent to vessels of Scottish build.

There was considerable noisy excitement through the country, the Jacobites ever striving to rouse the people in the great towns to riot and sedition, and when they found that impossible, spreading exaggerated accounts of the effects of their efforts. A mob was raised in Edinburgh, but it was appeased without the loss of a life, and with no other casualty save the frightening of the provost's wife. There were some eccentric movements among the Cameronians, rendered all the more grotesque by the Jacobites taking the leadership in them; and some of the more vehement clergy betook themselves to their own special weapons in the holding of a day of humiliation and prayer. Ere the whole came to a conclusion, a point was yielded to the Presbyterian Church of Scotland. It was passed as a separate Act before the Act of Union was passed—the separate Act stipulating its repetition in any Act adopting the Treaty óf Union. It provided for the preservation of the discipline, worship, and ecclesiastical government of the Establishment. It was further provided, that every sovereign of the United Kingdom, on accession to the throne, should make oath in terms of this Act. Hence it happens that this oath is taken immediately on the accession, the other oaths, including that for the protection of the Church of England, being postponed till the ceremony of the coronation. On the 16th of October 1706 there came a vote on the passing of the "Act ratifying and approving the Treaty of Union." This was carried in the Scots Parliament by 110 to 69.

It was the determination of the queen's ministers for England, to carry the Treaty as it came from Scotland, word for word ; and they employed all their strength to do so. It was the policy of the English Government and their supporters in the matter of the Union, to avoid a parliamentary debate upon it clause by clause at St Stephen's. To this end there was an endeavour to give it, as much as in the peculiar conditions could be given, the character of a treaty between two independent powers, each acting through its executive, that executive acknowledging the full power of Parliament to examine, criticise, and virtually judge the act done as a whole, but not admitting parliamentary interference with the progress of the details. If there were an illogicality in the essence of a treaty where the executive—the queen—was the common sovereign of both realms, the difficulty could be discarded as a pedantry in a constitutional community where the sovereign acts through responsible advisers. Some slight touches of apprehension were felt in England when it was seen that the Scots Estates were not only voting the separate articles, but in some measure remodelling them. The Estates were taking the privilege naturally claimed by the weaker party to a bargain in protecting themselves while it was yet time. When all was adjusted, England, as the vast majority, could correct whatever had been done amiss in the preliminary adjustment of her interests, but poor Scotland would be entirely helpless. There was another reason for tolerating the alterations, in their being directed to the safety and completeness of the legal institutions left in the hands of Scotland untouched, as matters of entire indifference to England; still it weakened the hands of those who desired to evade a parliamentary discussion on the several articles in England that this had been permitted in Scotland, and had become effective in the shape of amendments. John Johnston, who had been for some time Secretary of State for Scotland—a son of the celebrated covenanting hero Archibald Johnston of Warriston—was then in London carefully looking at the signs of the times. He wrote to Scotland, saying, "You may, I think, depend on it that the alterations you have hitherto made will not break the Union; but if you go on altering, it's like your alterations will be altered here, which will make a new session with you necessary, and in that case no man knows what may happen." All is well as yet —on the 4th January—and if there be no more serious alterations the English ministers will be able to give effect to their resolution "to pass the Union here without making any alterations at all." [1]

By what had been usually called a message from the throne, the attention of Parliament was directed to the Treaty as it had come from Scotland, but the matter being of supreme importance the queen was her own messenger. From the Commons she had to ask for a supply to meet the Equivalent. To both

[1] Jerviswood Correspondence, 178.

Houses she said : "You have now an opportunity before you of putting the last hand to a happy union of the two kingdoms, which, I hope, will be a lasting blessing to the whole island, a great addition to its wealth and power, and a firm security to the Protestant religion. The advantages that will accrue to us all from an union are so apparent, that I will add no more, but that I shall look upon it as a particular happiness if this great work, which has been so often attempted without success, can be brought to perfection in my reign." [1]

The opportunity was taken to imitate the Scots in a separate preliminary Act "for securing the Church of England as by law established." There was a desultory discussion in both Houses, with a result showing the overwhelming strength of the supporters of the Union. In the House of Lords there were some divisions, and among these the largest number of votes mustered by the Opposition was 23, bringing out a majority of 47 by 70 votes for the ministry. The conclusion of the discussion was a vote of approval by each House.

The Opposition, however, did not adopt their defeat. They were preparing to fight the battle over again, clause by clause, when a bill was brought in to convert the Articles of Union into an Act of Parliament. The English House of Commons has always been supremely tolerant to troublesome, and even mischievous, members, so long as they adhere to the forms of the House—forms to be zealously guarded, since they were framed for averting hasty legislation and the possible domination of an intolerant majority.

[1] Parl. Hist., vi. 558.

It was determined, however, that the impracticals and impedimenters should not have their swing on this occasion, when the descent of a French army to gather to its centre the Jacobitism still lingering in the country, darkened the political horizon. Both Houses had a full opportunity for discussing the merits of every word in the Treaty, and the risk of national ruin was not to be encountered because they had not expended all their loquacity, having expected another opportunity.

The tactic for evading the danger was credited to the ingenuity of Sir Simon Harcourt, the Attorney-General. The two Acts of Ecclesiastical Security and the Articles of the Treaty were all recited in the pre-amble of the bill under the command of the mighty "Whereas." The enacting part of the Act was dropped into a single sentence, shorter than statutory sentences usually are. The Opposition might throw out the measure, and the Ministry with it, if they had strength to do so; but there had been sufficient dis-cussion on the clauses, and there should be no more. In the descriptive words of Burnet, "This put those in great difficulties who had resolved to object to several articles, and to insist in demanding several alterations in them, for they could not come at any debate about them; they could not object to the recital, it being more matter of fact; and they had not strength enough to oppose the general enacting clause; nor was it easy to come at particulars, and offer provisos relating to them. The matter was carried on with such zeal that it passed through the House of Commons before those who intended to oppose it had recovered out of the surprise under

which the form it was drawn in had put them."[1]
There was thus but one question, that the Bill do
pass, and the Opposition had not reaped encouragement to resist so great an issue. The Lords had in
their usual manner of dignified repose managed to
discuss the clauses, but it was rather a conversation
to see that all was in right order, and that no accident
had happened to a measure of so vital moment, than
a debate.

On the 6th of March 1707 the queen came to the
House of Lords, and in a graceful speech gave the
royal assent to the Act.

[1] Parl. Hist., v. 296.

END OF THE FIRST VOLUME.

Printed in the United Kingdom
by Lightning Source UK Ltd.
92993